THAT
SEASON
IN PARADISE

Alex Gordon

Foreword by Sandro Mazzola

CQN BOOKS

Published by CQN Books, Scotland.

Copyright Alex Gordon 2016. All rights reserved.

First published in the United Kingdom in 2016 by CQN Books
ISBN 978-0-9934360-6-2

A catalogue for this book is available from the British Library
and the Irish Library in Dublin.

Cover & page design and typesetting
by Stephen Cameron for CQN Books.

Edited by David Faulds, Publisher,
CQN Books (Email: david@cqnpublishing.co.uk)

Printed by Gutenberg Press, Malta

A special thank you to everyone in the
Celtic Quick News community and the wider Celtic family.
CQN has published books on Lisbon Lions Willie Wallace,
Tommy Gemmell, Charlie Gallagher and John Hughes
alongside Caesar & The Assassin and
The Winds of Change by Alex Gordon.

Please visit
www.celticquicknews.co.uk and www.cqnbookstore.com

DEDICATION

This is for my wonderful and understanding wife Gerda
and our special friend Ziggy.

ACKNOWLEDGEMENTS

Thank you to the many former players who helped put this book together.
There are too many to name, but you know who you are.

A round of applause is due to Editor David Faulds for his sterling work yet
again in presenting this tome. Tough shift, but he got there!

Once again, a cheer for Paul Brennan, founder of Celtic Quick News, for
his professionalism and support throughout.

A special pat on the back for Kevin Hughes for his kind assistance in
arranging the Foreword with Inter Milan legend Sandro Mazzola. And, of
course, a big thank-you to Sandro for his words.

All the others, too, who were happy to give their time reflecting on such
a marvellous and historic season in Paradise. Much appreciated, my
friends.

Celtic supporters worldwide and to all the posters and readers on
www.celticquicknews.co.uk. Keep the faith.

And, of course, eleven individuals who are now embedded in the annals
of fame at Celtic Football Club: Ronnie Simpson, Jim Craig, Tommy
Gemmell, Bobby Murdoch, Billy McNeill, John Clark, Jimmy Johnstone,
Willie Wallace, Stevie Chalmers, Bertie Auld and Bobby Lennox.

The 'support cast' during the unforgettable campaign of 1966/67 - John
Hughes, Charlie Gallagher, Joe McBride, Willie O'Neill, John Fallon, John
Cushley, Ian Young, Jim Brogan, Davie Cattenach and Bent Martin.

And, naturally, a gentleman by the name of Jock Stein.

CONTENTS

SANDRO MAZZOLA

Honours: 70 caps for Italy. 2 European Cup medals,
1 Intercontinental Cup medal, 4 Serie A medals.

Helenio Herrera, our Internazionale Milan manager, went to Scotland to check on Celtic in person. He returned with a tape of the game.

The players watched the film of them in action and we weren't particularly impressed. I thought, 'These guys are mediocre.'

So, we possibly did not give them the full respect they were due. Remember, we had won the European Cup in two of the previous three years and we had beaten Real Madrid, the 1966 winners, en route to Lisbon. Also, we were favourites.

In fact, we believed it would be an easy game. That was the biggest mistake we could possibly have made! When I scored with my penalty-kick early in the match we thought that would allow us to slow the pace of the game and dictate the tempo. We did this every week in Italy.

The Celtic players would not allow us to do this. They refused to let us play our normal game.

Celtic were superhuman and I have never known a team with so much energy. You could say they took us by surprise. However, we had no complaints about the result.

They beat us fair and square in the European Cup Final in Lisbon in 1967.

Sandro Mazzola, Milan, June 2016

AUTHOR'S NOTE

The title of this book is 'That Season In Paradise'. However, it could so easily have been 'A Tale Of Two Seasons' (with apologies to Charles Dickens).

At the very onset of putting this tome together, it was my sole intention to concentrate wholly on the truly awesome 1966/67 campaign when Celtic were spectacularly triumphant, winning every single trophy for which they competed in sublime style.

The pinnacle of achievement, of course, was the breathtaking attacking performance that swept a manager, eleven players and a football team towards deserved legendary status when they pulverised Inter Milan into submission in the European Cup Final on an unforgettable May evening in Lisbon. The League Championship was claimed for a second successive year and it was joined in the Parkhead trophy cabinet by the League Cup, the Scottish Cup and, just for good measure, the Glasgow Cup.

As David Coleman, the respected BBC TV commentator, put it so famously and so laconically, 'Celtic would have won the Grand National and the Oxford/Cambridge Boat Race, too, if they had entered.'

Yes, it truly was a season in Paradise.

And yet...

One notable name was missing from the Roll of Honour at the end of a stupendously successful sweep through Scotland and beyond.

Joe McBride.

Jock Stein's first signing for the club - at £22,000 from Motherwell in June 1965 - was in unparalleled goalscoring form as 1967 loomed into view. The unfussy, up-and-at-'em, old-fashioned centre-forward had fearsomely bulldozed his way to a phenomenal thirty-six goals before injury so cruelly and callously ended his previous seemingly-unstoppable surge towards the record books.

McBride, without warning, was knocked out of his stride during a 1-1 draw against Aberdeen at Pittodrie on December 24 after aggravating a knee problem. It would be a miserable Christmas 1966 in the McBride household.

The player, following an agonising process to regain the strength in his stricken joint, returned to the first team almost a full year later - on December 23 - and, remarkably, fired in a hat-trick as Celtic beat Morton 4-0 on a mudheap at Cappielow. His previous goal had come in a 6-2 triumph over Partick Thistle on December 17 the year before.

In the twelve months the team were robbed of his services, Celtic continued their charge towards success in Lisbon, another First Division title and a Scottish Cup. However, there was misery beckoning when Jock Stein's side missed the opportunity of being crowned world champions after three brutal encounters with the disgraced Argentines of Racing Club of Buenos Aires in the so-called Intercontinental Club Championship.

The European Cup was surrendered at the first stage, losing 2-1 in the east end of Glasgow before gaining a 1-1 draw in Russia against Kiev Dynamo with ten men after the referee, an Italian by the name of Antonio Sbardella, inexplicably sent off Bobby Murdoch and also ruled out what looked a perfectly legitimate solo goal from John Hughes. Even today Yogi, as he was known to his team-mates and fans after the famous TV cartoon character Yogi Bear, shakes his head at the decision and insists, 'How could I have been offside when I beat about three of their players before I battered the ball past their goalkeeper?'

Tommy Gemmell, demonstrating some gallows humour, will often add, 'Maybe the referee was an Inter Milan fan.'

The League Cup was reclaimed, however, when Stevie Chalmers, with a double, and singles from Willie Wallace, Bobby Lennox and Hughes shared the goal-gathering responsibilities in a thrilling 5-3 encounter against Dundee at Hampden on October 28. Four days later, Celtic were involved in their return leg against Racing Club in South America and three days after that debacle they lost 1-0 in the Uruguayan capital of Montevideo during what has since become known infamously as 'The Second Battle of the River Plate'.

An anguished Joe McBride watched all three tussles from the stands, unable to assist his team-mates.

It would be well-nigh impossible to discover the utter frustration and the dark despair the player endured in the depth of those moments.

The 1966/67 campaign, that season of unsurpassable excitement and plentiful reward, had kicked off with the League Cup competition and Celtic had triumphed 2-0 over Hearts at Tynecastle. McBride put down his marker for what was to follow by rifling in both goals. He added an astonishing eleven in the next four games in the tournament, with four strikes coming against the unfortunate and vulnerable St Mirren in a rollicking 8-2 win in Glasgow. McBride was also on target when the defence of the newly-won league championship got underway, with Clyde being dismissed 3-0 at Shawfield. He continued in the same vein as the months rolled by and the goals flew in with joyous regularity.

And then, on a freezing December afternoon at Pittodrie, fate, an unforgiving opponent, interrupted to dismantle a dream.

Years later, Joe McBride reflected on that traumatic period in his career. He said, 'Bayern Munich's Gerd Muller won the Golden Boot as Europe's top goalscorer in season 1966/67 and he admitted at the presentation that the award would have gone to me but for the damage that was done to my knee. The doctors thought I needed a cartilage operation, but the problem was caused by flaking bone behind my knee and it took a year out of my playing life. The pain of being denied the opportunity of seeing what kind of goalscoring figure I could have achieved will live with me until the day I die.'

Without even a scintilla of bravado, McBride added, 'Sixty goals would have been a possibility.'

On a July evening around seven o'clock in 2012, I received an unexpected telephone call at home. It was from Tommy Gemmell. There was no need for preamble. 'Joe McBride has passed away,' he said. Minutes later, I phoned Bertie Auld who had also just received the sad news.

Moments shared with two Celtic greats who, at that point, were mere human beings stripped of status, individuals with heavy hearts coping with the news of the passing of an old pal who would always be more than just a team-mate.

I hope, then, that you understand I couldn't have written this book without Joe McBride receiving the accolade he so richly deserved.

He may have missed some of the acclaim and the applause, the cheers and the congratulations, the eulogies and the exaltations, but the fact he was a Celtic man right to the end could never be denied him.

Joe McBride has every right to a place in 'That Season In Paradise'.

PROLOGUE

Celtic Park was bathed in kaleidoscopic splendour as sunshine gaily bounced around the famous old ground on the Saturday afternoon of August 6 1966. At precisely three o'clock, the pre-match frenetic atmosphere generated by sixty thousand eager supporters was punctured by a shrill from referee Bill Anderson's whistle which set in motion the most epic season in the history of Celtic Football Club.

Those in attendance that day could never in their wildest dreams have imagined how the following ten months would develop; how a glorious jigsaw would come together with such extraordinary perfection.

The sheer preposterousness of Celtic winning the most glittering prize European football had to offer would not have been entertained or the ludicrous thought voiced by anyone with a double digit IQ.

Manchester United, the most glamorous of all English teams, provided the opposition and on show were three of the most flamboyant performers to grace the beautiful game. There was strutting, stylish Scotsman Denis Law, the aptly-named George Best, a rare combination of Irish guile and grit, and the dashing, debonair Bobby Charlton, winner of a World Cup medal with England only the previous week.

In the middle of the park, there was another of Sir Alf Ramsey's Wembley heroes, gap-toothed Nobby Stiles, a notoriously combative performer, and United's captain-for-the-day Pat Crerand, the accomplished former Celt whose right foot was the baton that conducted the United orchestra.

The Old Trafford line-up was not a disintegrating collection of all-stars. These were full internationals in their prime in an assembly which also included Northern Ireland's iconic goalkeeper Harry Gregg as well as tricky and elusive left-winger John Connelly, who had also figured in England's World Cup sortie.

This was to be no friendly confrontation. Back then, these encounters were treated like mini-internationals and Scottish and English teams tended to go head to head with frightening verve and relish. Besides, Celtic and United were led by two men, Jock Stein and Matt Busby, who were never comfortable with anything else other than first place. They were close friends, an allyship brought about during their days in the Lanarkshire mines, but there was to be no love lost on the field of combat where men had to prove themselves.

After fifteen spellbinding minutes, Celtic had thumped in three goals on their rumbustious way to a stunning 4-1 success. Eyes were opened and hopes were raised by all who witnessed the spectacle. Expectation levels, though, were not heading for stratospheric boundaries; not at this embryonic stage, anyhow.

Ironically, it was Bobby Lennox who got the ball rolling with the opener in the seventh minute as he first-timed a devastating drive that left Gregg groping helplessly on its unstoppable way towards the rigging. It was Lennox, of course, who had got the final goal of the previous campaign when he netted in the last minute against Motherwell for a 1-0 triumph to ensure twelve years of wandering aimlessly in the championship wilderness had, at last, come to a thankful halt. And it was Lennox who would score the goal against Real Madrid that gave Celtic a 1-0 victory in Alfredo di Stefano's Testimonial Match in front of 120,000 approving supporters at a Bernabeu Stadium which was engulfed in rapturous applause for the new European champions.

In between the encounters with Manchester United in August 1966 and Real Madrid in June 1967, Celtic's journey through football had been fairly memorable.

On a bright and clear afternoon in the east end of Glasgow against the Old Trafford luminaries, Bobby Murdoch clattered in a second three minutes following Lennox's strike and, after David Sadler had pulled one back, Joe McBride zipped a third low in at the left-hand post. A confused Bill Foulkes, United's veteran centre-half, tucked the ball into his own net just after the hour mark for the fourth.

The final scoreline was immaterial. Simply put, Celtic had been imposingly majestic; a structured unit playing with skill, pace, sophistication, cohesion and penetration against strong opponents who would prove their qualities that season on the way to winning the English First Division title. However, on this day, Manchester United were discovered to be inadequate against a blisteringly imaginative Celtic side, who, on the evidence of this supreme showing, had sent out a message only the foolish in football would choose to ignore.

Nine of the players wearing green-and-white hooped jerseys that afternoon would realise the joy of becoming part of the first British team to win the European Cup on another sumptuous occasion in Lisbon on May 25 1967: Ronnie Simpson, Tommy Gemmell, Bobby Murdoch, Billy McNeill, John Clark, Jimmy Johnstone, Stevie Chalmers, Bertie Auld and Bobby Lennox.

Willie O'Neill dropped out when Stein moved Gemmell to left-back to accommodate Jim Craig on the right flank. Alas, McBride, after rampaging to thirty-six goals before Christmas, was forced into submission with a persistent knee problem. Willie Wallace, bought for £30,000 from Hearts before the turn of the year, effectively took his place.

Ronnie Simpson, the weathered and worldly old pro, had begun his career at the age of fourteen and eight months as an enthusiastic amateur for Queen's Park in a Summer's Cup-tie against Clyde at Hampden in June 1945. Just over twenty-one years later, and across his home city of Glasgow, he was patrolling the Celtic goal-line and sensing something special might be around the corner. He put it this way, 'Manchester United were an experienced European Cup side which could be brilliant in its day, but played most of its football off the cuff. We hit them hard. We won 4-1 and what a starter for our fans. They thoroughly enjoyed themselves, sang the whole afternoon and really let themselves go every time we put the ball in the United net.

'The appetite had been whetted. We were running freely, taking our scoring chances, playing with plenty of method, strength and confidence and had shown that our close-season tour of the United States, Canada and Bermuda had only made us a closer-knit team. We looked 1967 straight in the eye with nothing but confidence.'

Many years after the ruthlessly-efficient disassembling of the acclaimed Old Trafford line-up, Bobby Lennox observed, 'I thought that win would help to kick-start what would be a wonderful season.'

Who would have believed such a breathtaking gift for the masterly understatement had been bestowed upon the wee chap from Saltcoats?

CHAPTER ONE
A GUY NAMED JOE: PART ONE

"I have been asked to name the best Celtic centre-forward I have ever seen play and the man I choose may surprise you. He's Joe McBride. He was a tremendous header of the ball and could take half-chances on the ground. And his heart was in the right place!"

- Jimmy McGrory,
Celtic's record goalscorer with 472 goals in 445 games.

Pain is a faithful companion. And thousands of Celtic supporters would most assuredly have testified to that solemn sentiment in the dark days of the late fifties and the formative years of the sixties.

Jock Stein marked his magisterial return to Celtic with the 3-2 triumph over Dunfermline following an exhausting Scottish Cup Final on a nerve-wracking afternoon of Saturday April 24 1965 watched by a frantic Hampden audience of 108,800. It was such a crucial breakthrough victory, Stein, in years to come, observed, 'Things might not have gone so well without that win.'

It was the triumph Bertie Auld insisted was more important than lifting the European Cup in Lisbon two years later. 'It proved we could win trophies again,' said the former midfield schemer.

One man, however, who did his utmost to scupper a triumphant comeback for the legendary manager was a robust journeyman centre-forward whose career had begun with Kilmarnock Amateurs and had travelled through the Junior ranks at Shettleston Town and Kirkintilloch Rob Roy before a step up to the seniors with Kilmarnock, Wolves, Luton Town, Partick Thistle and Motherwell. He was born in Govan, two hundred yards from Ibrox stadium, home of Celtic's historic rivals.

His name was Joe McBride.

And he came extremely close to being the destroyer of Big Jock's dreams and desires.

Joe McBride was never anyone's remotest idea of how a typical athlete should be portrayed. He was square-shouldered with a bolted-on neck, the possessor of a solidly-built trunk with sturdy legs and he stood a mere 5ft 8in at a stretch. His meanderings through football's maze saw him fail to settle at clubs on either side of the border. However, his demeanour and presence masked one indisputable fact; he was a goalscorer. The powerfully-structured character had fired in thirty-one goals in fifty-nine appearances during his two years at Firhill before moving to Motherwell in 1962 for a modest £5,000. By the time he took his place in the Fir Park selection for the Scottish Cup semi-final against Celtic on the afternoon of March 27 1965, he had notched over half-a-century of goals in three years for the claret-and-amber outfit.

McBride was three months shy of his twenty-seventh birthday and the burly forward, never afraid to mix it in packed penalty areas when the boots were flying, realised he was at the peak of his condition. Although he never hesitated in admitting his affection for the team based in the east end of Glasgow, McBride refused to shirk in his professional task of making life as difficult as possible for Billy McNeill and Co when they were on a collision course.

And that was the case while grey skies gathered and the wind picked up momentum as Jock Stein took charge of Celtic in a Scottish Cup-tie for the first time. Clearly, it was his most important game after returning from Hibs earlier in the month. Remarkably, he had already guided the Edinburgh side to a 1-0 win over holders Rangers in the previous round of the competition. On that same day, Celtic, managed for the last time by Jimmy McGrory, ploughed through the mud at Parkhead to overcome an excellent Kilmarnock side who would go on to win the league title that season on goal average, as it was then, from Hearts.

Forty-eight hours after the 3-2 victory over the Ayrshire team, Jock Stein, on Monday March 8, was installed as Celtic's new manager with McGrory taking over the post as the Parkhead side's first Press Relations' Officer. It's doubtful, though, if the club's greatest goalscorer ever got around to preparing a Press Release.

Big Jock watched Bertie Auld, with the assistance of two penalties, score five goals in a 6-0 victory over Airdrie at Broomfield two evenings later. Curiously, Celtic prepared for their semi-final against Motherwell with three league games against St Johnstone, Dundee and Hibs - and were proved not to be adequate enough to be successful in even one of them. Into the bargain, keeper John Fallon had conceded eight goals and the defence had looked far from secure. The Perth Saints won 1-0 in Glasgow, there was a 3-3 stalemate at Dens Park and then Stein's former team travelled through from Edinburgh and trounced the home side 4-2 on a Monday evening, the game played throughout in driving sleet and rain. Stein, alarmed at the deficiencies in his defence, had dropped Tommy Gemmell after the defeat against St Johnstone and reinstated stalwart Jim Kennedy, who hadn't played at left-back for two years.

'Thankfully, it was a return to the drawing board for Big Jock after conceding those seven goals in back-to-back fixtures against Dundee and Hibs,' recalled Gemmell. 'He never bothered giving me any reason why I was being left out. I discovered that was Jock's style during our years together. Possibly, he wanted to bolt the back door because The Pres, as Kennedy was known to everyone at the park, was never going to become famous for crossing the halfway line when he wore the No.3 shorts. He used to joke he would get a nosebleed if he ever ventured into our opponents' half. I realised the new manager actively encouraged his players to get forward, but he also made it clear it was our responsibility to be in place whenever the other team was on the offensive. So, without preamble, I was out and The Pres was in. Clearly, I hadn't made much of an early impression on Big Jock.'

There was a smirr of rain as Celtic arrived at the national stadium an hour-and-a-half before kick-off against Motherwell and Stein, very clearly, realised this was a confrontation he and his team could not even contemplate losing.

The league had long since been blown before his arrival after a sequence of dreadful results and awful performances and the Scottish Cup presented itself as the solitary opportunity for the team to pick up its first piece of silverware following eight years of near-drowning in a stormy ocean of embarrassment and torment for the support.

After a mere four games in the Celtic dug-out, an encounter of gargantuan proportions had presented itself to Stein, who realised he had to prove equal to the task of navigating the team to a place in the Scottish Cup Final. The launch pad to a new era in a proud club's history was so temptingly near and yet so agonisingly far away. Stein had to get his team selection absolutely spot on or face the consequences against dangerous opponents who were free of any relegation worries and had everything to play for. And they had a centre-forward who knew his way to goal in Joe McBride.

'I had played against Joe several times before this game, of course,' remembered Billy McNeill. 'I have to say I never had much pleasure in facing up to him. Joe was like a bull, charging around everywhere. If the ball was in the air, you knew you were about to be dunted. I don't mean to even infer he was a dirty player, but he was just so strong and courageous; a particularly lethal combination. He was completely single-minded when he went onto that pitch. Joe wasn't the tallest, but he was spring-heeled and his timing in the air was nigh on immaculate.

'If my recollection is correct, we had already beaten Motherwell home and away in the league that season and Joe hadn't managed to get on the scoresheet. That meant I was doing my job because Joe would have been my immediate opponent in both those meetings. But I also realised that would mean absolutely nothing at Hampden in the Cup semi-final. No centre-half could be complacent with a guy such as Joe McBride around. Take your eye off him for a split second and - bang! - your keeper's in trouble and so is the team.'

As was normal, Stein named his line-up shortly after arriving at the stadium; Tommy Gemmell was in, Jim Kennedy was out. John Hughes - Big Yogi to everyone - was chosen to lead the attack and Charlie Gallagher came into midfield alongside Bertie Auld. Stevie Chalmers made way for Jimmy Johnstone on the right wing.

Gemmell recollected, 'It was a bit of a relief to get the nod to play against my hometown team and, admittedly, my boyhood favourites. If I had been left out and Celtic had won, there was every chance Big Jock would have gone with the same formation again for the Cup Final. It was imperative I got the chance to show the Boss what I could do on the big occasion. Motherwell weren't doing particularly well in the league that season, but I knew they still had some excellent players in Bert McCann, Willie Hunter, Pat Delaney and, of course, Joe McBride. We realised we were in for a real fight that afternoon.'

And so it proved. Two goals from the lively, bustling McBride, who made life extremely uncomfortable for Billy McNeill, propelled Motherwell to a 2-1 advantage at the interval. The Celtic skipper owned up, 'The first goal came in the tenth minute and I have to confess it was all down to a moment of hesitation from myself. Once again, though, it showed how deadly Joe McBride could be. I mistimed a clearance as the ball came straight down the middle and that was all Joe needed. He wasn't the fastest over a distance, but he was quick to anticipate and seize on situations. He could put on a short burst that gave him daylight between defenders and the goalkeeper. I looked round to see him gather the ball and go directly towards John Fallon.

'My heart was in my mouth and I thought he had passed up the opportunity when it appeared our keeper had managed to divert the ball as Joe attempted to slide a shot under his body. As luck would have it, the momentum of the effort kept the ball rolling towards goal and, unfortunately, there was no-one there to get back and boot it to safety. Hands up, it was my mistake.'

It took eighteen taut minutes before the bulk of the crowd, fast approaching 60,000 with the arrival of latecomers delayed by the adverse weather conditions, could sigh with relief. Jimmy Johnstone scampered along the right touchline before slinging over a cross which was pushed away by anxious goalkeeper Alan Wylie. The ball dropped to the feet of the unmarked Bobby Lennox who fired it towards the gaping net. Defender Matt Thomson, making a desperate attempt to clear, only succeeded in helping it on its way. All-square - for four minutes, anyway.

The Celtic defence failed to deal with a swirling, awkward corner-kick and, unfortunately, the ball dropped at the feet of the last person Billy McNeill wanted to see left unattended. McBride smashed a vicious left-foot drive at goal which hammered against the chest of the flailing Fallon. His effort broke clear, but once again the penalty-box predator reacted more quickly than anyone else to batter the rebound into the roof of the net.

Jock Stein, sitting in the sunken dug-out, grimaced. It remained that way until referee Archie Webster blew his whistle to bring an eventful and fraught first-half to a halt. There was much work to be done by the new Celtic manager in the next ten minutes as he prepared his players for a rousing second-half.

'I recall Big Jock actually being quite calm,' said Bertie Auld. 'The man had a presence, even back in the early days, and when he spoke it was normally in a matter-of-fact manner. There was no gobbledygook, there was no time for that. He had to get his message across and he never wasted a moment during these interval observations. People have said all sorts of things about the so-called psychology of Big Jock. Call it what you like, but he was shrewd. He instinctively knew when he had to put an arm around a player's shoulders to give him a wee gee-up. He also knew when it was time to give someone a rollicking. There was little point in him shouting at someone and leaving them without a shred of confidence for the remaining forty-five minutes. He just seemed to know which buttons to press.

'I've said it before and, undoubtedly, I'll say it again, but the Boss was never interested in winning popularity contests among his players. His ambition was to win football games - and win them well while entertaining our supporters. He wanted his Celtic team to be a blend of winners. If you didn't match up, you were out the door. It really was as simple as that. So, you can be sure he would have got us pumped up for that second-half against Motherwell.

'He was also the master of saying something devastatingly simple just as the bell went to let you know your presence was required in the tunnel. As you prepared to go out again, he would offer, "We've got forty-five minutes to score just one goal. You lot should be able to score three or four in that time against this lot." Or. "One goal will change this game. Watch them try to come back after that. They'll throw in the towel." He always managed to inject confidence into his players. By the time the referee restarted the game, our sleeves were rolled up and we were ready to go.'

It took Celtic until the hour mark to get the required equaliser and it was Auld, who had just returned to his spiritual home from Birmingham City two months before Stein's comeback, who seized the opportunity to keep the plan on track. The clever, astute playmaker had started his senior career at Parkhead as an outside-left where, by his own admission, his sole job was 'to get down the wing and deliver crosses into the box'.

However, during his four-year spell in the English top-flight, Auld was encouraged to come inside by his manager Gil Merrick. 'Suddenly, things were opening up for me,' said Auld. 'I could switch play from left to right, I could play balls to feet and take return passes in dangerous areas. I've no doubt my stint across the border enhanced my game. I think Celtic got a better player when they bought me than the one they sold. And they made a £3,000 profit!'

Auld's experiences as a touchline operator worked for him when he decided to venture inside. He had an electrifying burst of pace to get away from hesitant defenders and he demonstrated that skill against Motherwell on that fateful afternoon at the national stadium. Celtic had dominated in the first fifteen minutes of the turnaround with Billy McNeill showing signs of things to come by menacing Alan Wylie on two occasions with his aerial ability at corner-kicks. The Fir Park side survived until Auld took a touch and sped away from three startled opponents. Defender Cameron Murray was late with a crude challenge and Auld went sprawling in the penalty box. The match official, who had earlier enraged the Celtic following by waving away their howls of appeals after Jimmy Johnstone had been decked in similar circumstances, had no hesitation, though, on this occasion to point to the spot.

'After hitting two against Airdrie a few games earlier, I was the designated penalty-taker,' said Auld. 'I was happy to take the responsibility and I was always certain I could score from twelve yards. If you can't hit the target from that range, you're in the wrong game. I realised it was such an important kick. If I missed, it would give Motherwell a helluva boost and goodness only knows what might have transpired. However, if I scored, well, we were on the front foot, weren't we? I knew there was still something like half-an-hour to play and, on top of that, we had a fairly stiff wind at our backs.

'On those occasions, I liked to let the opposing keeper know he had no chance of saving my shot. Gamesmanship, kidology, whatever you choose to label it, but I admit I would get involved if I thought it gave Celtic an edge. I would point to the goalie's left or right and say, "Hey, keeper, that's where the ball is going, straight into that corner." It gave them something else to think about as I began my run up to the ball. I tucked that one away and we didn't need to look over at Big Jock on the touchline. He wanted a winner and everyone representing the club that day totally agreed. We had Motherwell on the ropes and we were looking for the knock-out punch.

'I remember cracking a shot past the keeper in the final minute. Wee Jinky Johnstone picked me out with one of his wonderful, inch-perfect crosses and I hit it sweetly. Can you imagine my joy when I saw the effort fly into the net? Can you imagine my annoyance when the referee ruled it out? I was fuming because I knew I was onside. Again, all my years as a winger taught me to always look along the line, to make sure I didn't drift ahead of the last defender before the ball was delivered. The ref was having none of it. Eventually, we discovered the goal was ruled out because Jinky had been in an offside position when he crossed the ball. I doubt that, too. However, we didn't have the technology in the sixties that is readily available today. And, back then, that was certainly a good thing for a lot of the match officials who made some dodgy decisions without fear of reprisals or recriminations. Still, being positive, we had a Scottish Cup semi-final replay to look forward to after being out of the competition forty-five minutes earlier.'

'Keep an eye on McBride,' was Jock Stein's final words to Billy McNeill as he filed past his manager on the way out of the Hampden dressing room four days later. The Celtic skipper smiled and reflected, 'Big Jock rarely wasted his breath with needless remarks. After the way Joe McBride had played against me in the previous encounter, I didn't really need any reminding to watch him like a hawk.'

As it turned out, the Motherwell attack-leader was starved of service throughout a one-sided affair. Prior to the tie, Stein had talked about how important Jimmy Johnstone would be to his game-plan for the replay and, even in the mid-sixties, he was psyching out his opponents. His opposite number, Bobby Ancell, may well have structured the left-hand side of his team to deal with the menace of the mesmeric winger, but he would have realised he had made an error of judgement as soon as he was handed the Celtic team line-up thirty minutes before the game. There would be no sign of Jimmy Johnstone on the right wing. There would be no sign of Jimmy Johnstone anywhere except in a seat in the stand. Stevie Chalmers wore the No.7 shorts and, although he, too, kicked off his career as an outside-right, utilising his exceptional pace, he wasn't in the same mould as his diminutive team-mate. Chalmers preferred to come inside and that's exactly what he did all evening against Motherwell - and to great effect.

With a crowd of 58,959 looking on, Celtic, all power and aggression right from the first whistle, stormed their way to a 3-0 triumph with an opener from the roaming Chalmers, just before the half-hour mark, and two in a six-minute second-half burst from John Hughes and Bobby Lennox.

'You could say Big Jock worked extremely hard with the players as we prepared for this game,' said Tommy Gemmell. 'He took the defenders aside and laid it on the line. The fact that John Fallon had now shipped ten goals in four games was never going to be tolerated by the Boss, who had played all his career as a no-nonsense centre-half. He readily admitted he had never thought twice about hoofing the ball into the stand if he believed the situation warranted it. "No-one ever scored a goal from Row A," he would often remind us. Big Jock emphasised the need for a clean sheet. "That's your foundation," he said constantly. We were getting organised like never before.

'Jimmy McGrory was a lovely man - too nice to be a football manager, that's for sure - but he was no tactician. We never saw him in a tracksuit and he never took training. Everything was off the cuff. Jock was changing our outlook and our development. We were beginning to look at the game from different angles. "Use the midfield," he instructed. "Give the ball to Bertie Auld, Bobby Murdoch and Charlie Gallagher. Let them earn their wages, get them to open up the opposition. It's their job to pass the ball." He would drum it into you.

'Then he would go to the midfield players and work on them. They were told to make themselves available for passes out of defence. In the past, a lot of the players simply raced into an attacking position and the defenders would put their laces through the ball to belt it downfield. Now our team-mates were being told to drop short, collect and carry passes before distribution. Jock would then set to work on the front players such as John Hughes, Stevie Chalmers and Bobby Lennox.

'He would hammer home the importance of clever, intelligent running and not just haring around for the sake of it. They, too, knew when they had to drop deep to allow room for midfield players to come through and support the attack or even have a pop at goal themselves. It was a simple enough tactic that allowed Bobby Murdoch, in particular, the opportunity to show off his fabulous range of shooting skills.

'Big Jock went into extra-time with Jinky, but no-one could be too sure how much our wee extrovert took in. He would nod his head at the right times, of course, but even our manager must have known that, more often than not, Jinky would just go out and do what came so naturally to him. You can't coach the sort of ability Wee Jinky possessed into any individual. The main thing, though, was that each and every player had an idea of what was expected of him within the structure of the team. We knew what to do when we had the ball and, just as importantly, we knew what to do when we didn't have the ball.

'And, remember, Big Jock had to figure out our best formation and how to get the best out of his players in the space of only five games leading up to the replay. Or, put another way, around seven-and-a-half hours of actual playing time. That he managed to convey his thoughts in such a convincing manner within that time frame is a testimony to the man.'

Motherwell may have been dismantled and dismissed, but Joe McBride remained in Jock Stein's thoughts. The fourth manager in Celtic's history had already selected his first transfer target for the club.

First of all, though, there was the Scottish Cup Final meeting with Dunfermline at Scotland's grey, old football fortress in April 1965. With the greatest of ironies, the two clubs had squared up in the Final of the competition only four years earlier - with Jock Stein in command of the East End Park outfit. The outcome, back then, was an absolute shocker for runaway favourites Celtic. They were held to a goalless draw in the first game and the consensus of opinion was that the Fifers would have been thrashed out of sight if it hadn't been for their inspired goalkeeper

Eddie Connachan, who picked that afternoon to manifest into an uneatable barrier. He had just quit his job as a miner to go full-time in football and, on this showing, proved he had made a sound decision.

Celtic were still enormous favourites to wipe the floor with the East End Park side in the second game. Once again, Connachan would not be denied his only medal in football and two breakaway goals from David Thomson and Charlie Dickson, after a terrible gaffe by Celtic's No.1 Frank Haffey, took the trophy to the Kingdom of Fife. Celtic chairman Robert Kelly, in his guise as Scottish Football Association President, watched as his wife presented the trophy to Dunfermline captain Ron Mailer while his team-mates celebrated. Kelly had done nothing to keep Stein at Parkhead when he let it be known he was prepared to leave his job as reserve team coach.

Billy McNeill, among others, beseeched the Parkhead supremo to keep the innovative young strategist, but Kelly paid little heed to his or anyone else's pleas or opinions. As Stein held aloft the spoils of war, the Celtic chairman, fairly magnanimously, told an SFA colleague, 'What a friend gets is no loss.' Five years later, Stein was the Celtic manager and, unlike his predecessor Jimmy McGrory, made it clear he would not brook any interference in his running of the football side of the club.

Emphatically, on the day of his appointment, he publicly declared, 'The responsibility for all team matters is down to me; the selection of players, the training, the coaching and how we play. I will make those decisions and no-one else.'

Kelly, though, was a stubborn individual who was highly unlikely to fade into the background. Before one of Stein's first games, the chairman, as was his wont, entered the dressing room to have his say to the players. After his little sermon, Stein shut the door behind him and said, 'Right, you can forget all that for a start!' Kelly's pre-match visits became rare events after that.

The Scottish Cup, of course, was duly delivered following a nail-biting ninety minutes against a splendid Dunfermline team which only missed out on the First Division championship after finishing on forty-nine points, one adrift of Kilmarnock and Hearts. The Fifers' Irish manager Willie Cunningham, who had succeeded Stein, was a thoughtful, even intense, character who had continued the good work of his predecessor.

Dunfermline, who were, quite rightly, installed as favourites for the Cup, had a compelling blend of skill and strength with individuals such as future Celt Tommy Callaghan, a tireless midfield worker, and his brother Willie, typical of the breed of the time, a determined, little full-back. Jim Herriot was a more than capable goalkeeper who would go on to represent Scotland, while Jim McLean was an old-fashioned centre-half who took no prisoners. There was pace and grace in the shape of wingers Alex Edwards and Jackie Sinclair and they also possessed a typical battering-ram centre-forward in John McLaughlin.

One player who missed getting the nod to play was a certain Alex Ferguson, who was left out of the team following a poor performance during a 1-1 draw with his former club St Johnstone. The centre-forward, by his own admission, 'had a series of misses in the second last league game of the season that was reckoned to have denied us the championship because we had better goal figures than either Kilmarnock or Hearts. If we had got two points instead of one against St Johnstone, Dunfermline would have won the league.'

But Ferguson, the club's top goalscorer, still believed he was a shoo-in for the meeting against Celtic after playing well in the 2-0 victory over Hibs in the semi-final at Tynecastle on the same day Joe McBride was attempting to derail Jock Stein's aspirations at Hampden. Ferguson, an ungainly, inelegant raider, discovered only fifty minutes before kick-off that he wouldn't figure in the Cup Final and, in the days before substitutes, the nearest he got to the Hampden pitch was a seat in the stand beside his father. As Willie Cunningham read out his line-up and Ferguson's name was missing, the future Manchester United manager exploded. 'You bastard!' he exclaimed. A transfer demand swiftly followed from the irate Ferguson.

Immediately after the Fife outfit's battling defeat at the national stadium, Cunningham sought a new centre-forward. Joe McBride was the man he targeted.

Many years later, McBride admitted, 'I knew Celtic wanted me and then in came Dunfermline. I had asked for a transfer and Motherwell were not about to stand in my way. Through various routes, I was told what the Fifers were willing to pay in a basic wage and it was a lot more than what was on offer at Celtic. Big Jock told me he would sort things out. He didn't need to reassure me. Celtic were my club and, corny though it may sound, it had always been a dream and an ambition to pull on those green and white hoops. Now I was being given that opportunity and nothing was going to prevent me from making that move. Money was never my prime consideration.'

And McBride, like so many before and after him, ignored the financial incentives elsewhere to sign on the dotted line. Another who followed his heart and not his head was Bertie Auld. He recalled in his autobiography, 'A Bhoy Called Bertie', 'Clyde offered me £60 to sign professional forms for them in 1955. Partick Thistle offered me £50. Celtic offered £20. So, of course, I joined Celtic!'

It was Auld, performing with all the gallus swagger of a typical Glaswegian, who was so instrumental in Jock Stein's first piece of silverware success. Harry Melrose scrambled in the opening goal for the Fifers in the fifteenth minute, but, just after the half-hour mark, the Maryhill man levelled with a brave header from under the crossbar after a well-struck shot from Charlie Gallagher had thumped against the woodwork. Just before the interval, Dunfermline struck again when John McLaughlin, Ferguson's replacement, accepted a short free-kick and walloped a twenty-five yard effort wide of John Fallon. Back came Auld and Celtic, though, in the fifty-second minute when he finished off a well-worked move with a rare right-foot drive beyond Jim Herriot. That set up a grand finale to top the lot and bring eight years of hurt and suffering to a welcome, shuddering and spectacular halt.

Nine minutes remained of a thrilling encounter when the artful Charlie Gallagher gracefully arced a left-wing corner-kick into the penalty area. Jim Herriot would have required the assistance of stepladders to thwart Billy McNeill as the Celtic captain outjumped friend and foe to meet the cross squarely with his forehead and the ball pummelled the netting with a fair degree of ferocity. Hampden, in an instant, was transformed into a green-and-white wonderland.

'Instinctively, we knew that triumph would be the start of something good for everyone connected with Celtic,' said matchwinner McNeill. 'I had played in two losing Cup Finals before that and, naturally enough, the disappointment leaves you wondering if you will ever win anything. It was the same for John Hughes and Stevie Chalmers. They were also in the teams that had lost in replays to Dunfermline in 1961 and Rangers two years later. You feel sickened for yourself, your team-mates and, of course, the man on the terracing. On days like that, you know you have failed them, you have let them down and haven't matched their expectations. It does get to you, believe me.

'Beating Dunfermline changed everything. Suddenly, Celtic supporters were smiling and wearing their colours with pride. The players didn't have to duck and dive when they were out in public. It was a pleasure to be stopped in the street and talk about actually winning something.'

Some special days lay ahead for Billy McNeill and his Celtic colleagues. And, of course, a guy named Joe.

CHAPTER TWO
A GUY NAMED JOE: PART TWO

"I leave the Fancy Dan stuff to guys such as Jinky and Yogi. I concentrate on doing what I think I do best and that is scoring goals."

- Joe McBride,
Scorer of 86 goals in 94 games.

Myths and reality have gone hand-in-hand as willing, if unusual, partners in the world of football since the first pig's bladder was booted around a village somewhere back in time. It is widely believed Jock Stein bought Joe McBride for £22,000 shortly after gathering his breath following the trailblazing Scottish Cup Final triumph over Dunfermline. Not so. In fact, McBride didn't sign on the dotted line for his boyhood idols until June 5, fully forty-one days after the Hampden epic.

It had nothing to do with the centre-forward swithering about joining Celtic or trying to squeeze an extra fiver out of the Parkhead coffers with Dunfermline willing to pay considerably more to the player they had earmarked as the ready-made successor to fill Alex Ferguson's No.9 shirt. With Joe McBride involved, you could be certain there would be no such acts of skulduggery. However, with continued reports of his boyhood favourites, following a puzzling and interminable delay, showing an interest, he had tabled a transfer request at the end of the 1964/65 league season and Motherwell were prepared to sell their top asset.

The truth of the matter is simple; the barrel-chested frontman was persuaded to stay at Fir Park for a little longer with the club involved in the revived, but ultimately short-lived, Summer Cup tournament. Ironically, Jock Stein had masterminded Hibs' win in the competition the previous year when the Edinburgh outfit defeated Aberdeen 3-1 in the play-off decider after a 4-4 stalemate following the two-legged Final.

Motherwell had gone thirteen years without a major trophy success - they had won the Scottish Cup in 1952 when they overcame Dundee 4-2 - and they had reached the home-and-away Final of the ill-fated tourney that endured for only two years. They hammered holders Hibs 6-4 on aggregate in the semi-final and were due to face Dundee United, with the first meeting at Fir Park scheduled for Saturday May 29 and the return at Tannadice in midweek. McBride led the Lanarkshire line-up to a 3-1 home victory and, although United won 1-0 on Tayside, the Fir Parkers just edged it 3-2 on aggregate.

So, on June 2 1965, the Motherwell fans had something to celebrate following an end to their favourites' prolonged and barren years and, three days later, McBride became Jock Stein's first signing for Celtic. As is often the quirky manner in the beautiful game, Alex Ferguson withdrew his transfer request, remained at Dunfermline and was joint top league scorer with thirty-one goals at the end of the 1965/66 season alongside...Joe McBride.

During the summer, Jock Stein was ruthless as he plotted to build on the Scottish Cup success. He wanted to work with a smaller first team squad and over twenty youth players were shown the door at Parkhead. Big Jock wouldn't have lost a wink of sleep following the instigation of such a dramatic cull of young talent.

Davie Hay recalls, 'I think I might have been Big Jock's first signing for the club. He took over in March and I arrived a month later. Prior to that, however, I had been asked to train at Celtic on Tuesday and Thursday evenings. Coming from Paisley, I was a St Mirren fan, but there was no looking back when Celtic came calling. Tommy Docherty attempted to take me to Chelsea and made an excellent offer. However, it was always going to be Celtic for me. As I arrived, one of the first things I noticed was that Big Jock was pruning the playing staff. He wanted the coaches to concentrate on smaller groups of players.

'He reckoned they should spend more time with certain individuals and, of course, it worked. I was lucky enough to get the nod. Many of our group were allowed to move on and, if fortune had smiled on them, they might have gone on to do wonderful things at Parkhead. Jim Holton, for instance, trained with Celtic while I was there. He was a big, raw centre-half, but he wasn't taken on. Jim went to West Bromwich Albion, kick-started his career, spent a year at Shrewsbury and was signed by Tommy Docherty for Manchester United in 1972. He was also a team-mate in the Scottish team in the World Cup Finals in West Germany two years later that returned home unbeaten, the first nation to be knocked out without losing a game. Jim was proof a few will slip through the net. No-one is going to realise the potential in every youngster, that's just not possible. Some take longer to mature than others. Some can bloom overnight after struggling for so long. It just happens.'

As Stein looked to the future, Hay, of course, arrived alongside the likes of Kenny Dalglish, Danny McGrain, Lou Macari, George Connelly, Vic Davidson and Paul Wilson, an eager bunch of skilful teenagers who earned the nickname 'The Quality Street Gang'. The Celtic manager's immediate target in the close season in 1965, though, was the Scottish First Division Championship. Conquering Europe was not in his thoughts; not at that point, anyway.

Interestingly, Celtic kicked off their nine-in-a-row championship-winning surge with their smallest squad of players in years with a mere nineteen full-timers and nine part-timers with only two groundstaff as back-up.

To bolster the squad, Stein turned his attention to the exotic and intriguing Brazilian market. Ayrton Ignacio and Marco di Sousa, inside-forwards from Sao Paulo, were jetted in for a two-month trial period. Another two exciting prospects, Jorge Farah and Fernando Consul, were being lined up to join them at the Scottish Cup winners. It was no gimmick, as many sceptics glibly claimed. In the late fifties and early sixties, a fair percentage of South American talent - mainly from Brazil and Argentina - made its way to Italy. However, a transfer embargo slowed down the influx and Italian club sides were limited to a certain number of foreign signings. Agents, mainly based in Portugal, were forced to look elsewhere to place their clients in Europe. Jock Stein, always innovative, tapped into the market in the hope they might have something to offer Celtic.

I watched Ignacio and Di Sousa in a reserve game against Motherwell at Parkhead - over 11,300 fans turned out that evening - and, from the little knowledge I had of football, I was hugely impressed by Ignacio. He scored a bewildering, swerving right-foot shot from an angle that almost tore a hole in the net and, at the age of thirteen, I left the stadium that evening convinced Big Jock had unearthed 'the new Pele' for Celtic. Didn't happen that way, of course, but it was a gamble worth taking.

Celtic's record in the league since winning the title in 1954 was nothing short of diabolical. Jock Stein must have been alarmed at the lack of belief and conviction among the players he had just inherited. Even Billy McNeill accepted the club's best chance of success would be in a knock-out competition rather than the marathon that was the league.

'We were ambitious enough as a set of players,' said the club legend. 'We were realistic, as well. Most years, by the time January was out, we were nowhere to be seen, as far as the league was concerned. That was when our focus would be diverted to the Scottish Cup. Winning that competition was a major deal back then, probably a lot more so than it is today. We discovered that fact in 1965, of course. We finished a lamentable eighth in the table, winning only sixteen of our thirty-four games. And, even with Big Jock behind us, we had horrible results like losing 5-1 to Dunfermline at East End Park only days after the Cup Final and there was also a ridiculous 6-2 loss against Falkirk at Brockville on the countdown to Hampden. Yet, after our victory over the Fifers, our supporters celebrated all the way through the summer. Our abominable form in the league wasn't mentioned.

'However, the Boss changed our mindset. In his typical blunt, forthright manner, he gathered the squad around him one morning at Barrowfield before the campaign kicked off and told us, "Right, listen. Every team is at the top of the league at the moment. No-one has won, no-one has drawn, no-one has lost. We're all lining up together for a very long race and we've got to believe we will be first at the end. Celtic Football Club is all about winners. Let's not be standing here this time next year talking about failure and facing another season of chasing others; we want them chasing us." You could say Big Jock got his message across. Suddenly, we realised that the odd Cup success every now and again was never going to be acceptable to Jock Stein. He was looking for us to become the dominant force in the country. As a matter of fact, he was insisting on it.'

Joe McBride was ready for the challenge, determined and anxious to make up for time scoring goals for other teams elsewhere. It had taken him eight years as a professional - and 115 league goals for five different teams on both sides of the border - before he was invited to take his sledgehammer skills to the east end of Glasgow. He made his debut in the unlikely surroundings of a tiny football stadium on the Isle of Man in a Benefit Match for the Society for Handicapped Children. The game was played against Motherwell in a virtual downpour on a Wednesday afternoon on July 28 in front of 2,500 fans. It wasn't the most memorable baptism for McBride and it ended in the twelfth minute after a clash of heads with his former team-mate John Martis.

Stein might have wondered about the wisdom of taking only fourteen players - including two goalkeepers - for the flight that morning to the holiday island. Stevie Chalmers replaced McBride and, in fact, netted the late equaliser after Ian Thomson had given the Fir Parkers an improbable lead. Before the end, Bertie Auld limped off with a thigh pull and Johnny Divers came on in his place. Thankfully, the match came to an end before substitute keeper Ronnie Simpson was invited to display his outfield talent.

Normal service was resumed in the next friendly encounter, a meeting with Shamrock Rovers at Dalymount Park where Joe McBride walloped in his first hat-trick for the club as they thrashed their opponents 7-0. A crowd of 10,000 took in the action and, so typical of McBride's run-until-I-drop unselfish attitude, he was still battling away until two minutes from the end when he completed his trio. Bobby Lennox (2), Charlie Gallagher and John Hughes were the others to get on the scoresheet. The players didn't have to raise their game above a canter in Dublin and must have expected a more testing confrontation when they arrived at Roker Park four days later to take on a Sunderland side that had just paid £90,000 - a huge fee in those days - for Rangers' left-half Jim Baxter.

The elegant, ball-playing Fifer boasted an excellent record against Celtic while performing on the other half of Glasgow's Great Divide, but that meant nothing on this occasion. John Hughes, in particular, was in the mood and ran amok while playing through the middle. Yogi thumped two efforts behind Scottish keeper Sandy McLaughlin while Joe McBride, Bobby Lennox and Bobby Murdoch piled on the agony in a 5-0 landslide. The blasé Baxter had sallied and sauntered through one-sided Glasgow derbies to maximum effect in the past while the Ibrox fans taunted their Celtic counterparts on far too many uncomfortable occasions. This time, though, the chants of 'Easy! Easy! Easy!' were reserved for Sunderland's record signing who, by the way, just happened to be a very good friend of Billy McNeill.

It wasn't long before McBride's dream was shattered. Due to knee and ankle injuries sustained on Wearside, his competitive debut appearance had been delayed until the third game of the League Cup, the tournament which was utilised to spearhead the new season back then. Celtic had kicked off the competition with a 2-1 loss to Dundee United at Tannadice which prompted Jock Stein to say, 'We can do better. We know that and we will be trying to prove that when we play Motherwell on Wednesday. However, we're not blind here. We were beaten by a good team and the Dundee United players deserve credit for doing so well.'

In midweek at Parkhead, Stein watched his side scrape their way to an unimpressive 1-0 win over Motherwell. Stevie Chalmers led the line on both occasions, but had failed to score - Bertie Auld and Johnny Divers had been the marksmen in the respective games - and Stein took the opportunity to replace him with a fully-fit McBride. Dundee, with a strong line-up, arrived in Glasgow on August 21 and went home with a 2-0 victory, Kenny Cameron scoring both goals in the space of nine second-half minutes.

Tommy Gemmell played that day. He remembered, 'That defeat actually gave us a well-deserved boot up the backside. We hadn't performed well and we couldn't argue that Dundee deserved their win. As you might expect, Big Jock was fuming. He was eager to start the new season the way we had finished the previous one and that meant winning a trophy and, of course, the League Cup was the first one up for grabs. And, yet, we had started with two defeats in three games and we weren't too convincing in our win over Motherwell, either. It was fairly obvious we had to get our collective finger out. And fast!'

Rather bizarrely, the powers-that-be dictated the Scottish First Division should not kick off on a Saturday, but, instead, moved the opening fixtures to Wednesday August 25. Celtic were due to begin the campaign with a trip to Tannadice to take on a Dundee United side that had actually finished the previous league season one point adrift of the Glasgow outfit. They had been good enough, though, to inflict an opening-day League Cup defeat on Celtic and were confident of registering more punishment on their rivals. From nowhere, Celtic began firing on all cylinders. They eased their way to a 4-0 success with Johnny Divers scoring the first goal in the memorable procession to nine successive championship victories. He netted early on, but the loudest cheer from the travelling fans was reserved for the fifty-second minute when new boy Joe McBride slammed a pass from Stevie Chalmers, in for Jimmy Johnstone on the right wing, past keeper Donald Mackay from twelve yards. Four minutes later, Ian Young, a steady and dependable right-back, slotted in a penalty-kick after Bobby Lennox had been downed and Tommy Gemmell, the cavalier left-back, rifled in a twenty-yarder in the sixty-fifth minute to complete the scoring. It was a remarkable transformation in the space of only eleven days on Tayside.

A local sports reporter was moved to write, 'There was a champagne quality about the play of this latest Celtic blend. Victory was the product of teamwork and they were an impressive balance of speed, skill and spirit. The Parkhead forwards, backed by a defence that moved swiftly out of retreat, performed with a directness that eventually told on their opponents.'

Praise indeed. So, it was one down and thirty-three to go in pursuit of the club's first Scottish crown in twelve years.

The following Saturday, though, it was back to the League Cup and the crazy soccer calendar saw Dundee United provide the opposition for the third time in a fortnight. John Hughes, the juggernaut forward blessed with almost balletic balance, had missed the start of the season due to a suspension held over from the previous campaign, but Stein wasted no time in thrusting the powerhouse raider straight into the first team as soon as he was available. Big Yogi, playing on the left wing, was unstoppable. Celtic were already two goals ahead via efforts from Ian Young, sinking another penalty-kick, and Stevie Chalmers when the game was petering out with only three minutes left on the clock. And that represented plenty of time for Joe McBride to double his competitive goal haul for the club. Chalmers set it up with a speedy run and deft pass and the centre-forward touched the ball to one side of the outrushing goalkeeper, Donald Mackay, as he went around the other to catch up with it before rolling it over the line.

Jock Stein declared himself 'satisfied' with the win. However, he added, 'We have to remember there are two halves to a football match. I couldn't fault the lads in the first-half, but I feel they eased up a little after the interval. The fans come here and pay their money to see ninety minutes' worth of football and I'll be reminding the players of that fact.' The words were accompanied by a stern expression. Clearly, gone were the days when a Celtic manager would complacently accept a victory under any circumstances.

Unfortunately, McBride had taken a knock against the Tannadice outfit and was forced to miss the return League Cup encounter against his former side Motherwell at Fir Park. Celtic went into the tie in the realisation that a win would put them on top of their section. They duly got their two points, but they made heavy weather of the task. John Hughes took over McBride's duties in the middle of the attack and scored a penalty-kick in a 3-2 triumph. Bobby Lennox claimed the others. Jock Stein's men had a one-point advantage over Dundee United, Dundee and Motherwell going into the sixth and final group stage game.

Dundee, after their 2-0 stroll in Glasgow in Joe McBride's debut, stood between Celtic and a quarter-final place. Hughes switched again to the left wing to accommodate the fit-again McBride and Big Yogi once more put on a spectacular show with an astonishing solo goal in the team's excellent 3-1 success at Dens Park. Celtic were already leading with an eleventh-minute effort from Johnny Divers when Hughes ignited the 28,000 crowd and decimated the Dundee defence when he latched onto a pass, nimbly raced away from international right-back Alex Hamilton and, with a posse of opponents chasing after him, simply thundered an unstoppable thirty-yard drive that clattered into the net before keeper Ally Donaldson had a clue what was going on. Andy Penman pulled one back before the interval, but it was that man McBride who again applied the killer touch with a strike five minutes from time. Hughes and Chalmers combined and McBride, like any self-respecting goal thief, was unmarked when the ball came into the penalty area and, from close range, he nodded it beyond the exposed Donaldson.

Joe McBride's mantra was simple. 'I leave the Fancy Dan stuff to guys such as Jinky and Yogi. I concentrate on doing what I think I do best and that is scoring goals. When I see the whites of the goalposts the other guys know they are wasting their time shouting for a pass, it's just not going to happen. The way I figure it is simple. I just let fly and try to make sure I get my effort on target. Look, I can have my back to goal when I receive the ball, but I will know where the goal is, those frames don't move. So, if I'm doing my job properly, I should at least make the keeper work. I won't always hit the target, of course, but that is always my ambition. And if I don't score and the keeper fumbles the ball, then we've got nippy, alert players such as Bobby Lennox and Stevie Chalmers who are sure to punish him. Jock Stein didn't buy me to set up goals. He bought me to score goals. That's my game and he laid it on the line when he paid a fair chunk of money for me. If I continue to score goals, I know I've got a reasonable chance of staying in the team.'

The centre-forward, in fact, made a total of twenty-four appearances on the journey to the turn of the year. With McBride leading the line, Celtic won twenty-one games, drew two and lost one - the striker's debut against Dundee. Just as impressive was the goal return from Jock Stein's historic first purchase for Celtic. McBride clubbed in twenty-four goals, averaging one-per-game, as he single-mindedly went about his business. He fired in fifteen in fourteen league games - failing to score in only three - as well as seven goals in seven League Cup-ties, missing out on two occasions, and twice in three European Cup-Winners' Cup confrontations, lapsing only in the second round return leg against Aarhus when Celtic won 2-0 in Glasgow after McBride had claimed the only goal of the first tie in Denmark.

Remarkably, McBride scored in five successive League Cup encounters after drawing a blank against the Dens men at the start of the adventure. He had missed the 2-1 defeat against Rangers in the league earlier in the season with an ankle injury, but he was fit for the League Cup Final against his club's oldest foes at Hampden on October 22 - ludicrously only five days after Celtic had beaten Hibs 4-0 in the semi-final replay on a sea of mud at Ibrox. If Jock Stein's men were supposed to be tired following their exertions against a very good Easter Road side, their fatigue wasn't obvious against the Ibrox outfit.

Two John Hughes penalty-kicks had Celtic 2-0 ahead at the interval. The first award was for an obvious handball from centre-half Ronnie McKinnon for no apparent reason as a long cross was sailing out of play for a goal-kick. Yogi tucked it away as keeper Billy Ritchie, diving to his right, went the wrong way. Number two came shortly afterwards when the little bundle of tricks that was Jimmy Johnstone was flattened by an anxious left-back, Davie Provan. There was a little piece of brinksmanship from Ritchie as Hughes ran up to take the kick. The goalie swiftly removed his cap and threw it into the corner of his goal. It mattered not a jot as Yogi blasted the effort to his right. Ritchie got a hand to it, but the sheer velocity of the drive carried the ball into the net.

Years later, I mentioned the little bit of gameship from his Old Firm opponent. Had it put him off even slightly, I wondered? In typical Yogi fashion, he returned with a deadpan expression, 'I didn't even notice. He could have been swinging from the crossbar for all I cared. I just wanted to hit the ball with everything I had and get it on target.'

There was a scare near the end when right-back Ian Young, under pressure from John Greig, diverted a header beyond the startled Ronnie Simpson, but there was no way back for the team who saw the Cup wrenched from their grasp and removed from their trophy room to find a new home across the Clyde. Joe McBride celebrated his first piece of silverware with his new team-mates in a Glasgow hotel later that evening and probably wasn't too perturbed that he hadn't scored on the occasion of his Old Firm baptism; Celtic, after all, had won the League Cup and that was the main objective.

What would most certainly have concerned him, though, would have been the knowledge he would play against the age-old rivals on another seven occasions and never know the joy of thumping the ball into the Rangers net.

Years later, McBride said, 'I was unlucky I didn't score against Rangers in a Celtic jersey. I did for the reserves, but never in the eight games for the first team. We won six of those games, drew one and lost one and I didn't get a solitary goal. I was reminded often I had failed while wearing the green-and-white hoops, but my answer was that I didn't need to score a goal because my mates took care of that task. Having said that, I would have loved to have scored for Celtic against Rangers. It just wasn't to be.'

The next Glasgow derby was scheduled for January 2 at Parkhead, only twenty-four hours after the first league game of 1966 against Clyde at Shawfield where Celtic won 3-1 and McBride took his goalscoring form into an exciting new year with two strikes. Rangers were destroyed 5-1 in the east end of Glasgow on a bitterly cold afternoon with the action taking place on a sparkling white, flint-hard surface. The visitors scored in only ninety seconds when a whiplash effort from Davie Wilson skidded in front of the diving Ronnie Simpson and found a place in the far corner of his net. Remarkably, despite an onslaught on Billy Ritchie's goal, that effort still separated the teams at half-time.

It's now imbedded in Celtic folklore what happened after the turnaround. John Hughes put it this way in his autobiography, 'Yogi Bare'. He reflected, 'As ever, Big Jock had something to say in the seclusion of our dressing room at the interval. Like the rest of us, he was not happy. "This is more important than a Cup Final," he observed. "This is the league championship. Win this and they'll never catch us. Get out there and get the job done."

'We had forty-five minutes to change things around. I spotted a pair of discarded white training shoes lying in the corner. They had suction pads and were used for training indoors. I think they were Billy McNeill's gear, I'm not sure. I had been wearing rubber studs in the first-half and they were as useful as a chocolate fireguard. I decided to give the other shoes a try and, thankfully, they fitted. What had I to lose? Kai Johansen, the Rangers right-back, would have been more than delighted with his performance up to that point. I had to give him something else to think about. I discarded my normal boots and replaced them with the shoes. Could they make a difference? We would find out soon enough.

'The game was merely four minutes into the second-half when I combined with Tommy Gemmell and our left-back sent a dangerous low cross into the Rangers penalty area. Joe McBride dummied the ball and that was just perfect for someone with the speed and courage of Stevie Chalmers. He darted into the danger area and turned the ball past Billy Ritchie. Game on!

'I was beginning to get into my stride on the left wing. The shoes were doing their job and definitely helped me maintain my poise and balance when I was running with the ball. Suddenly I was leaving Johansen in my slipstream. My pace was beginning to tell and he was mistiming his tackles. Thirteen minutes after the equaliser, we were ahead. It was Stevie again with a header from a left-wing corner-kick. Rangers were on the ropes and we knew it. So, too, did they. Time to go for the jugular and finish them off.

'Seven minutes later, I got away from Johansen again and saw Charlie Gallagher taking up a great position about twenty-five yards out. Charlie could strike a beautiful ball, that was undoubtedly his forte. He wasn't a tackler, but Charlie had other strengths. He was a lovely passer of the ball to unlock the meanest of defences and he could hit a shot with a lot of venom, too. I beat another couple of defenders before looking up to make sure Charlie was still unmarked and slipped the ball as expertly as I could in front of him. Charlie simply lashed an unstoppable drive in the direction of Ritchie's goal. The ball exploded against the underside of the crossbar before bouncing down over the line. The Rangers keeper didn't move a muscle.

'The fourth goal in the seventy-ninth minute from Bobby Murdoch was a collector's item. Not because of the awesome power and flawless accuracy from our midfielder; he displayed those qualities often enough in an exceptional career. No, it was the role referee Tiny Wharton played in it. Jimmy Johnstone and Gallagher combined on the right before Charlie sent the ball across the Rangers defence about twenty-five yards out. The pass was actually heading straight for Tiny when he suddenly opened his legs and let the ball go through them. It was a consummate dummy any pro would have been proud to claim. Bobby read it perfectly and hit a devastating left-foot drive that almost took the net away. I have watched a video rerun of that game and I was hugely impressed by Billy Ritchie. He was left lying on the brick-hard surface, beaten for the fourth time, the game lost and, amazingly, he got to his knees and applauded Murdoch. That didn't often happen in the heat of an Old Firm duel, but it did display the keeper's unbelievable sportsmanship.

'It was all over for the Ibrox side when I moved the ball over from the left. Wee Jinky got involved and the ball dropped perfectly for Stevie to launch a low drive past Ritchie. It was the end of a perfect day played in hellish conditions. The fog continued to descend and about an hour after the game you couldn't see a hand in front of your face. How, the Rangers contingent in the 65,000 crowd must have hoped it had fallen earlier in the afternoon.'

As Big Yogi pointed out it was, indeed, a 'perfect day', but there was one Celtic player who could have been happier at the end. 'We won, got the points and scored five goals. We could - and should - have scored more and I would have dearly loved to have marked my first Old Firm league game at Celtic Park in front of our own fans with a goal. That would have capped it for me.' The words belonged to Joe McBride.

Charlie Gallagher had an interesting recollection of the match official's excellent skills when he dummied his low ball across to Murdoch for the fourth goal. 'I had enough time in the build-up to shout at the referee and tell him he was in the way of my pass. Believe it or not, he yelled back, "Don't worry Mr Gallagher, I'll get out of the way!" Big Tiny always called the players 'Mister'. And, thankfully, he was as good as his word. He did get out of the way and Bobby did the rest.'

Upon reflection, that was another extremely important victory for Jock Stein and his players. At the end of the league season, they picked up their first title since 1954 by only two points, Celtic in pole position on fifty-seven points with Rangers on fifty-five. The champions scored one hundred and six goals and conceded thirty while their Ibrox challengers claimed ninety-one strikes and lost one fewer on twenty-nine. After trouncing Scot Symon's side, Celtic had seventeen league games still to play and surrendered on only three occasions - at Aberdeen, Hearts and, against all odds, Stirling Albion.

After firing two blanks against the men from Govan, Joe McBride would get the opportunity to rectify the situation on the most glamorous of platforms - the Scottish Cup Final at Hampden in front of 126,599 fans on April 23. Celtic went into the gala encounter as massive favourites. What could go wrong?

CHAPTER THREE
A GUY NAMED JOE: PART THREE

"Joe McBride was my first hero. I idolised him as a boy. He lived in the next close to me in Govan. I used to play with him in kickabouts. He was a natural goalscorer, two-footed, quick off the mark and a really good finisher."

- Sir Alex Ferguson

Joe McBride drilled a thirty-second minute penalty-kick beyond St Johnstone keeper Mike McVittie in a hard-fought 3-2 win for Celtic on March 12 1966. He could never have guessed it would be his last goal at Celtic Park that season.

The club's top scorer collected two goals in a 7-1 destruction of Hamilton at Douglas Park the following week and another double in a 3-0 victory over St Mirren at Love Street on April 5, but, after those two romps, he was firing blanks. The goal supply dried up as abruptly as it was unexpected.

The muscular frontman's progress hit an invisible brick wall. He was still barging around with controlled aggression and making a general nuisance of himself, but the rewards had now diminished alarmingly. Four days after his double in Paisley, McBride was up against the same opponents in the east end of Glasgow. It was a frustrating afternoon for the striker and his team-mates. McBride, noticeably, was bereft of his usual snap in the penalty-box. On this occasion, Celtic had to rely on Charlie Gallagher to open the floodgates in the fifty-fourth minute. With three minutes to play, Celtic were cruising 5-0 ahead with Bertie Auld and Stevie Chalmers pitching in with two apiece.

A few days later, Celtic took on Liverpool in the first leg of their European Cup-Winners' Cup semi-final at a sold-out Parkhead, with 76,446 in attendance. I was fortunate enough to be there to witness Celtic 'massacring' the mighty Anfield outfit 1-0 with a second-half goal from Bobby Lennox. It is no exaggeration to say Jock Stein's side could - and should - have won by four or five goals that evening. Ronnie Simpson had so little to do throughout the entire ninety minutes, he could have joined me and my Dad in the Jungle.

There could be no debate that a fully-functioning Joe McBride would have given Celtic the edge and, possibly, a passage to a prestigious European Final, a year ahead of Lisbon. It wasn't quite a case of switching from prolific to profligate, but the assurance and penalty box poise that had been so evident at the start of the season had, in general, evaporated. And, to be fair, McBride was the first to admit it. He failed to convert a pinch against the Anfield side during the siege of Tommy Lawrence's goal you would have put money on him knocking over the line in his sleep a month or so previously.

He said, 'The game at Parkhead was terrific, but I missed one from under the bar. Heading was a strong point of mine, but I passed up a certainty. The ball came across from the wing and I got under it and headed over the bar instead of under it. It was a horrible miss.'

Although McBride was misfiring, Jock Stein kept faith with the forward who had notched forty-three goals in all competitions until that stage of the campaign. To put that total in perspective, it was seventeen more strikes than the highest tally of the previous season by Stevie Chalmers. Alas, it simply looked as though McBride had run out of goals at the so-called 'business end' of the season. A goalless draw against Hibs at Easter Road followed the Liverpool tie and then it was onto Anfield for the second leg. Again, the record books show Celtic failed to register a goal in a 2-0 defeat on a Merseyside quagmire on an evening of wildly deteriorating conditions.

The game ended in uproar and controversy in the last minute when Bobby Lennox turned the ball behind the grounded Tommy Lawrence and left-back Gerry Byrne, who was on the goal line. 'Offside,' said Belgian referee Josef Hannet to the surprise of everyone. Billy McNeill's take on the incident years later can be filed in the philosophic category. 'Obviously, it was impossible for Bobby to be offside with two opponents between him and the goal. Later, we discovered Hannet had watched the highlights of the game on television that evening and realised he had made a mistake. He actually owned up to his error. Thanks, referee, just a wee bit too late for us to take our place in the Cup-Winners' Cup Final at Hampden the following month. Liverpool lost 2-1 in extra-time to the West Germans of Borussia Dortmund and there was the widespread belief among my Celtic team-mates that they had used up all their good fortune against us. That wasn't sour grapes. The fact is they had contributed so little against us over the two legs. We dominated in Glasgow and we were comfortable all the way through the first-half at their place. Then they scored two goals inside five second-half minutes to turn the tie on its head. We had a legitimate goal ruled out and we were out and they were in the Final. It was a sore one to take.'

McBride recalled the no-goal decision years later. 'It was a shocker from the referee,' he claimed. 'It was impossible for Bobby to be offside. Quite apart from the fact there were two opponents in front of him, he was actually behind me when I passed the ball in front of him before he took it on and stuck it in the net. I was well onside - their centre-half Ron Yeats was around the vicinity, as well - so, that being the case, Bobby had to be onside, too. It was a mystifying decision by the match official. If we had got through, I'm certain we would have won the Cup-Winners' Cup at Hampden. I'm convinced we would have had too much for Borussia Dortmund in what would have felt like a home game.'

Privately, Jock Stein fumed at the Anfield defeat. Publicly, though, he preferred not to go into detail. He merely observed, 'It's history. What we need to do now is concentrate on the next game which is the Scottish Cup Final against Rangers on Saturday. That's the only thing that matters. Europe has gone for this season, but we have the immediate opportunity to win a trophy and that has got to be our priority.'

The Celtic manager, though, had problems before the Hampden date with the Ibrox club. Bobby Lennox had sustained an injury at Anfield and had no chance of playing at the national stadium. That was more of a blow than Stein would care to admit. Lennox's terrifying acceleration was a massive weapon against a fairly pedestrian Rangers central defence that relied solely on the strength of captain John Greig and anticipation of centre-half Ronnie McKinnon. Neither was a speed merchant and Lennox had enjoyed encounters at their expense. However, Stein was informed by the medical staff at Parkhead he would have to strategise his plans for the Scottish Cup Final without Lennox. It didn't help his mood, either, when he realised Bertie Auld, who thrived in the often-toxic Old Firm atmosphere, would also sit it out after picking up an SFA suspension following three bookings. Jimmy Johnstone and Charlie Gallagher came into the team in their places.

The notorious Hampden Swirl was in evidence on the Saturday afternoon of April 23 1966 on the south side of Glasgow. A crowd of 126,599 turned out to witness a fairly drab and unenterprising encounter where both teams appeared far too tentative and negative. The nearest to a goal came from a header by Billy McNeill that soared high over keeper Billy Ritchie before banging off the face of the crossbar and being hastily booted clear by a frantic and relieved John Greig. There was a singular scare for Celtic when the normally-reliable Ronnie Simpson left his line to deal with a long diagonal cross from the left wing. To the veteran's consternation, the ball appeared to hold up in the wind. His timing was off and he was actually coming back down from his leap when the ball arrived in the penalty box. Rangers forward Jim Forrest, with an extraordinarily good strike rate against Celtic, raced in as he attempted to take advantage, but, thankfully, Simpson recovered his composure and grabbed the wayward object at the second attempt.

Joe McBride put in his usual ninety minutes' worth of dexterity, but, once more, had precisely nothing to show for his raw effort. The Glasgow Herald observed, 'McBride had a header brilliantly touched away by Ritchie, but Celtic's leading scorer was, for the most part, an anonymous figure.'

For the first time in Jock Stein's tenure as Celtic manager, the team had gone three consecutive matches without scoring a goal. He knew he would have to rectify that dire situation against Rangers in the Cup Final replay the following Wednesday. Once again, Stein was convinced his centre-forward would answer the call and Joe McBride led the line alongside Stevie Chalmers with an unfit Bobby Lennox again sitting in the stand.

Bertie Auld, free of suspension, came back into the midfield at the expense of Charlie Gallagher, who, rather bizarrely, played for the reserve team against St Mirren on the same evening at Parkhead.

A crowd of 96,862 turned out at Hampden while Charlie performed in front of two men and dog across Glasgow. At least, the 'attendance' in the east end of the city watched the Celtic second string win 7-0. Gallagher recalled, 'Jock could do these sort of things. One minute I was good enough to play in an Old Firm Cup Final in front of over 100,000 fans and the next I was packed off to play at a deserted Parkhead where you could hear the grass grow. That was Jock, though. After awhile you ceased to be surprised by his reasoning and just accepted it and got on with it.'

Remarkably, at the national stadium and for the fourth game in succession, the Celtic forwards couldn't put the ball in the opposition's net. It must be said, though, that Billy Ritchie's goal led the most beguiling of charmed lives. How the Rangers keeper survived the bombardment will forever remain a mystery to anyone who witnessed the spectacle, this author included. Bertie Auld was shimmying this way and that, strutting around while skipping away from clumsy challenges and creating havoc with his exceptionally astute deliveries. He was in the mood to introduce his opponents to a carnival of chaos and all he required was for his team-mates to respond.

In the first-half, Stevie Chalmers passed up two opportunities and John Hughes was also culpable after being set up by the midfield craftsman. After the turnaround, Billy McNeill headed narrowly past the upright, Ritchie held on well to a shot low down at his left-hand post from Jimmy Johnstone and McBride put Chalmers in the clear with a neat knockdown, but his frontline partner carelessly lofted the ball over the crossbar. A goal just had to come.

A newspaper reporter described it this way, 'The vital goal was scored by Rangers' Danish right-back Kai Johansen twenty minutes before a relentless, at times ruthless, battle would have had to go into extra-time. It was a goal worthy of winning any trophy and its quality was matched only by its unexpectedness. Willie Johnston wriggled his way to the byeline on the left and when George McLean missed the ball a few yards out, it ran to Willie Henderson. The winger's shot was cleared off the line by Bobby

Murdoch out to Johansen, who let fly from twenty-five yards and the ball flew low and hard into the corner of the net. Thus are Cups sometimes won and in this instance the deed was done by a defensive member of the side whose forwards, compared with the opposition, had given little indication that they were capable of doing such damage by themselves.'

From Bobby Lennox's vantage point in the stand, he observed, 'I remember Celtic storming straight back at Rangers after that goal. If I recall correctly, Big Yogi ran down the left wing and pitched over a peach of a cross. In the busy penalty area, Joe McBride was first to react and thumped in a ferocious header. Billy Ritchie hadn't a clue where the ball was. It struck him on the shoulder, flew upwards, came down, ran across the top of the crossbar and, with what looked like half the Celtic team queuing up on the goal line to knock it in, suddenly veered in the wrong direction, as far as we were concerned, and flopped on the roof of the net. That just about summed up Celtic's luck in both of their matches against the Ibrox side.'

McBride completed the game limping on the left wing with John Hughes taking over his role in the centre of attack. In those unenlightened days before substitutes, managers were reluctant to render their line-up a man short and deployed an injured player to a role on the wing where they could at least be a pest to the opposition. McBride, without complaint, did as he was ordered, but, at the same time, also did so much damage to a pulled muscle that his season ended as soon as referee Tiny Wharton placed the whistle between his lips and blew for full-time. It had been a bad night all round for Celtic and Joe McBride.

Celtic were now three games - and four-and-a-half hours - away from winning their first championship since 1954 and Jock Stein was aware he would have to plot the way ahead without the services of his most resolute goalscorer. McBride was in the stand at Cappielow when Celtic took the first of the trio of hurdles against Morton on Saturday April 30 which followed swiftly on the disappointment of the Scottish Cup capitulation. The first of Stein's trophies at Celtic had been surrendered negligently against inferior opponents. However, the title was within the team's grasp and it was reckoned the most glittering prize the country had to offer would be more than acceptable as a fair consolation.

Bertie Auld said, 'No-one should mistake what losing the Scottish Cup to Rangers meant to Big Jock. Us players, too, of course. The win the previous year against Dunfermline was so important to this club and our fans. I've said that often enough. For me, it was the absolute foundation for everything that followed. You can be certain we had every intention of retaining that particular piece of silverware. We knew we were a better team than Rangers. In one hundred and eighty minutes of football against them at Hampden, I think they might have had two shots on target and they scored with one. Goodness only knows how many we had in the replay alone - double figures, at least. But the better team doesn't always win for a variety of reasons. Sometimes it's a fluke bounce of the ball, a lucky shot that could go anywhere, an individual error or a referee's decision. Fates decreed the Scottish Cup would be removed from our trophy cabinet and we didn't like that one bit.

'It was a learning curve, of course. Expectation levels among the fans had risen as the team's performances reached higher levels. However, in the space of just over a week, the players had to contend with the bitter disappointment of going out of Europe after being only half-an-hour or so from a place in the Cup-Winners' Cup Final and also losing the Scottish Cup. But we had to concentrate on the main prize, the First Division championship. I didn't always see eye to eye with our manager, but I have to say he was outstanding around that period. With the Big Man in our dressing room and in our corner, there was no chance of an individual being allowed to feel sorry for himself. And he knew just how to gee us up.

'He gathered the players around him before we got down to the nitty gritty of training at Barrowfield a day after the Cup Final loss. "Look," he said, "what trophy did we all want to win at the start of the season? The league title, right? Now we're three games away from our priority target. All we need to do is win the remaining three games and it's all ours. It doesn't matter what anyone else does. Forget what's happening up the road. If we win, we're the champions. And we all know we deserve that trophy. Our name is on it. Win it for yourselves, your families, your friends and every Celtic supporter. Win it for football's sake. We're the best team in Scotland. Now go and prove it." How could you fail to respond to that? How could we let anyone down? Suddenly, our chests were puffed up again.

'Big Jock could knock you down sometimes, but there were other occasions when he could lift you towards the clouds. Around that time of the defeats from Liverpool and Rangers and the subsequent bitterness of knowing we were the better team than both of them over the games, Big Jock showed a lot of character. He would have been as disappointed as the players, maybe even more so because he was such a perfectionist and a winner, but he stood up to be counted. I admired him for that. Maybe in the past, our heads might have gone down and stayed down, but he wasn't having any of that.'

Dame Fortune, though, continued to scowl in the direction of Stein and Celtic. John Hughes would have been the ideal replacement to lead the line in place of Joe McBride, but he, too, had taken a knock against Rangers and had to be ruled out. The Celtic boss thought long and hard about his line-up to face a Morton team desperately trying to remain in the top division. The Greenock side had lost their previous six games and realised another defeat would consign them to the old Second Division. They were prepared to fight to the end. Stein announced his team just before the kick-off and, remarkably, it contained ten of the names that would conquer Europe in Lisbon just over a year later. Charlie Gallagher wore the number eight shorts and, of course, he was replaced by Willie Wallace against Inter Milan in the Portuguese capital almost thirteen months later.

Tommy Gemmell recalled, 'Obviously, it was a massive game for us, but I was only too aware what the contest meant to Morton. I was told the players had been offered a helluva lot of money to stay in the top division. I knew their basic wage wasn't great and that would take a hit if they were relegated, so the players we faced that day at Cappielow were scrapping for their very livelihood. You could say it was a fair incentive for them to beat us.'

Celtic's lack of goals followed them to Greenock and Morton keeper Erik Sorensen wasn't unduly perturbed during a tentative opening period. And, in the thirty-first minute, Morton had the ideal opportunity to break the deadlock when the referee awarded them a penalty-kick while indicating Jimmy Johnstone had tugged Allan McGraw's jersey. En masse, the Celtic players protested and insisted the infringement had taken place at least a yard outside the box, but the match official stood firm and pointed to the spot. The sun smiled radiantly on a perfect afternoon on Inverclyde, but the disposition of the travelling supporters among the 18,000 crowd didn't quite match the natural elements as Flemming Neilsen placed the ball twelve yards from goal. Could it be possible that another Danish import would wreak havoc on Celtic for the second consecutive game? Neilsen strode forward purposefully while Ronnie Simpson did his best to second-guess his opponent. Cappielow was hushed as Neilsen's boot made contact with the ball and the serenity was shattered in an instant with the whoops of the Celtic fans as his attempt flew wildly over the crossbar.

A minute from the interval, Jimmy Johnstone scored his team's first goal in almost four-and-a-half games. It was no classic, but there wasn't a solitary complaint among the Celtic contingent present in Greenock as the outside-right reacted quicker than everyone else in a thickly-populated penalty area to strike a shot beyond Sorensen. It was tense and taut throughout a nerve-riddled second-half with both sets of players displaying an energy and robustness as they met the challenge that offered the possibility of the title to one team and certain relegation to the other. In the fading moments, Johnstone swung over a cross and his good friend Bobby Lennox headed the second and decisive goal. The league table showed Celtic and Rangers in joint top position on fifty-three points, but the Ibrox side had played one game more on thirty-three.

Dunfermline, who had lost 2-1 to the Ibrox side the previous Saturday, revisited Glasgow and Parkhead for the penultimate encounter on Wednesday May 4. Again, Celtic made life tough for themselves. Jock Stein had little option but to go with the same line-up that had carved out the victory against Morton. Joe McBride and John Hughes were again spectators in the stand, their powerful goal threat frustratingly removed with the finishing tape in sight. Over thirty thousand fans were at Parkhead in the hope of watching Celtic clinch their first title in twelve years. Rangers were playing Clyde at Ibrox on the same evening and transistor radios appeared to be compulsory items for most of the fans. Strong hearts were required in Glasgow that evening.

On the twenty-nine minute mark at Parkhead, Celtic fell a goal behind. Alex Edwards, the Fifers' tricky little outside-right, swung in a corner-kick that somehow eluded every swinging boot until it dropped nicely for Alex Ferguson, totally unmarked at the far post. He didn't quite connect sweetly, but his effort had enough oomph to elude the dive of the startled Ronnie Simpson and crawl over the line. It was an absolute gift for the Dunfermline striker. Jock Stein emerged from the dug-out, waved a clenched fist and growled at his players. Tommy Gemmell recollected, 'It was just your bad luck if you were playing on the wing next to Jock on the sidelines and he was giving it pelters. I haven't a clue how many times I was on the receiving end. It didn't matter if the place was packed, a complete sell-out, Big Jock always made himself heard. And he wasn't happy with our defending, I can tell you that. If the defence conceded a goal from a setplay, it normally meant we would be held back at Barrowfield the following day in training and Big Jock would go over and over how it was lost and what we had to do to make sure it didn't happen again.'

Bobby Lennox, within five minutes of Ferguson's goal, levelled with a brave header into the roof of the net after some nice interchanging between Jimmy Johnstone and Charlie Gallagher. Just before the hour mark, it was bedlam in Paradise when Johnstone snapped up a typical opportunistic effort. Lennox, with that short backswing that surprised most goalkeepers, caught out Eric Martin with a low drive from just outside the box. The goalie, who had been performing heroics, managed to parry the ball away, but the Celtic winger was onto it in a green flash and rammed it into the net. It remained that way until the final whistle when news filtered through from Govan that Rangers had eased to a 4-0 triumph over Clyde. That result was met with derision among the Celtic support as they danced and sang and cavorted with unrefined glee. They were convinced Celtic's trek through the labyrinths of failure in the championship were at an end.

One man remained to be convinced - Jock Stein.

He refused to allow his players to accept the invitation from the supporters to go out for a lap of honour. It was mathematically possible for Rangers to win the league on the old equation of goal average if Celtic lost by a certain margin in their last game against Motherwell at Fir Park. Jock Stein, a well-known gambler among the bookmaking fraternity in the West of Scotland, was taking no chances, his cards still firmly held to his chest. A well-meaning member of the Press extended his hand to the Celtic manager at the aftermatch conference. 'Congratulations, Jock,' said the newspaperman. Stein shot a withering glance in his direction. He could do sarcasm with the best of them. 'Oh, so you know Saturday's score, do you?' he snapped. 'Would you like to fill in my coupon, too?' The Pressman stepped back. Jock's mood lightened a little and he said, 'What happens if we lose 4-0? Let's celebrate when we know it's in the bag - and not before.'

It didn't prevent one national newspaper scribe from penning, 'Celtic are beyond reasonable doubt Scottish League champions again at last. After an interval of twelve years and, surprising though it may seem, only the fourth time in forty years, they virtually assured themselves of this most elusive honour by their victory over Dunfermline Athletic at Celtic Park.'

Bertie Auld recalled, 'It wasn't an act from the Boss. I've no idea what the odds would have been for us to lose by four goals to anyone, never mind Motherwell, but he absolutely insisted on his players remaining professional right to the very end. "You can do what you want after Saturday," he said, more or less telling us to refrain from cracking open a few bottles of champagne or even sneaking in a solitary can of beer. Big Jock's aversion to alcohol was well documented and he really never understood the drinking culture among players. "What good does that stuff do you?" he would ask over and over again. And the players knew when it was time to shut up.'

Emotions abounded with wondrous abandonment on a fantastically sunny afternoon at Fir Park on Saturday May 7 with the Celtic players taking a colourful curtain call as they celebrated their first championship success in twelve years; the long-term hurt swept into the dark recesses of history as the players enjoyed a lap of honour in front of gleefully celebrating followers, more than a few actually dancing on the roof of one of the stands. Billy McNeill and Bobby Murdoch lifted veteran goalkeeper Ronnie Simpson shoulder high; his incredible personal story almost as sensational as that of the club. The First Division title had been delivered with a late winning flourish. As the clock ticked down to its exorable conclusion on an extraordinary football season, Bobby Lennox, from almost underneath the crossbar, turned in a low right-wing cross from Jim Craig for the only goal of the game. The Scottish game's most coveted honour was heading for the east end of Glasgow with Celtic completing the marathon on fifty-seven points, two ahead of Rangers.

One national newspaper scribe reported, 'The final word of a lengthy campaign was written on Saturday with a timing as symmetrical as the signing of an armistice. For in the last minute of the last game of the last day of the season, Bobby Lennox scored the goal which beat Motherwell and made Celtic the Scottish League champions on points instead of by the much less satisfying margin of goal average. And, so, as Celtic became champions again after an interval of twelve years and for the twenty-first time in the club's history, they made sure of their first venture into the most prestigious of competitions which was inaugurated after their last success in the league.'

The article continued, 'There was never the slightest suggestion that Motherwell would score enough goals to deprive Celtic of their right. No-one would surely deny that Celtic, having suffered the disappointment of recent Cup defeats by Rangers and Liverpool, do not deserve to hold the leading position in Scottish football which has escaped all their efforts for an inordinately long time.'

Drama, the like of which had never been witnessed before in Paradise, awaited in the new season. Naturally, Joe McBride was eager to play his part.

CHAPTER FOUR

THE GREAT AMERICAN DREAM

"The pre-season tour of the States should never be underestimated in what it meant to Celtic."

- Bobby Lennox,

scorer of nineteen goals on the trip

It seemed that no sooner had Bobby Lennox's close-range drive nestled in the Motherwell net, than the Celtic players were packing their bags for the football trip of a lifetime. There were a few who questioned the wisdom of Jock Stein ushering his newly-crowned champions on an eleven-game one-month tour of the United States, Canada and Bermuda a mere four days after an exhausting and gruelling domestic and European campaign.

The dissenters should have known better.

Quite simply, Stein, with that uncommon commodity of common sense, reckoned he would find out a lot more about the depth of personality within his players on a prolonged trip as opposed to a scattering of pre-season games. Seventeen professionals were among the Celtic party who flew out from Abbotsinch Airport - now Glasgow International Airport - on the Friday morning of May 11 1966. Jim Craig remained at home for dental exams, a situation which left Stein doubting his commitment to the club, and young Frank Carron was brought in as his replacement. Ian Young and Jimmy Johnstone were involved, but had been given permission to return with two games still to play to attend their respective weddings.

It became a voyage of discovery and players have repeated over the years that it could very well have been the axis around which the Celtic success story revolved in the developing twelve months. As an exercise, it served as an extraordinary bonding factor among the individuals. The Parkhead side returned in the early hours of Wednesday June 12 with a record that showed eight wins, three draws and no defeats. A remarkable forty-seven goals had been racked up with the concession of only six. A foundation had been put in place for what lay ahead.

Bobby Lennox was the goalscoring star of the roadshow with nineteen strikes. He reflected, 'I have often stated that Celtic really gelled and came together months before we even thought about playing in Lisbon. I am talking about our American tour in 1966 and it was a masterstroke to take us away for four weeks. The players got to know one another even better than is possible when you are just turning up for training and, of course, playing on matchday.

'We all enjoyed the experience, but we also realised we were there to work. This was no holiday and Jock Stein, even after a full season, was still getting to know the squad of players he had inherited. We all wanted to impress him and I think I did well enough - I managed to score nineteen goals in eleven games!

'Okay, we did play a few select teams from Bermuda, New Jersey and St.Louis, but we also took on Spurs three times. The London side were a really top outfit at the time and they went on to win the FA Cup in 1967, beating Chelsea 2-1 in the Final. Of course, they had also won the European Cup-Winners' Cup in 1963 when they walloped Atletico Madrid 5-1 in Rotterdam. But I think they were a bit annoyed that they couldn't put one over on us. We beat them 1-0 and then 2-1 before we played them for a third time and they managed to get a 1-1 draw. These were important games for us. They were taking us to another level and it didn't do our confidence any harm, either.'

Tommy Gemmell agreed that it was not all fun and games on the trip. 'Big Jock became our social convener for a month and that drew us all together, but there was never any doubt who was the Boss. There was a line that was never crossed. I don't want to paint a picture of a control freak because that wouldn't be fair or accurate. But he let you know who made the final decision and would never be swayed.

'I pestered him on the trip to let me play up front in a game against one of the local sides. "If I can score all those goals as a left-back, gaffer, how many do you think I'll get if I play as a centre-forward?" It was all a laugh, of course. However, our first game was in Bermuda against the Hamilton Select and he cut me some slack. We won 10-1 and I scored two. I was completely eclipsed by Bobby Lennox, though, as he got four and my wee mate Bertie Auld claimed a hat-trick. Billy McNeill got the other and I recall their scorer was a Scot by the name of Jimmy Copland who used to play for Kilmarnock.'

Three nights later, Celtic took on the Bermuda YMCA and Lennox had to be content with a hat-trick in another one-way confrontation. Gemmell rattled in two and Joe McBride matched that in a 7-0 victory. Stein, though, was raging before the match when he was told Jimmy Johnstone, Ian Young and Frank Carron couldn't play because of sunburn. He gave the three of them a verbal dressing down and the manager remembered the incident a year later when Celtic were domiciled in Estoril before the biggest game in the club's history.

After two days' rest, Lennox, with praiseworthy consistency, fired in another treble in the 6-0 victory over New Jersey All-Stars at the Kearney Stadium and McBride added two with Bobby Murdoch joining in the net-bulging frolics. A reporter noted, 'It was all very easy, all very pleasant - even for the American fans, who were shown a brand of football entirely new to their eyes. Indeed, but for a mountain of a man, goalkeeper Gary Grantz, who looked as though his huge bulk would make him as agile as a sloth, the score would have been well into double figures. Grantz was astonishingly deceptive. He made an entire series of super saves and, although he was beaten with relentless monotony, he still ended up with the title of "Star of the All-Stars". Deservedly so, as well.'

Lennox couldn't stop scoring and, three days afterwards, got the only goal of the game to defeat Spurs in front of 20,000 fans at the Varsity Stadium in Toronto. The voracious little forward struck sixteen minutes from time and Jock Stein's dedication to winning - even friendlies far from home - was demonstrated when he put on Jimmy Johnstone for John Hughes in the seventieth minute. The White Hart Lane club's assistant boss Eddie Bailey, with manager Bill Nicholson remaining in England, was incensed at the substitution. He believed there had been a pre-match agreement that fresh players would only be introduced to replace an injured colleague.

Stein remained completely po-faced as he replied, 'Yogi had a knock and, in fact, shouldn't even have played in the first place.' Bailey was rendered speechless; no-one had noticed Celtic's giant winger in any distress during his hour-plus performance. In fact, Hughes was in the starting line-up for the next outing four days later against Hamilton Primo in Ontario. Bobby Lennox, as anticipated, took centre stage with a four-goal spree in an 11-0 walkover. Bobby Murdoch knocked in a hat-trick, Joe McBride, two, and Tommy Gemmell got others, but the individual who took the spotlight on this occasion was the unassuming quiet man of Parkhead, dependable sweeper John Clark. Lennox recalled, 'I scored four goals, but John got all the plaudits after that game because he, too, netted with the help of a penalty-kick. John didn't score an awful lot, so the players made a fuss of him afterwards.'

Two evenings later, Celtic played Italian opposition in Bologna who had finished the season as runners-up to Inter Milan in Serie A, only four points adrift after their thirty-four game campaign. The game was organised by the large Italian community in New Jersey and the occasion was marred by bottle-throwing from raging fans after star winger Giancarlo Merrone was sent off for persistent fouling in the sixty-eighth minute. It finished goalless accompanied by a cloud burst throughout the second-half and veered close to a roughhouse on occasion. Billy McNeill missed the next game after receiving stitches in a gash on his brow. The entire episode wasn't aided by the fact it had been played on a surface at the Roosevelt Stadium that was more suited for baseball.

It was on to St Louis next for the Scottish champions and a game on the Sunday evening against their All-Stars' line-up. It was played in suffocating temperatures of eighty-five degrees and Celtic weren't extended as they eased to a 6-1 win. There had been an agreement between the clubs that substitutes could be used at any stage. Joe McBride and Stevie Chalmers both scored in the opening two minutes and that was the signal for the home coach to begin putting on substitutes. He utilised his entire squad of eighteen throughout the ninety minutes. Nevertheless, McBride added another and Bobby Lennox, inevitably, Bertie Auld and John Hughes brought the total to six.

Lennox remembered, 'San Francisco was next and again Spurs were the opposition. They were determined to get revenge for losing in Toronto, but we triumphed again, this time 2-1 and I got the winner. Actually, I was beginning to feel a wee bit sorry for the Spurs lads by this time. Whenever we were in town the Scottish and Irish exiles would abandon the London team and start following us everywhere.'

Bertie Auld thumped Celtic into the lead in the twenty-fifth minute in the Kezar Stadium, but the opposition were awarded a penalty-kick within sixty seconds. Dave Mackay, the club's rugged Scottish midfielder, blasted the ball goalwards and was stunned to see Ronnie Simpson dive full-length to push his effort away. Unfortunately, Mackay reacted quicker than the defenders and he managed to squeeze the rebound over the goal-line. Lennox lashed in the clincher just before the hour mark.

There was a worry, though, for Jock Stein when Auld was carried off with an ankle injury. By this stage of the tour, John Cushley and Frank Carron were also sidelined with similar knocks. Jimmy Johnstone and Ian Young were now in a position where the club might have requested they gave serious thought to cancelling their nuptials! Stein was swiftly running out of fit players. Johnstone, though, was still available for selection for the next game on June 4 and Spurs were given a third opportunity to prevent a Celtic victory. This time they managed a 1-1 draw, but Johnstone was involved in an incredible melee with only five minutes to go following the London side's equaliser.

Bobby Lennox had zipped his eighteenth goal behind Northern Ireland keeper Pat Jennings in the nineteenth minute before his best pal Jinky saw red at the opposition's equaliser. Terry Venables appeared to push Bobby Murdoch in the back as he took possession before belting the ball past Ronnie Simpson. The wee winger was raging and delivered a stream of verbals at local referee John Webber. Obviously, some of Jinky's observations hit a raw nerve and the match official immediately pointed to the dressing room. The Celtic star continued to remonstrate with the American and Dave Mackay, Johnstone's international team-mate, intervened on his behalf. Jock Stein, too, appeared on the scene. After much gesticulating and arm-waving, Webber backed down and, remarkably, Jinky remained on the pitch until full-time. Afterwards, he took his leave and flew home to an altogether more convivial situation by marrying fiancée Agnes the following Saturday.

Celtic returned to San Francisco on June 8 to take on Bayern Munich only four days after a side consisting of legendary players such as Franz Beckenbauer, Gerd Muller and Sepp Maier had won the German Cup. It ended 2-2, but the game was held up for seven minutes after another astonishing incident. Tommy Gemmell recalled, 'They had a full-back by the name of Adolph Kuntswald and he must have had some sort of death wish. He had been kicking Stevie Chalmers for most of the game and I could see our boy was getting a little fed up with the treatment. Just for good measure, the Bayern player delivered a punch straight to Stevie's jaw. Someone had just lit the touch paper; Stevie, a fairly mild-mannered bloke, just lost the plot.

'It was like something out of the Keystone Kops as our player chased the German around the pitch. Herr Kuntswald looked horrified when he realised he had overstepped the mark just a bit. Before he could take to his heels, Stevie smacked him one in the eye, but obviously wasn't quite content with that. He sought more retribution and the 12,000 fans were given some extra entertainment for their four dollars. That was amusing enough, but at one stage a fan raced onto the pitch to try to pull Stevie off the Bayern player so he could get a couple of punches in himself! Thankfully, peace was restored and the game came to a conclusion without any more fisticuffs.'

Celtic, in fact, had to come back from two goals down to salvage a draw at the Kezar Stadium. Rainer Olhauser scored the opener with a blistering shot behind John Fallon in the twenty-second minute and he added a second in the sixty-seventh minute. Back came Celtic, though, with their never-say-die spirit and Bobby Lennox pulled one back in the seventy-fifth minute and Joe McBride levelled eight minutes from time.

Jock Stein's men were the walking wounded for their final game of the tour against Mexican champions Atlas at the Los Angeles Memorial Colliseum on a Sunday evening on June 12. Celtic were so strapped for players that trainer Neil Mochan, aged thirty-nine, who last played for Raith Rovers in 1964, was told he might have to get stripped. John Fallon was in goal and

Ronnie Simpson was the team's only substitute. Joe McBride played with one thigh heavily strapped and Willie O'Neill was clearly half-fit. Into the bargain, there were the conditions of 80 degrees heat.

Remarkably, Celtic, against all odds, won 1-0 when Tommy Gemmell, ignoring the oven-like heat, galloped down the right wing and flashed over a low cross which was expertly turned into the net by Charlie Gallagher with only two minutes remaining. Bobby Lennox remembered, 'Our opponents were obviously a bit more used to those sort of temperatures and I recall they were a good side. John Fallon made a handful of decent saves, but we eventually wore them down. We were so happy to return home undefeated.

'The pre-season tour of the States should never be underestimated in what it meant to the club. There was a real sense of camaraderie among the players and I still believe that's what laid the foundation to make 1967 such a memorable year.'

CHAPTER FIVE
AUGUST
AND SO IT BEGINS

*"Jock liked to move his forwards around to confuse the opposition.
I found myself playing at outside-right every now and again."*

- John Hughes,
Celtic's seventh-highest goalscorer in history with 189 goals.

Undeniably the most significant season in the monumental history of
Celtic Football Club kicked off in earnest in the nation's capital city when
Jock Stein's men were required to initiate the defence of their League Cup
trophy against Hearts at Tynecastle on Saturday August 13 1966.

The previous week, the newly-crowned Scottish champions had
annihilated Manchester United 4-1 in an extremely competitive challenge
game which was played throughout in welcoming sunshine, possibly not
enjoyed as much by the exposed participants on the field of play as the
short-sleeved audience on the terracings. A week later, demonstrating the
need for adaptability in their chosen sport, the players of Celtic and Hearts
were asked to perform on a surface which was swiftly transformed into a
something resembling a swamp as heavy rain, driven by a near-gale force
wind, incessantly lashed down from the slate-grey skies over Edinburgh.

Interestingly, Hearts decided to field a player at centre-forward who had
resolutely refused to sign a new deal. His name? Willie Wallace. The stocky
and versatile frontman had turned down several attempts to persuade him
to agree terms to extend his contract at the club. Despite the dispute, the

Edinburgh outfit retained his registration and, back in the days before anyone had heard of a Belgian footballer by the name of Jean-Marc Bosman, there was little the player could do about it. He was Hearts' property. Wallace took his place in attack, but it was his opposing number, Joe McBride, who commandeered the headlines.

Diligently throughout the summer months, McBride had worked on his fitness following the frustration of the previous campaign when he had been forced to miss the last three games in the run-in to the club's first title success in twelve years. Jock Stein's initial buy for the club completed the campaign with the impressive total of forty-three goals, but he admitted he was disappointed he didn't get the opportunity to reach the half-century.

Bertie Auld recalled, 'Most strikers would be happy with the return of twenty goals in a season, but Joe was a different breed. When he realised fifty goals was within range, he made up his mind to go for it. Seven goals in our remaining three games against Morton, Dunfermline and Motherwell wouldn't have been outwith the bounds of possibility for Joe. Sadly, he never got that opportunity, but I also realised he was determined to hit the ground running in the new term. Every day in training, he told me he was feeling good and he was ready to go. He came out the blocks at full pelt.'

McBride's first competitive goal of the season arrived in the eighteenth minute via the penalty spot after Bobby Lennox had hared onto a long ball from Billy McNeill and was in the act of shooting when he was crudely dumped to the sodden turf following a rash challenge from Hearts skipper Alan Anderson. McBride placed the ball on the spot, took a couple of paces back, measured his stride running forward and blitzed a ferocious drive into the net with keeper Jim Cruickshank left without an earthly.

After the long-awaited change of rules, each team were now allowed a substitute in season 1966/67 and Charlie Gallagher was the first to be bestowed the 'honour' at Celtic. The clever midfielder didn't get off the bench, although Jimmy Johnstone took a knock in the first minute following a robust tackle from left-back Davie Holt. Jock Stein stuck with his original formation and was rewarded when the outside-right set up the second goal in the eighty-eighth minute with a low cross that was tucked away without ceremony by McBride.

Four days later, McBride smashed in a hat-trick, including a spot-kick, as Clyde were taken apart 6-0 in the east end of Glasgow. Bobby Lennox, with two, and Stevie Chalmers completed the rout against a Shawfield side that had appointed Davie White as their manager in March that year when John Prentice left to take over the Scotland international team. At thirty-three years of age, he was the youngest team boss in the UK and earned deserved plaudits when he guided the club to third spot in the league by the end of that campaign. Later in his career, he would come face to face with Jock Stein in the heat of Old Firm battles.

McBride's goalscoring run continued unabated in the next League Cup outing when he thrashed four beyond St Mirren keeper Jim Thorburn as Celtic romped their way to an enthralling 8-2 win. Bobby Lennox added two more and there were singles from Bertie Auld and Stevie Chalmers as the Parkhead men continued to coast through their section towards the knock-out stages of the tournament. Billy McNeill recalled that game for one very good reason. 'Big Jock was raging when we got back to the dressing room,' he said. 'We had just scored eight goals and had been applauded off the pitch by a crowd of over 30,000, but our manager was upset that we had conceded two late goals. He made the point our concentration had dipped a little during the second-half. To be fair, we were seven goals ahead at the time!

'There were only twelve minutes left to play when one of their players, a young forward by the name of Frank Treacy, scored. He plonked another behind Faither, Ronnie Simpson, about four minutes later. I looked over at the dug-out and, sure enough, there was Big Jock waving his arms about, clearly not happy with his defence. Stevie got our eighth in the closing moments, but it wasn't enough to deflect the ire of our manager. Once again, he made it abundantly clear that we were there to do a job for every minute of the ninety. Fair enough. However, I can't think of too many teams who would score eight goals and still get a rollicking off their boss!'

The next game was due on Wednesday August 23 - the little matter of a Glasgow Cup-tie against Rangers at Ibrox. The pedigree of the competition meant little; this was a showdown between the two juggernauts of the Scottish game and presented Jock Stein with an early opportunity for reprisal following the Scottish Cup Final disappointment in late April.

It was not a chance he was ever remotely likely to overlook. The Ibrox side may have won the silverware, but no-one among the club's hierarchy was being fooled; it was very much a case of Celtic losing the Scottish Cup rather than Rangers winning it. The superiority of their Glasgow neighbours had been obvious in the league and their manager, Scot Symon, had been given a blank chequebook during the summer.

He spent £100,000 - a serious amount of money in the sixties - on two players he believed would strengthen his team. He paid £50,000 to Aberdeen for Davie Smith, an elegant ball-playing left-half. This transfer might have surprised Jock Stein. Around this period, he had made tentative enquires about one of the Pittodrie side's emerging youngsters, a skilful inside-right by the name of Jimmy Smith, a Glaswegian with a known affection for a team which performed in the east end of the city. The Celtic manager was assured by his opposite number at Aberdeen, Eddie Turnbull, the Dons would not sell any of their first team squad to either member of the Old Firm. A month or so later, Davie Smith pitched up in Govan. Symon also liked the look of yet another Smith - none of them related - Alex, of Dunfermline. He was a clever, old-fashioned inside-forward who was known to nick a goal or two. He also cost £50,000. So, the Rangers team which faced Celtic in the Glasgow Cup-tie in August at Ibrox had been enhanced from the one that had beaten them in April at Hampden.

Jock Stein plotted the downfall with as much care to meticulous detail as he would a European tie. Bertie Auld recalled, 'Big Jock was only too aware of the fuss that had been made of Kai Johansen after his Cup Final goal against us. The gaffer believed the Rangers right-back would be enticed to play further forward up the pitch in the hope of getting another goal and the adulation that would go with it. Remember, Johansen had been slaughtered by Big Yogi in the January game when we won 5-1 at Parkhead. He had been heavily criticised for not being able to cope with our outside-left when Yogi ran amok in the second-half. But he was given all the credit for his Scottish Cup winner and it was easy to see he might just fancy some more of that. Big Jock laid his plans accordingly.'

Tommy Gemmell also remembered the instructions from the Celtic boss prior to kick-off. 'I thought I was hearing things. Big Jock was actually telling wee Bobby Lennox to stay up the pitch. Normally, he would tell every player to be mindful of their defensive duties. Even Wee Jinky was told to get back and cover. Bertie still tells people he could have played at least another five years at Celtic if he hadn't had to spend so much time running around and covering behind me! No truth in that, of course. But Big Jock was quite clear before this match. Bobby Lennox was given a free reign and was practically ordered not to come into our half. Naturally, Wee Bobby was more than delighted to do as the Boss ordered.'

Celtic cantered to a landslide 4-0 triumph at the home of their bitterest rivals and Bobby Lennox helped himself to an exceptional hat-trick while Billy McNeill played the captain's part and got the opening goal with a shot beyond goalkeeper Billy Ritchie. McNeill's effort had historians researching furiously to discover when he had last scored a goal for the club with any part of his anatomy other than his head.

The legendary captain recalled, 'Aye, it was a bit of rarity. In actual fact, I was running up the field to take my usual position in readiness for a header after we had been awarded a free-kick about thirty yards out. However, Wee Bertie decided to take a quick one and slipped the ball short to Charlie Gallagher. Charlie skipped past a challenge, saw me on the left out of the corner of his eye and slid a pass in front of me. It was perfect for my left peg and I first-timed it towards goal. Ronnie McKinnon, the Rangers centre-half, raced out to block the shot, but I followed up with the rebound and just hammered an angled drive towards goal. Their keeper was at his near post and looked bemused as the ball zipped through his legs into the net. Maybe not one of my best, but I was still happy to claim it. It came inside ten minutes and set us up nicely for the rest of the evening.'

Auld added, 'I had kept it in mind what Big Jock had said and, as soon as we were awarded the free-kick, I glanced to see if Johansen was in his right-back berth. He had been lured infield leaving a lot of space on their left wing. I quickly passed it to Charlie and he was clever enough to skip away from Greig and, suddenly, everything opened up for Caesar. With Johansen out of position, McKinnon had to race out of central defence and, although he did well to get a foot to the initial shot, our skipper kept going and got his reward. It was a well-executed goal, but it was all down to the forward thinking of our manager. He had read the situation perfectly. Neither Rangers nor Johansen twigged all night as we picked them off down the left.'

The first of Bobby Lennox's goals was intoxicating, a spectacular finish that would have graced a World Cup Final. Many years later, I asked Bobby to name some of his favourite goals. Considering he netted 273 in 571 games, I reckoned he might be spoiled for choice. But, sure enough, that effort at Ibrox was high up in his ratings. He saw it this way, 'One that means something to me came against Rangers in a Glasgow Cup-tie in 1966. The tournament might not have been the most prestigious, but that didn't matter and we were all aching to get at our old rivals to make up for our Scottish Cup defeat against them.

'I was fortunate enough to score three in an emphatic, one-sided triumph. The one I can recall vividly was our second goal - my first ever against the Ibrox side. That would have been memorable enough, but I am glad to say it was a real belter. I got the ball about thirty-five yards out on the old inside-right position. I just took off, got away from John Greig and hit a left-foot effort from the edge of the box. Billy Ritchie had the good grace not to bother even going for the ball as it rattled high into the roof of the net. That was a sweet goal.'

And the man known as 'Buzz Bomb', the original fox in the box, claimed two more in the second-half. As Jock Stein had prophesied, Johansen was elsewhere, distracted, no doubt, by the possibility of bright lights and large headlines. Charlie Gallagher set up Celtic's third with a piercing long pass which created a problem for Greig. He lost the flight of the ball and, with no defensive cover from either Johansen or McKinnon, Lennox swooped to take control and, with the utmost impudence, calmly flicked the ball away from Ritchie with the outside of his boot. His trio was completed when he came in from the left, unhindered by the Danish right-back who had been drawn once again to the ball elsewhere. Auld, with that cunning, quick brain, slid a delightful pass wide to Lennox, who took a touch, picked up momentum, cut inside and smashed a drive low past the keeper at his right-hand post. A crowd of 76,456 was in place to watch the destruction of the Scottish Cup winners by the Scottish League champions. Twenty-four days later at Parkhead, Rangers would have that old familiar sinking feeling in the first league meeting of the rivals of the season.

Before that, though, it was back to League Cup business for Celtic when, only four days after the Govan sojourn, Hearts arrived in Glasgow. Joe McBride, once again, was immense and his deadly finishing was the difference between two teams willing to slug it out in a tense encounter. It was scoreless at the interval before McBride moved up a gear, scored two, set up another and Celtic completed the tie as reasonably comfortable 3-0 winners. Bobby Lennox, after his laudable exertions at Ibrox, was given a rest by Jock Stein who brought in John Hughes for his first competitive outing of the campaign.

Yogi had fallen foul of his manager by delaying signing a new contract with the club during the summer. 'Of course, it was all about money,' admitted the seventh-highest goalscorer in the club's history. 'It was ALWAYS all about money. I wanted to stay at Celtic and Big Jock and everyone else knew it. I was a Celtic player and, at the same time, a Celtic fan. I think the club played on that loyalty and passion sometimes. I reckon they believed a player would sign any contract that was offered to them. That summer, though, I held out for what I thought I was worth. A compromise was reached, thank goodness, but I actually didn't sign on the dotted line until a couple of hours before our friendly against Manchester United. I wanted to play in that one, but Big Jock had other ideas and I got a seat in the stand.'

And Hughes remained persona non grata with the Celtic boss for the opening three League Cup-ties and the Glasgow Cup set-to with Rangers. 'It was a relief to get the nod to play against Hearts,' recalled Hughes. 'It can be more than just a little frustrating when you train all week and you get yourself into peak condition and then be told you won't be required. So, when I realised I was playing in that one I was ready to go.'

Hughes was equally adept while leading the line or playing wide on the left and he was given the touchline role against the Edinburgh team. The first-half came and went with little to note apart from a dreadful miss by a Hearts forward. Willie Wallace would do a lot better when he performed on the same pitch later in the year. Nine minutes into the second-half, Hughes, not known for his tackling prowess, took the ball off Roy Barry, an uncompromising defender, and shifted at commendable pace down the wing. He sent an inviting low pass into the tracks of McBride who shot strongly past Jim Cruickshank. With the barrier broken, the Hearts resistance disintegrated to rubble and Stevie Chalmers flashed in the second after a good strong surge on the right flank by McBride. It was all over with seventeen minutes still to go when the flustered Barry handled in the box and McBride gleefully battered the penalty-kick award past Cruickshank.

Stein shuffled the pack again for the midweek visit to Shawfield for the game against Clyde and Lennox returned in place of Hughes. Yogi recalled, 'Back then, when Big Jock said he was about to freshen up the team, it normally meant he was about to change the attack. He rarely touched the defence, that was almost sacrosanct. I suppose, being a centre-half during his playing days, he understood the merits of a solid and reliable back-line where everyone knew each other's styles, strengths and even weaknesses. Faither always made the point he enjoyed playing behind Caesar because he knew exactly how our skipper would deal with high balls into the box. It was rare for our keeper to venture too far from his line such was the commanding aerial ability of our centre-half. It was different up front, though. Jock liked to move his forwards around to keep the opposition guessing and I even found myself playing at outside-right every now and again.'

Joe McBride went into the tie with Clyde with eleven goals from four League Cup outings and it didn't take him too long in hoisting that remarkable total to thirteen before half-time. The scourge of Scottish custodians got the opener in typical opportunistic fashion in the sixteenth minute. However, with a crowd of 18,000 watching from the ramshackle 'stadium', Joe Gilroy, a slick-moving striker, momentarily halted the singing from the visiting fans with an equaliser fashioned out of thin air. McBride replied within two minutes with another ferocious spot-kick and Tommy Gemmell made certain the points were heading out of Rutherglen and across to the east end of Glasgow with a powerful long-range drive that zipped beyond veteran keeper Tommy McCulloch.

The flamboyant left-back recalled, 'Joe McBride was unstoppable at that point. People were saying he was boosting his tally with penalty-kicks and the award against Clyde was his fifth in as many League Cup-ties. Just in case anyone is wondering, Celtic did not have a lot of followers among the refereeing community back then. Far from it. But the reason we received so many spot-kicks was quite simple; we were practically playing all our football in the opposition's half. Big Jock demanded we were on the front foot all the time. I can look at today's defenders and see them pass the ball square inside or even backwards. Our manager would have gone crazy if I had done that. He hammered it home that my first touch was to go forward. If you watch old footage on videos or DVDs, you'll see this to be the case. Same with whoever was playing at right-back, Ian Young or Jim Craig. We were urged to always be on the offensive.

'The manager didn't complicate the game. He would say, "Look, if you pass it inside, you're giving them time to filter back and get into position. You give the ball to Big Billy or John Clark and you're passing the buck. Take responsibility at all times. The ball's at your feet, so do something positive with it. Get down that line, play it foward and inside to Bertie and then go and look for the return. Keep their players turning, make sure they are always running back towards their goal and not going forward towards ours. If you can see the numbers on the backs of their jerseys, then you're doing your job. That's the way to win games. And that's why you're at Celtic; to win games, score goals and entertain the man on the terracing. Football without fans is nothing." It was a phrase he often used.'

History was made in the final League Cup group match when Willie O'Neill became the first substitute to make an appearance for Celtic when he came on in the sixty-fifth minute for Jimmy Johnstone against St Mirren at Love Street. Gemmell laughed, 'Wee Jinky had a clash of heads with a Paisley defender, but, after a spot of treatment, remained on the pitch. I was upfield for a corner-kick when the Wee Man said to me, "Tam, I'm feeling a bit groggy. Maybe I've got one of those concussion things." I felt like asking him, "How would you know, Jinky?", but I refrained. In truth, though, Jinky was brave beyond belief and it would take a lot for him to admit defeat. Eventually, he had to be helped to the touchline and on came Willie O'Neill for his landmark appearance.

'Willie was an out-and-out left-footed defender and rarely ventured into the other team's territory. When Jinky went off, I wondered where Big Jock would place him in the team. Willie trotted over to me and said, "I'm playing left-back, Tam." What he said next surprised me somewhat. "The Big Man wants you to play outside-right!" I knew he wasn't joking. Willie had a dry sense of humour, but I realised he was deadly serious. Not a lot of people will know this, but I actually started my career as a right-winger with my Junior club Coltness United. So, it wasn't exactly knew to me, but, obviously, I had never played in that position in senior football.

'There were still twenty-five minutes to go and we were winning only 1-0 with a Bobby Murdoch goal about ten minutes after the interval. So, there was still much work to be done. It ended 1-0 and Jim Thorburn became the first keeper to shut out Joe McBride in the League Cup. Not bad when you consider he had conceded eight - and four to Joe - only a fortnight earlier.'

CHAPTER SIX
SEPTEMBER
THE FIRST STEP TO LISBON

"When you queried something, Jock would wave you away with that big left hand of his. 'Oh, just do as you're told,' he would say."

- Jim Craig

Scotland's footballing rulers, applying the identical reasoned judgement as that of General George Armstrong Custer at the Battle of the Little Bighorn, decreed that champions Celtic should kick off the new 1966/67 league season with the opening game against Clyde at Shawfield.

So, thanks to the muddled thinking of the decision-makers at Park Gardens, where common sense was a distinct rarity, Jock Stein's triumphant side were denied the opportunity of an afternoon of colourful celebration, a gala event for their loyal supporters following a twelve-year odyssey of First Division suffering and torment. There would be no opening-day acclaim at a sell-out 60,000 capacity arena with the fans eager to pay their rapturous respects to their heroes. The cherished league flag would remain unfurled and in mothballs for another day. Instead, the club were told they would begin the defence of their newly-won title with a confrontation against a collection of keen part-timers at a rusty, rundown ground that doubled as a dog track.

So much for pomp and ceremony.

When the action got underway, however, there was no mistaking the gritty combination of enthusiasm, passion, verve and zest displayed by the Celtic players. It was obvious they were in the collective mood to pour every ounce of energy into the creation of something wonderful. They were two goals ahead inside twenty minutes and didn't ease up throughout another lop-sided skirmish. The opening goal came in the tenth minute when Joe McBride, displaying his range of attacking skills, turned provider when he drew John Wright from his goal and passed neatly inside for Stevie Chalmers to sweep the ball into the inviting net. It was Celtic's tenth goal in three games against gallant opposition in the space of only twenty-four days following the League Cup romps.

Eight minutes later, McBride added another; a vicious effort from a cross from John Hughes following a good run down the left flank from the tantalising winger which exposed the Clyde rearguard. Surprisingly, the supporters had to wait until the seventy-fifth minute before they witnessed the third goal. Chalmers, demonstrating the fact he had started his career as a winger, got wide before hurling in a hanging cross and Hughes, who always insisted he wasn't particularly good in the air, got up superbly to launch an unsaveable header beyond Wright. In between the second and third goals, Celtic had struck the woodwork three times, had two efforts scrambled off the line and over-worked goalie Wright made a handful of decent stops. Everything had gone according to plan, but Bertie Auld had reason to feel a trifle tentative as the referee prepared to bring the contest to a halt. I co-authored the legendary player's autobiography, 'A Bhoy Called Bertie', and here's his memory from that game.

'So, there I am, pinned against the dressing room wall with Big Jock's massive left hand around my throat and he is threatening to wallop me with his right. If he was trying to get some sort of message across, it was working, take my word for it.

'We had just come off the pitch after beating Clyde 3-0 at Shawfield and I knew our manager wasn't greatly enamoured with some of my antics. My sin? I sat on the ball three times during the game. Okay, it's a highly unusual 'tactic' when you are hoping to tempt a team into your own half. Clyde, though, refused to budge that afternoon. We were three goals ahead and you might expect them to open up and have a go at grabbing some sort of salvation. Not that day. The Clyde players seemed wary of even crossing the halfway line. They appeared to be content to keep the scoreline as it was.

'I chased back to the eighteen-yard line to collect a throw-out from Ronnie Simpson. I looked up and, sure enough, there were the Clyde players refusing to come out of their own half. Quick as a flash, I decided to sit on the ball, hoping to spur at least a couple of their players into action. Nope, they weren't buying it. I got up, rolled the ball back to Faither and asked him to return it. He duly did and I sat on the ball again. Still nothing stirred from our opponents. I staged an action replay immediately and parked my backside on the ball for a third time. Still, Clyde didn't want to know.

'I looked around the Shawfield Stadium and the Celtic fans were cheering and applauding. They loved this piece of showmanship, but I wasn't doing it to belittle our rivals. Genuinely, I wanted them to make a game of it and they just didn't want to know. I glanced over at our dug-out and that was when I saw Big Jock in full ranting mode. Not a pretty sight. Now whoever designed the dug-outs at Shawfield would never win any award for services to architecture.

'For a start, you had to take a step down to get into them and that left you getting a worm's-eye view of the action. All you could see were the ankles flying past and there is no way you could actually witness the game unfolding. It was the worst view in the house. But there was Big Jock, with all his bulk, trying desperately to clamber out of that small, confined space. There was a slab of concrete across the top of the dug-out that acted as a roof. Jock slammed his head off it - not once, not twice, but three times - as he attempted to climb his way onto the track.

'He was furious and I thought, "You're for the high jump here, Bertie. Let's hope he calms down at full-time." I could always hope. There wasn't a chance of that happening. Once Big Jock went up like Vesuvius it took an awful long time for him to come back to earth. Maybe a week or two!

'When the final whistle blew, I took a gulp and headed for the away team's dressing room. I wondered if there was any chance I could get a shower, get changed and get on the coach before Jock emerged. I prayed for someone to stop him and have a chat before he could get into the dressing room. Headbutting a speeding train would be preferable to incurring the wrath of Jock. I knew I was in for an ear-bashing, but I didn't anticipate what happened next.

'Jock, with that heavy limp from the injury that ended his career, stormed in behind me as fast as he could. Now, the pegs in the changing area at Shawfield must have been put up by some fairly tall joiner. They were so high up the wall we used to have to put Wee Jinky on our shoulders when he was hanging up his gear!

'Big Jock must have thought it would be a good idea to hang yours truly on one of those pegs that afternoon. He grabbed me with that massive mitt of his and lifted me off the floor. "Put me down, boss," I squeaked, as his clenched right fist looked a wee bit too close to my nose for comfort. "Don't ever treat a fellow-professional in that manner," he growled. My feet were dangling by this stage as I attempted to plead my case. Jock wasn't interested. "Do that once more and you'll never play for this team again as long as I am the manager." Thankfully, after a while, he released his grip and I slumped to the floor.

'Then he turned to Faither, who thought he was going to get away with his part in my impromptu 'tactics' of trying to entice our opponents to cross the halfway line. "The same goes for you," said Jock. "You encouraged him." At least, our veteran goalkeeper was spared being suspended by the throat for a minute or two.'

Following his 'tete-a-tete' with Auld, Stein met the Press to sum up the contest. 'I was delighted with the team and the way we played,' he said. 'What pleased me most was the way we controlled the game. That's what I want to see because it pleases me more than individual brilliance. We've got a lot of tough games coming up and that's the standard I'm looking for.'

It was just a pity a mere 16,500 could pack into ramshackle Shawfield to witness the action. Joe McBride, incidentally, had scored a hat-trick three evenings earlier as the Scottish League overwhelmed their Irish counterparts 6-0. Bobby Lennox claimed two and Tommy Gemmell, Bobby Murdoch and John Clark also represented the Select. The inter-league meetings were abandoned due to lack of public interest in 1980. The Scots played the Irish on sixty-two occasions and were victorious on fifty-six of the meetings. The fans eventually grew tired of the lack of competition in these fixtures.

One encounter that would have certainly packed them in at Parkhead was the possibility of world-renowned Brazilian side Santos, with the acclaimed Pele in their line-up, performing in the east end of Glasgow on October 12. Santos were the footballing equivalent of basketball's Harlem Globetrotters as a massive draw wherever they played. The news spread quickly among excited fans who were hoping for a glimpse of the player who was rated the most expert exponent of a football on the planet; the incomparable Pele. One observer likened a defender attempting to contain the South American genius as 'trying to capture a shaft of light in a matchbox'. As ever, there had to be a snag; the Brazilians were demanding £50,000 in appearance money and expenses. Celtic chairman Robert Kelly politely declined.

Next up for Celtic in the harrowing early-season schedule, with the club's first-ever performance in the European Cup against Zurich only a fortnight away, was an intriguing meeting with Dunfermline in the League Cup quarter-finals with the first game at Parkhead on Wednesday September 14. A crowd of 36,000 were in for a soccer treat as the players strutted their stuff throughout a first-half of an exceptionally well-drilled exhibition. Even the demanding Jock Stein couldn't have asked for any more from his players during a forty-five minute display of near-perfection. Celtic were 5-1 ahead at the interval and heading for a complete wipe-out of the Fifers, rendering a second leg redundant. However, the manager would have words after a second-half dip that saw the opposition, almost on the floor in the first period, score twice with the final scoreline revealing a 6-3 triumph for the trophy holders.

For most of the evening, though, Celtic's football was simply breathtaking, an absolute joy to witness. Five goals thundered behind the powerless Davie Anderson, Dunfermline's up-and-coming prospect, in twenty-three flawless minutes from the home side as they rendered the opposition impotent in their feeble attempts to stem the merciless tide that flowed relentlessly towards their nineteen-year-old goalkeeper. He was picking the ball out of his net after only thirty seconds following a trademark soaring header from Billy McNeill following Jimmy Johnstone's right-wing corner-kick. Anderson and his defensive colleagues hardly had time to recover before John Hughes clubbed in a long-range second in the fourth minute. The groggy Fifers, gasping for breath, were three goals adrift seven minutes afterwards when Bertie Auld scored the most spectacular counter of the evening. As ever, Bertie has a story to tell.

'The fans must have wondered about my celebration that night. I have to say, in all humility, it wasn't a bad goal. As I remember it, John Clark rolled the ball into my tracks around the halfway line and I was forced to veer to my right. Everyone knew my left foot was my stronger and I used to drive Big Jock potty by insisting, "Why do I need to kick the ball with my right when I've got a left as good as this? It does the work of two feet!" On this occasion, though, there wasn't any room to manoeuvre the ball back onto my left foot, so there was nothing else for it but to have a belt at it with my so-called standing foot from about thirty yards.

'The ball just took off like a rocket. I was as amazed as anyone when it arrowed high into the top left-hand corner of the keeper's net. He made it look even more special with a fabulous, acrobatic leap across his line as he tried to paw it away. Some hope! That was a goal as soon as it left my boot. I raced over to the Boss in the dug-out and waved my right leg at him. There are some fairly crazy goal celebrations around these days, but that one has got to be up with the daftest. At least, Big Jock got the message and permitted himself a smile. Mind you, the fact we were now three goals up after eleven minutes might have had something to do with it, too.'

There was brief respite for the visitors, though, when Alex Ferguson pulled one back with a header, but normal service was restored when Joe McBride rattled in a penalty-kick in the twentieth minute after Jim McLean had handled in the box. Three minutes later, young Anderson was helpless when Johnstone sneaked in an angled drive between the rookie keeper and his near post. It had been forty-five minutes of sheer splendour which was lapped up by the fans, myself included. What did the second-half hold in store after such a persuasive presentation from the men in green?

Apart from another fine strike from Auld - this time with his left foot - Celtic never touched the heights of the opening period. To be fair, Dunfermline, no doubt with the words of a furious manager Willie Cunningham ringing in their ears, showed a determination hitherto undetected in the first-half of this particular visit to the east end of Glasgow. They stuck another two beyond Ronnie Simpson to close the gap, but no-one at Parkhead that evening believed a dramatic fightback would be on the cards in the second leg, due at East End Park the following midweek.

Celtic had an important home meeting with Rangers in between the League Cup-ties and Jock Stein displayed Nostradamus-like qualities when he looked ahead to the visit of the Ibrox side. 'It would be ideal to get off to the same sort of start that we enjoyed against Dunfermline,' he said. 'But you can never budget for these things in football.'

Inside four minutes, Celtic were leading 2-0 and the game was practically over. It was one of the most remarkable commencements in an Old Firm duel anyone could remember. Rangers had been humbled in Govan during the Glasgow Cup-tie the previous month and had made noises of retribution in the league. They didn't even get out of the starting blocks. The occasion had barely got into motion when John Hughes sent Bobby Lennox scurrying into a dangerous area. Lennox, who helped himself to a hat-trick at Ibrox, became goalmaker on this occasion, flashing low ball across the penalty area. Joe McBride, unmarked smack in front of goal, swung a boot at the ball and connected with nothing more menacing than fresh air. Bertie Auld, however, was following up behind his good personal friend and he thumped a first-timer low beyond the stranded Billy Ritchie from ten yards, the ball ricocheting into the net off the base of the upright.

The hands on referee Tiny Wharton's watch nudged just beyond three minutes played when Celtic doubled their advantage. And it was a masterpiece of precision, ingenuity and innovation by the masterful Bobby Murdoch. Jimmy Millar, the man dubbed the 'Old Ibrox Warhorse', banged into McBride to give away an obvious foul twenty-five yards out. Lennox touched it sideways to Murdoch who elected for power. His shot, though, bounced off the defensive wall and what happened next summed up the mindset of the peerless midfielder. Without breaking stride, the multi-talented Murdoch flighted an impeccable and delicate ball high towards the keeper's top left-hand corner. Ritchie threw himself frantically at the attempt, but it was futile; the Celt's improvised effort gracefully glid towards its destination. Parkhead erupted. A fair percentage of the 65,000 in attendance appeared to be enjoying the fare on offer. There were still eighty-six minutes to play, but, as everyone realised, the game was over as a contest.

Jock Stein took the team to his old stomping ground in the Kingdom of Fife for the return leg of their League Cup quarter-final and teenager David Anderson, the goalkeeper bombarded and traumatised in Glasgow only a week earlier, was left out with the unpredictable Eric Martin recalled. Celtic were forced to wait until the thirty-second minute to score on this occasion and, remarkably, it was the blond head of skipper Billy McNeill that again administered the punishment on the Fifers. Jimmy Johnstone swung over a right-wing corner-kick and, uncannily like the effort at Parkhead only seven days before, McNeill rose to bullet the ball beyond Martin. Caesar smiled, 'I could have been the club's leading goalscorer if we played Dunfermline every week!'

Stevie Chalmers sent in a swerving drive that completely confounded Martin as Celtic doubled their lead three minutes before the interval to move into an unassailable 8-3 aggregate lead. And the perplexed custodian must have wished his manager had kept faith in Anderson in the fifty-fourth minute when he fumbled the ball and that was all the invitation Chalmers needed to claim No.3 on the night. No-one seemed to notice - or care - that George Fleming had scored one for Dunfermline late on; by that time the holders were sailing towards the semi-finals. Rocks were ahead, though, in the league game against Dundee at Dens Park three days later.

Andy Penman, a thoughtful, old-fashioned inside-right, was the first player to send Celtic into unknown territory by going a goal behind in this most memorable of seasons. Penman, a genuine craftsman who never fulfilled his potential, also possessed a cannonball shot and he demonstrated this ability with the utmost perfection to Ronnie Simpson and Co's annoyance in the twenty-eighth minute of a keenly-contested affair. Penman was allowed to line up an effort twenty yards out and he struck a devastatingly-accurate drive high over the Celtic keeper's left shoulder into the roof of the net.

Tommy Gemmell recalled, 'That goal was our fault. We had seen Penman hit those shots before and we should have closed him down immediately. Faither wasn't too happy that we didn't get out in time to charge down his shot. And I can assure you our goalkeeper would spare no-one's feelings when he described our lack of defensive qualities is such instances. Thankfully, though, we were only behind for four minutes.'

The majestic Billy McNeill, matchless in aerial battles, towered above the Tayside defenders to nod on an astute free-kick from Bertie Auld, the ball bending beautifully to pick out the advancing run of the centre-half. McNeill headed it down, there was pandemonium in front of goalkeeper Ally Donaldson and Bobby Lennox thrived in this panic-stricken environment. As the ball bobbled around, he thrust out a foot and prodded it beyond Donaldson. It was never going to be a contender for Goal of the Season, but it was crucial on an afternoon when Celtic's opponents were clearly in the mood to halt the progress of the green-and-white machine.

Only twelve minutes remained when the visitors claimed the winner after they were awarded a penalty-kick following defender Doug Houston's handball in the box. It was a stick-on spot-kick, but there was a problem - Joe McBride had sustained an injury and had remained behind in the dressing room at the interval with Stevie Chalmers taking his place. So, who was going to take the award? McBride had tucked away five in flawless fashion and now it was someone else's turn to take the responsibility.

Up stepped John Hughes, who had knocked in more than a few earlier in his career, including two in the 2-1 League Cup Final win over Rangers the previous year. Alas, Hughes' accuracy deserted him that afternoon. Donaldson, a goalie who, throughout his career, had been linked with

Celtic, got down athletically to push the ball away. Chalmers, however, saved the blushes of his team-mate and raced in to smash the rebound into the net. The strike put him into the history books as the first substitute to score a goal for Celtic, but Chalmers would be better remembered for another goal later in the same season.

However, before the date of May 25 1967 bore the slightest significance to anyone of a Celtic persuasion, there was the business of playing the club's first-ever tie in the European Champions' Cup against FC Zurich at Parkhead on the evening of Wednesday September 28 1966. The players had become used to Jock Stein producing the magnetic tactics board by this time, but, more often than not, the manager ignored the device when he was dealing with domestic games. He reckoned he was going over old ground discussing the merits of opponents' systems and one thing Stein detested with a passion was having to repeat himself.

John Clark recalled, 'When the Boss was talking tactics, I found I had to listen intently. He would speak fairly quickly in a lot of detail and if you didn't catch what he had said first time around there was no chance of him backtracking. It was always the individual's fault for not paying attention, according to Big Jock. So, we were normally a fairly hushed group of players when the magnetic board was produced.'

Jim Craig admitted, 'I had an inquisitive mind and I would ask questions. This was something that was new to Big Jock and something he didn't embrace with any enthusiasm. I was the guy who would query this, that and the next thing while most of my colleagues bit their tongues and kept quiet. He would point to the tactics board and go through a lengthy routine. Some of us took it in and others didn't. How could you tell Jimmy Johnstone how to play?

'I would ask a few questions, make a point or two and Big Jock, plainly, didn't welcome such intrusions. He was a meticulous planner and would go through our line-up and tell us exactly what he expected us to do. I thought it was only right and proper that I should ask a question or two just to clear up any possible misunderstanding. If Plan A wasn't working, what was Plan B? Jock didn't like that. He was a big fan of the master/servant relationship and, naturally, I didn't agree with that mode of thinking. So, when you queried something, Jock would wave you away with that big left hand of his. "Oh, just do as you're told," he would say. Okay, he was the manager, but that didn't mean I had to touch my forelock every time I spoke to him.'

Tommy Gemmell said, 'As I've mentioned countless times, Big Jock was scrupulous in his preparations. When he got the tactics board out we knew we would have to sit through half-an-hour or so of instructions as he moved the little magnetic dots around. He simplified everything for us as usual, and, as you would expect, he had done his homework on our opponents. Their biggest name was their player/coach Laszlo Kubala, who had been a player for Barcelona at the height of his ability. However, to be honest, the Hungarian was now forty-one years old and his best days were in the past. We knew, though, they had had six players in the Switzerland squad for the World Cup Finals in England that summer and, as champions of their country, they would be no mugs.

'So, by the time the kick-off came around to our first leg in Glasgow we were fairly well primed as to what to expect from our first opponents in Europe's blue riband competition. Or so we thought. What Big Jock hadn't legislated for were the Swiss being a team of cloggers. They set out to kick us off the park that night and Wee Jinky, in particular, got some heavy treatment. To be honest, we didn't see it coming and Jock hadn't anticipated it, either. There were some nations that would produce so-called nasty pieces of work, players and teams who concentrated on the physical side of the game. No-one predicted FC Zurich from Switzerland being one of those teams.'

Kubala, a clever and astute forward who scored 194 goals in 256 appearances for Barcelona between 1951 and 1961, had transformed the Swiss team after taking over earlier in the year. They were quite brutal in their treatment of opposing players which was in direct contrast to the way Kubala performed as a footballer. Danish referee Frede Hansen allowed a lot of challenges to go unpunished and there can be little doubt the Celtic players were knocked out of their stride by the unexpected approach by the Swiss.

The wiles and promptings of Bobby Murdoch and Bertie Auld in the middle of the park were being suffocated, Joe McBride and Stevie Chalmers were getting little joy in the centre of the attack against a defence that employed a sweeper, still a relatively new ploy outside Italy at the time, and Jimmy Johnstone and John Hughes were making no progress on the flanks against tenacious full-backs who stuck to their task with grim ferocity. As the contest unfolded, the 47,604 audience realised competing in the upper echelons of European football was a lot different from performing in the domestic game. It may have been even worse because Ronnie Simpson had been forced into action to produce a stunning stop shortly after kick-off.

In his 1967 memoirs, 'Sure it's A Grand Old Team To Play For', the keeper recalled, 'I had probably my best save of the entire European Cup competition in the early minutes. Zurich's Italian inside-forward Rosario Martinelli came through fast and hit a shot at goal which swerved in flight. I had to change direction as I went for the ball and was fortunate to get one hand to it to save the troublesome effort.'

It was still goalless after the hour mark and the crowd was beginning to get more than just a little bit anxious. The Swiss players swarmed around the pitch as they nullified the threats of the opponents who had been clearly pinpointed by their player/coach Kubala, sitting only yards away from Stein on the trackside. Someone, though, must have overlooked the pulverising power Tommy Gemmell possessed in both feet, mainly his right. The clock ticked towards the sixty-fourth minute when John Clark, tidy and efficient as ever, halted a rare Swiss attacking foray and knocked a neat ball out to Gemmell, playing at right-back that evening with Willie O'Neill on the left.

The defender with the cavalier attitude, a few yards inside enemy territory, nodded the ball forward and must have been surprised - and delighted - there wasn't a posse of opponents immediately surrounding him as he moved into attack. The Zurich defenders made their biggest mistake of the evening and backed off as Gemmell continued his surge forward. Celtic fans, with a reasonable certainty of what was about to transpire next, held their collective breath in anticipation. The adventurous Celt took a swift look up, got his eye-to-ball co-ordination absolutely spot on, and swung his mighty right boot at the spherical object that simply took off from twenty-five yards and blazed its way into the keeper's top left hand corner of the net. Steffen Iten hardly moved a muscle as the missile zeroed in on its target.

Celtic Park bounced with the combination of joy and relief as the fans welcomed their team's first-ever goal in Europe's top-flight competition and, a mere five minutes later, they were hugging each other again as Joe McBride doubled the advantage. Clark, once more with his uncanny anticipation, broke up a Swiss raid and rolled a short ball to Gemmell who knocked it inside to McBride. The striker, who had been shackled up until that point, sensed danger. He played a swift one-two with Auld, who wrong-footed the Swiss defenders with a snappy back-heel to his team-mate. McBride, from the edge of the eighteen-yard box, whacked the ball and it took the merest of touches off a lunging defender as it swept beyond the bewildered Iten. Cue pandemonium in Paradise.

The game ended on a controversial note, though, when it looked as though McBride had claimed a third goal. Certainly there was nothing wrong in the manner in which he scored and there was no question of him being offside. However, referee Hansen signalled the game was over and thousands of puzzled supporters emptied out of Celtic Park wondering if their favourites had won 2-0 or 3-0. It transpired the over-fussy match official had blown his whistle just as the ball had been crossing the line. The Swiss, with their obsession for precision timing, would no doubt have applauded the intervention of the punctilious Dane.

The FC Zurich players left Glasgow the following morning naturally grateful their task at overturning the deficit at their Letzigrund Stadium the following Wednesday had been rendered a lot less difficult by a highly dubious decision by the referee. It was only a matter of time before they would become Celtic's first European Cup victims on the Glasgow club's invigorating march towards history.

CHAPTER SEVEN
OCTOBER
ON THE VERGE OF SOMETHING SPECIAL

"We won the Cup and that was what we set out to do. Naturally we are delighted."

- Jock Stein,
After 1-0 League Cup Final triumph over Rangers.

The first piece of silverware in Celtic's all-conquering season arrived after Bobby Lennox's whiplash strike had defeated Rangers in the League Cup Final on October 29 1966. The Hampden triumph brought down the curtain on an astonishingly successful month for Jock Stein's side.

They had played eight games in four different competitions, had won the lot and had scored an extraordinary total of twenty-seven goals throughout their ruthless rampage. Ronnie Simpson had been required to fish the ball out of the back of his net on only five occasions - and three of them were conceded in one rollicking encounter against Hibs.

It was clear this Celtic team were on the verge of something special even this early in what was developing into a stellar campaign.

The players underlined their intentions on October 1 when they overwhelmed St Johnstone 6-1 at Parkhead to hoist their goal tally to the season to fifty-one. During this outing, Joe McBride could even afford to miss his first penalty-kick for the club, but atoned for a lack of accuracy from twelve yards with two second-half piledrivers. The Perth side erected a doughty defence in front of keeper Jim Donaldson, but Jimmy Johnstone pierced the barrier in the eleventh minute and Bobby Lennox did likewise seven minutes before the interval. Both were on target in the second-half before McBride walloped in the fifth in the sixty-fifth minute and added No.6 ten minutes later.

Four days afterwards, Celtic took their crusade on the road when they played their first-ever away tie in Europe's premier tournament against FC Zurich in Switzerland. It would be the first - and only - time the players disagreed with their manager. They chose the occasion of Stein's forty-fourth birthday to voice their united disapproval of his tactics before the second leg as they prepared to defend their advantage obtained in Glasgow seven days earlier.

Ronnie Simpson said, 'In the pre-match tactics talk, the Boss told us that Zurich would play a 4-4-2 system and would continue to use a sweeper despite the fact that they were down two goals. Not one player agreed with him. I chipped in and said, "They must come at us. They are bound to play an attacking style of game and try and get the goals they need. But I was wrong and so were the rest of the lads. Jock Stein had read the game perfectly. He told us, "They haven't got the guns to do any damage. They haven't the power we have. They'll try to get the score down." None of his players saw it that way and we told him.'

Not even one of Jock Stein's best friends, Glasgow bookmaker Tony Queen, was in accord with the manager's thinking. The well-known Celtic supporter was on the club flight to Zurich when Tommy Gemmell cheekily asked him what odds he would lay on an away win. Queen thought for a moment and offered 7/2. Gemmell immediately put on a few quid. The player passed on the information to Stein and he, too, didn't hesitate in putting on a wager.

'I have to say that was a most unusual situation,' admitted Gemmell. 'We were aware Big Jock liked a flutter, but it was mainly on the horses. I was a bit of a fan of the gee-gees myself and I would bump into the Boss every now and again at meetings at Hamilton, Musselbrough, Perth and the like. We would compare notes and then work out what we were prepared to gamble. I haven't a clue what Big Jock placed on the nags. For me, it was a bit of fun. I liked a day-out at the horses, but I rarely went anywhere near football, as far as punting was concerned. I reckoned that particular sport was far too unpredictable!

'I didn't throw money at the bookies, either. Remember, I was always good with figures, so I had a budget and I kept to it. Some days, I won; most days, I lost. I was never hooked, but when I asked Tony for odds on Celtic winning in Switzerland, I realised that was just too good a price to overlook. A quick calculation in my head told me it was definitely worth a wee punt. It was a private bet struck between two individuals, so I didn't see it as any sort of problem, as far as football authorities were concerned. Obviously, Big Jock thought the same way. But I have to say the bet meant nothing when the game got underway. I can say in all honesty the thought didn't enter my head until well after full-time and Tony Queen turned up at the rather opulent Dolder Grand Hotel, on the slopes overlooking Lake Zurich with the Alps beyond. It was the perfect setting to take money off a bookie. All that and we were in the draw for the next round of the European Cup!'

The European football officials had received a report with details of the first game that informed them it could have got out of hand. They reacted with commendable speed to change the referee. They gave the tie to hard-liner Concetto Lo Bello, a Sicilian policeman, who had been in charge of the USSR v West Germany World Cup semi-final earlier in the year. Lo Bello, of course, would be the referee when Celtic lost 2-1 to Feyenoord in the 1970 European Cup Final in Milan, but that is an altogether different story for another time.

Tommy Gemmell, the Swiss side's torturer-in-chief in Glasgow, belted in another screamer for the opener in the twenty-second minute and it was all over when Bobby Lennox flicked on a right-wing corner for Steve Chalmers to fire low and hard under the keeper's body. Gemmell crashed in a penalty-kick shortly after the turnaround for his third goal in a 5-0 aggregate win. Keeper Stefan Iten, after facing a virtual one-man firing squad in Gemmell, must have had enough of the bombardment by this stage and dived the wrong way as the defender lashed the ball unerringly into the net.

The returning heroes were given a rousing reception from the majority of the 43,256 crowd as they ran out onto an Easter Road pitch bathed in sunshine the following Saturday for one of the most electrifying encounters of the season. As they had achieved against Dundee at Dens Park the previous month, the Parkhead men took one on the chin before getting off the floor to administer some fearful punishment in gleeful retribution. This, remember, was against excellent opponents with many fine players such as Pat Stanton, who would enjoy an Indian Summer late in his career at Celtic, astute defender Alan Cousin, cultured left-back Joe Davis, clever midfielder Peter Cormack, flying left-winger Eric Stevenson and Colin Stein, a centre-forward with all the delicate touches of a wrecking ball. It made for compelling viewing.

Celtic's marking at a corner-kick in the tenth minute would have had their manager sucking out his fillings as Cormack, practically unhindered, placed the ball beyond the exposed Ronnie Simpson, who, once more, had some choice words for his dozy team-mates. Five minutes later, it was all-square when Joe McBride responded to the task at hand and fired one low past Thomson Allan at his far post. It seemed only a matter of time before the visitors scored again and they duly obliged on the half-hour mark when Stevie Chalmers swept in the rebound after a McBride shot had struck the woodwork. Edinburgh defender Davis, who rarely missed from the spot, was given another opportunity to display his expertise seven minutes later after Billy McNeill had rashly floored Stevenson. The full-back left Simpson stranded with a flawless execution.

McBride then struck twice in four minutes as half-time beckoned and he collected his fourth of a satisfying day in the seventy-fourth minute as Celtic dominated proceedings following the turnaround. Allan McGraw's strike in the fading moments was deemed an irrelevant intrusion in a fine display from the visitors. John Rafferty, a veteran journalist with the Glasgow Herald and a good friend of Jock Stein, extolled the virtues of the champions to his newspaper's readers the following Monday. He wrote, 'The well-known noisy partisan who sits behind the Press seats at Easter Road bravely faced the moment of truth. In unusually subdued tones, he said, "You've got to admit they're a good team." It was like saying the rain was wet.'

The scribe added, 'There was individual brilliance from Celtic in the impish Auld, the sweeping precision of Murdoch's passing, the exciting shooting of McBride, the jinking of Johnstone, the galloping of Hughes and the dashes of full-back Gemmell, but, at the end of the day, most admiration must go to the highly-geared team work.'

Queen's Park, the gallant amateurs from Hampden, were next in line as they visited Parkhead for the second stage of the Glasgow Cup and Celtic, just as they had done against Rangers in the previous round, cantered to a 4-0 triumph. Jock Stein shook things up a little and Ronnie Simpson missed his first game of the season with Danish keeper Bent Martin brought in. The Celtic gaffer had taken a liking to the blond, lithe and athletic shotstopper who had performed so well against the Parkhead side in the previous season's European Cup-Winners' Cup and was the main reason the aggregate advantage over Aarhus was pegged at a respectable 3-0. Although he had a shut-out, he never played again for Celtic and moved on to Dunfermline in December that year. Martin won a Scottish Cup medal with the Fifers in 1968 - after having defied his old team-mates at Parkhead in an earlier round as his team triumphed 2-0.

He wasn't exactly overworked on his first and last game for the club. It was an evening for Jimmy Johnstone to light up the east end of Glasgow with his unique repertoire of tricks and flicks. The defenders of the wonderfully-nicknamed 'Spiders' hadn't come up against his like in the old Second Division and, on the rare occasions when they did get within touching distance, they were normally found floundering after a shake and a shimmy from swivel hips took the flame-haired winger away from them and into dangerous areas. One scribe wrote, 'There could be no holding Johnstone, except, perhaps, by the jersey.' It was a routine night's work for Celtic with Joe McBride and Bobby Lennox scoring in the first half-hour and Charlie Gallagher and McBride adding two more after the interval.

Curiously, and at long last, 41,000 Celtic fans were given the opportunity to join in delightful and rousing harmony when the league flag was eventually unfurled on the afternoon of October 15 when Airdrie, unbeaten in the league up until that point, provided the opposition. Chairman Robert Kelly's wife conducted the ceremony in a carnival-like atmosphere and no-one ever explained why it took until the third home league game of the season before the ceremonial event took place. One resident of the

Jungle reasoned, 'Probably it's just because it's so difficult fitting in an extra celebration these days.'

Jock Stein, with an eye to playing the same opponents in the League Cup semi-final the following midweek, left Jimmy Johnstone on the substitute's bench and rested the midfield double-act Bobby Murdoch and Bertie Auld. John Clark was detailed to a more offensive role alongside Charlie Gallagher with Willie O'Neill coming in to partner Billy McNeill in the middle of the defence. In truth, the team struggled to discover a rhythm and fluency to upset a rugged Broomfield side who were more than satisfied to camp in front of keeper Roddie McKenzie, who had conceded nine goals at the same venue three years earlier. Capping a bizarre performance that particular day, he saved a penalty-kick from Celtic's often-erratic goalkeeper Frank Haffey with the game petering to a halt.

McKenzie and Co's resistance endured until twenty-five minutes from time when Joe McBride, with his eighteenth goal of the campaign, swept a Stevie Chalmers pass beyond the shotstopper with his customary aplomb and, three minutes later, Bobby Lennox diverted in a Tommy Gemmell cross for the second. Lennox put the finishing touches to another fine move three minutes from time to make the final score 3-0. Billy McNeill recalled, 'It's understandable for people to look back at our record in season 1966/67 and see a scoreline like this one and believe it was a walkover. However, very often we had to work exceptionally hard at getting the victories. Airdrie were never a flamboyant or particularly attractive team, but they could make life helluva difficult. The fact that they had been unbeaten when they played us tells you everything. That was the sixth league game of the season so they must have been doing something right.

'My memories of Airdrie back then are of some bitter, bruising battles, particularly at old Broomfield. No-one looked forward to these encounters in deep winter on their tight, uneven little pitch. A lot of teams back then favoured big, burly centre-forwards and Airdrie had a guy called David Marshall. King Kong would have thought twice before tangling with this character. I always knew I was in for a bit of a buffeting when Marshall was in opposition. That was the way it was then and it was okay, so long as they could take it back.

'I recall St Johnstone had this bloke by the name of Bill McCarry who had the nickname 'Buck'. I don't know if that had anything to do with bucking broncos, but he was another who liked to put it around. Buck, in fact, was normally a centre-half, but he was often switched up front and I admit my heart sank when I saw he was wearing the No.9 shirt against us. I knew the old rib cage was in for a battering. Stirling Albion also had a massive character who led their attack. His name was Jim Kerray and it was never a joy to face up to him, either. Ayr United had Alex "Dixie" Ingram and there were a few others. Don't get me wrong, I'm not saying they were dirty players. Let's just say they were enthusiastic - maybe overly-enthusiastic!'

The Celtic captain came face to face with Airdrie's human steamroller in the League Cup semi-final at Hampden only two days later. The luck of the draw handed the teams the Monday night fixture with Rangers and Aberdeen due to play their last-four encounter on the Wednesday at the national stadium. Once again, the team nicknamed 'The Diamonds' - known to most of the opposition by their unofficial monicker of 'Rough Diamonds' - camped in their own half, protecting Roddie McKenzie, and relying on high balls to the lumbering Marshall in the hope he could knock something down for a team-mate following up in an isolated breakaway. In fact, Ronnie Simpson had to look lively on two occasions to repel Airdrie with the game locked in goalless stalemate.

The tie followed the same pattern as the Parkhead match and it was still 0-0 after the hour mark. However, Celtic, with Bobby Murdoch, Bertie Auld and Jimmy Johnstone back in the line-up, continued to seek ways through the well-organised shield and the breakthrough goal arrived in the sixty-second minute - three minutes before the opener at Parkhead. It was Murdoch who provided the key to unlock the door leading to the Final. A Bobby Lennox free-kick was haphazardly cleared towards the edge of the box and fell with the utmost perfection for the midfielder who hit a howitzer-like attempt that screamed past McKenzie.

Tommy Gemmell had good reason to remember the strike. 'I picked up a first edition of one of the newspapers in Glasgow city centre that night,' he said. 'I was reading the match report of our game and I had to laugh when one sportswriter described Bobby's goal as "Gemmell-esque in its power". I had to show him the paper when we went through a light training session the following day. "Keep that up, mate, and you'll get yourself a good reputation," I told him. It was all in jest, of course. Bobby possessed ferocious power in both feet, although, like me, his right was undoubtedly his stronger.

'There was a friendly rivalry between us - and Big Yogi Hughes could give the ball a fair dunt, too - and we could never prove who had the harder shot. However, someone did rig up an electronic device and players from all over Scotland were invited to take part. I won when my shot measured 69.2 miles per hour and I was christened 'Scotland's Big Shot'. It didn't matter, though. As Big Jock continually reminded us, it was about Celtic the team and not anyone as an individual.'

Fifteen minutes from the end of an exacting, gruelling tie, Auld picked out Joe McBride, lurking with intent as always, and he headed the crucial second counter past the valiant McKenzie. In between the goals, Stevie Chalmers had two shots cleared off the line. It had been a workmanlike performance from the Parkhead side and Jock Stein observed, 'We had to grind out this win and you must give our opponents credit for that. They had a game-plan and they stuck to it. We had to break it down, we kept at it and eventually we got our reward.'

Stein and his players would have to wait, though, to learn who they would face in the Cup Final at the end of the month. Rangers and Aberdeen fought out a 2-2 draw in the first game, but the Ibrox side won 2-0 in the replay five nights later. So, for the third successive season, it would be an Old Firm head-to-head conflict to decide the destination of the League Cup at a damp, colourless Hampden Park on Saturday afternoon October 29.

Tommy Gemmell, John Clark, Jimmy Johnstone and Joe McBride headed for Cardiff three days after the victory over stubborn Airdrie to represent Scotland in a Home International Championship match against Wales. The quartet were 'invited' to perform on the glue-pot surface of Ninian Park and were heading for a shock 1-0 reverse after Ron Davies had flicked the ecstatic Welsh ahead in the seventy-sixth minute following a left-wing corner-kick. However, McBride played a huge part in the equaliser and facesaver two minutes from time when keeper Gary Sprake couldn't hold his low shot and the irrepressible Denis Law, with the well-deserved reputation as 'The Merchant of Menace', slid through the mud to toe-poke home from eight yards.

Unfortunately for McBride, he sustained an injury in a punishing game against the rugged Welsh and had to sit out the league match against Ayr United at Parkhead the following Monday. Gemmell had been injured, too, but overcame his ankle knock to take his place at right-back with Willie O'Neill still patrolling the opposite wing. Clark and Johnstone, thankfully, came through unscathed following their international experiences.

Celtic were expected to stroll towards their twentieth consecutive win of a pleasantly developing campaign, but they toiled and were being held 1-1 by the Somerset Park part-timers as the interval loomed. Bobby Lennox had got the opener in the second minute and the 21,000 crowd sat back and awaited an avalanche. However, inspired defending, slack finishing and wayward passing allowed Ayr United the platform to spring a shock and Bertie Black stunned the stadium when he levelled in the fortieth minute. However, John Hughes netted the second on the stroke of half-time and it was mainly one-way traffic in the second period with Johnstone claiming two and Gemmell powering in another for an ultimately handsome 5-1 victory.

Five days later, Celtic returned to Hampden, the scene of their Scottish Cup Final demise in April. Now the League Cup was up for grabs against the same opponents and Bertie Auld recalled, 'We had been tipped by many the previous season to win the national competition and, of course, the bookies rarely got it wrong. We just shaded the odds, but the favourites don't always win, as was the case that painful night in Mount Florida. So, the turf accountants once again put their mouth where the punters put their money and had us as odds-on to win the League Cup. I was acquainted with a few bookies, of course, and I didn't know any who had difficulty finding the cash to put petrol in their Rolls-Royces. They weren't wrong too often. They had confidence in us not to fall twice at the final hurdle. We were fairly confident ourselves, as a matter of fact.'

Rangers, following back-to-back embarrassing reversals from their venerable rivals, were in determined mode and desperate to turn events on their head. The Ibrox side were only too aware of the startling progress that was being made across the Clyde and realised the Jock Stein express had to be derailed; the sooner the better. Long-serving keeper Billy Ritchie, after conceding six goals in two Old Firm confrontations, was brutally axed to make way for Norrie Martin, who had played in the 2-0 replay triumph over Aberdeen. There were also indications that the new boys, Davie and Alex Smith, were beginning to settle into their roles within the team structure. The ever-dangerous Willie Henderson and Willie Johnston, two pacy flankers, were beginning to motor while a lot of the goalscoring onus was put on the unpredictable George McLean, the forward who infuriated the club's followers with his particular mixture of wonderful and woeful.

Tommy Gemmell reflected, 'I had a lot of admiration for Willie Henderson and, as a matter of fact, he is still a very good friend to this day. He was so fast and elusive when he got into his stride. I always tried to encourage him to go inside when we were face to face and I was playing at left-back. If I could coax him in there, I knew John Clark and Billy McNeill could take care of business. But you knew you were in trouble when Henderson got his head down and went straight for the bye-line. Big Jock was always happy to play Willie O'Neill against the winger. Willie's great strength was his tackling, his timing was excellent. Henderson would show him the ball and our man would jockey along beside him, refusing to rush into a rash tackle. If you did that, you would find yourself swiping at nothing and the wee Rangers player would be on his way, haring down the touchline. Big Jock again chose Willie O'Neill at left-back for the League Cup Final and I played at right-back. I was up against Willie Johnston and he could be real handful, too. Like Henderson, he was speedy, direct and could deliver a good cross. Willie O'Neill and I knew we had our work cut out that afternoon.'

And so it proved. Rangers rose to the occasion and performed diligently throughout, a fact acknowledged afterwards by Jock Stein. However, the Final was settled as early as the nineteenth minute when Bobby Lennox, with his usual lightning-swift reactions, put the Ibrox side to the sword. Bertie Auld clipped over a cross to the edge of the penalty box and Joe McBride back-headed the ball into the tracks of his striking team-mate. Lennox, racing at top speed, was perfectly balanced to receive the pass and fizzed an unstoppable drive past the helpless Martin from eight yards. The move had developed at such bewildering pace the Rangers defence resembled exhibits at Madame Tussaud's as it was speedily constructed around them.

That was the solitary goal of a tension-laden, rain-drenched, sodden afternoon at the national stadium. The nearest Celtic came to adding to Lennox's strike came when John Greig scooped away a shot from Jimmy Johnstone that had eluded Martin. Rangers claimed a goal when Bobby Watson battered the ball into the net, but referee Tiny Wharton blew for a foul after detecting a sly nudge by Alex Smith on Ronnie Simpson as the Celtic keeper came for a swinging high ball. Ibrox manager Scot Symon was asked for his verdict on the match official's call. He sniffed, 'The referee is the judge. What I think doesn't count.'

The nearest Rangers got to scoring a legitimate goal against Celtic in four-and-half hours of football that season arrived in the fading moments when Alex Smith scrambled the ball beyond the grounded Simpson. It was rolling, apparently inexorably, towards the net when Willie O'Neill arrived on the scene. Gemmell recalled, 'I got a good close-up view of the incident and I have to say I thought the ball was going over the line. Willie seemed to appear from nowhere. It called for a right-footed clearance, but we all realised Willie was all left foot. If he had swung at it with his right, goodness only knows where the ball would have landed! Thankfully, he slid in with his left and hooked it to safety. Willie normally shunned the spotlight and never bothered with praise, but that was an extremely important piece of defending from a very reliable professional.'

Stein accepted his team had not fired on all cylinders, but said with a measure of defiance in his tones, 'We won the Cup and that's what we set out to do. Naturally, we are delighted. We didn't play as well as we can and I think everyone who saw this game would agree with that.'

One newspaper reporter noted, 'If Rangers don't know where their trouble lies, they should all be using white sticks. At centre-forward, George McLean had no idea how to beat Billy McNeill without fouling him. Every high ball was the property of the Celtic centre-half and captain - and nearly every low one, too.'

One trophy down - and four to go.

The History Bhoys ...the Lisbon Lions pose before they take the field against Inter Milan in the Portuguese capital on May 25 1967. **Back row** *(left to right)*: Bobby Lennox, Tommy Gemmell, Ronnie Simpson, Jim Craig and Bobby Murdoch. Front row: Jimmy Johnstone, Bertie Auld, John Clark, Billy McNeill, Stevie Chalmers and Willie Wallace.

Skipper supreme ...Billy McNeill leads his team-mates on the lush turf at the Estadio Nacional. Also in the frame are: Ronnie Simpson *(half hidden)*, Tommy Gemmell, Bobby Lennox, Stevie Chalmers, Willie Wallace, Jim Craig and Bobby Murdoch.

Let the action begin ...the Bhoys prepare for battle. Left to right: Jim Craig, Willie Wallace, Tommy Gemmell, Jimmy Johnstone, Ronnie Simpson, Bobby Lennox, Billy McNeill, Bertie Auld and John Clark.

Penalty! Willie Wallace crashes to the ground as he is hauled down by Inter Milan keeper Giuliano Sarti *(out of picture)*. German referee Kurt Tschenscher astonishingly refuses the appeal while a grateful Italian defender hammers the ball to safety.

That winning touch ...Stevie Chalmers *(extreme left)* turns away after scoring his historic goal to bring the European Cup to Paradise. About to join in the celebrations are Jimmy Johnstone and Bobby Lennox.

Power and poise ...Willie Wallace escapes the attention of Inter Milan skipper Armando Picchi to fire a shot at goal. The remarkable Giuliano Sarti was there to repel another Hoops' raid.

The glory goal ...even Sarti is powerless on this occasion as Stevie Chalmers turns in Bobby Murdoch's low cross for the winner.

What a hat-trick ...Bertie Auld sports some natty headgear as he is flanked by Joe McBride *(left)* and Willie Wallace. McBride missed out on Lisbon through injury after claiming an astonishing haul of thirty-six goals before the turn of the year.

CHAPTER EIGHT

NOVEMBER

MYSTERY, MAGIC AND MAYHEM

"Critics made quite an issue over the amount of late goals we scored. I'll let you into a secret - Big Jock trained us for EVERY game going into extra-time."

- Bertie Auld

Entertainment was the watchword of Jock Stein; a mantra played out, relentlessly, forcefully and without fail, in the Celtic dressing room before every game. 'Remember,' he would tell the players, 'these people have worked all week to get money to come here and see you play. Get out there and show them what you can do. Give them something to shout about, go and put smiles on their faces.'

Bertie Auld recalled, 'Aye, Big Jock would hammer into us the need to win, but also to put on a show for the fans. He didn't have to go through that routine every week, of course. We all knew our responsibilities to the man on the terracing because we were fans, as well. For goodness sake, my dad Joe used to stand at the same spot in the Jungle at every game with his pals. I offered him complimentary tickets for the stand, but he always knocked me back. He preferred to be in that famous old, rickety pavilion with "real" fans, as he called them.'

The Celtic midfielder could afford a laugh as he looked back. 'Mind you, my dad took me aside one day and told me, "Listen, Bert, if you guys keep playing the way you are, my mates and I are going to have to leave the pub a lot earlier to make sure we can get in." Was that a complaint or a back-handed compliment? I'm fairly sure it was the latter. My dad would watch every home game from that same vantage point and I can also tell you he was fairly frank in his observations. He didn't hold back if he thought his son hadn't performed as expected. I didn't need Big Jock to keep me on my toes!'

Auld added, 'We all knew the Boss was the absolute master at the wind-up. Every time we played Rangers or any big game, he would make a point of standing with the players at the dressing room door before we went down the tunnel. He would wait for our opponents to line up alongside us and then he would say in a staged whisper, "You know you've got this game sorted, it's as good as in the bag, so all you need to do now is give our supporters something extra to cheer, put on a wee show for them. And you know you are good enough or else you wouldn't be here in the first place." I would sneak a glance at the face of an opponent and I knew we were a goal ahead without a ball being kicked.

'I would get involved myself, of course. I would go over to John Greig, the Rangers skipper, and say, "Hey, Greigy, what sort of bonus are you on today?" He would say, "Twenty quid for a win, Bertie. What about you?" I would answer, "Ten quid, Greigy." And before he could utter another word, I would chip in, "Mind you, I'm guaranteed to get mine!" And with that we would trot down the tunnel and onto the pitch to do battle in front of 60,000 or so fans who were, as usual, giving it pelters.'

One game that emphasised the drive in the Celtic camp to constantly charm and beguile the onlooker was a league meeting with Stirling Albion on a dreich, dank Wednesday evening on November 2, only four days after the 1-0 League Cup Final triumph over Rangers. Despite the unpleasant weather conditions, there was a carnival atmosphere at Celtic Park as a couple of ball boys paraded the newly-won silverware. As was the custom back then, the Cup was held aloft by the two fortunate youngsters selected for the duty, gifted their fifteen minutes of fame. They would walk slowly around the trackside, pause every now and again and milk the moment. The procession of the glittering prize would be guaranteed to get the supporters charged up for the spectacle that most assuredly lay ahead. This night in the east end of Glasgow wouldn't prove to be the exception.

In stunning, whirlwind fashion, Celtic rattled in six goals in thirty-seven first-half minutes in a bedazzling display. Poor Stirling Albion, a team in the wrong place at the wrong time without a hope of sanctuary. Jimmy Johnstone got the ball rolling with the opener in the sixth minute and the fans had to wait a mere four minutes before Joe McBride got on the scoresheet. Stevie Chalmers popped one in shortly afterwards and Bertie Auld joined the party in the twenty-fifth minute. Devastated Stirling defenders were hit by a two-goals-in-a-minute burst just before the interval with McBride and Chalmers again on target. No-one seemed to notice that the bedraggled visitors actually managed to get the ball behind Ronnie Simpson practically on the half-time whistle. The typhoon became a mere gust after the interval as McBride completed his hat-trick and the scoring for the champions in the forty-eighth minute. Two late goals from the Annfield outfit completed the 7-3 scoreline and the Celtic defenders, after a couple of momentary lapses, were aware they were about to be on the receiving end of a well-rehearsed sermon from their manager.

Charlie Gallagher limped out of the romp early on after picking up a sore one in a challenge from an over-zealous Stirling defender and Jim Craig came on as substitute. He went straight into Tommy Gemmell's right-back role and the attacking defender was moved forward into midfield with Bobby Murdoch taking up his former position higher up the field at inside-right. Gemmell joked, 'You could say I was "The Man for all Reasons". I was fairly versatile and Big Jock knew that. I also trained for half-an-hour at Barrowfield just about every day as a goalkeeper because I was stand-by if Ronnie Simpson picked up an injury. Remember, we only had a substitute shotstopper for European ties back then and John Fallon got that role.

'So, by the time we were only a week into November, I had played at both right and left-back, outside-right and in midfield. And with Caesar missing with his bout of flu, the manager turned to me and told me I was playing centre-half against St Mirren on the Saturday following our seven-goal show against Stirling Albion.

'That was fair enough, I never quibbled about where I played, just so long as I was in the first team. Someone once asked me if I fancied playing outside-left. I smiled and replied, "Have you not been watching me all season? I have been playing at outside-left!" Well, it just felt like that because I appeared to spend more time in the opposition's half than I did in my own. I suppose I was a handy man to have around, even if I do say so myself!'

The effervescent Gemmell also liked to remind everyone he was a rarity as far as Celtic goalkeepers go. 'How many can say they played more than one game for the team and never conceded a goal? I can lay claim to that one. I moved into goal when Faither, Ronnie Simpson, was injured in a Scottish Cup-tie against Clyde at Shawfield on a February afternoon in 1969. It was a perishingly-cold Wednesday, as I recall, with a 4.30pm kick-off because there were problems with the home side's floodlights. Faither dislocated a shoulder going down with typical bravery at the feet of a Clyde forward. If I remember correctly, the opposing player was Jimmy Quinn, who was actually on loan from Celtic!

'Our keeper departed the scene very early, after only fifteen minutes or so. We didn't have a substitute goalie, so Bertie Auld came on and I went between the sticks. My colleagues did their best to keep the ball away from me for the remainder of the game, but I recall making a decent save from Harry Hood, who, of course, would become a team-mate shortly afterwards. That game ended goalless and we won 3-0 in the replay. It was a vital match because we went all the way to win the Scottish Cup that season, giving Rangers a 4-0 hiding in the Final.

'And I stepped in after Faither had taken a knock on the same shoulder when we were playing Ayr United in a League Cup semi-final replay at Hampden in October 1969. It was 2-1 with only about twelve minutes to play when I took over the goalie's jersey and the score remained that way. Surprisingly, we had drawn the first game 3-3 when John Fallon had been in goal. But Ronnie came back for the league game against Airdrie at Broomfield on October 11 which just happened to be his thirty-ninth birthday. Big Jock made him captain for the day and we won 2-0.

'Unfortunately, it wasn't such a happy tale two nights later when we faced Ayr United again for the right to see who would play St Johnstone in the League Cup Final. Faither dived to push away a low shot at his post and he was in obvious distress when he landed on the hard surface. His shoulder had gone again and I realised in an instant that my game as an outfield player was over and I would be handed the No.1 jersey. Faither was helped off and that was the last we ever saw of him playing for Celtic. It was the end of an extraordinary career for one of the most remarkable characters I ever had the good fortune to meet, on or off a football pitch.'

Unexpectedly, Celtic stalled at the twenty-third examination of their skills and St.Mirren, after conceding eight goals during their last visit to Parkhead in the League Cup in August, stubbornly held on for a 1-1 draw. It was November 5, but, on this occasion, the fireworks were sparce from Jock Stein's side. It was an afternoon to forget for the champions when very little went according to plan. There were a few factors to be considered; two 'goals' chalked off in the first-half, a couple of goal-line clearances, a heroic display from the opposing goalkeeper and the fact Celtic were forced to complete the game with ten men following the mysterious dismissal of Bobby Murdoch. You get days like that and, being positive, it had been a long time coming. And Celtic still remained undefeated.

Billy McNeill missed his one and only game of the campaign after being stricken by a flu bug and Tommy Gemmell did, indeed, play in the pivotal role in defence alongside John Clark. 'As I said, I was always happy to fit in where Big Jock thought best,' admitted Gemmell. 'I had played at centre-half in bounce games and enjoyed the role to a certain extent. It helped that I was two-footed, which I would say is essential for a player in that position. The one restriction, of course, was that I couldn't be quite as adventurous so far as charging into attack was concerned. Wee Luggy, John Clark, was used to the way Caesar played and he rarely abandoned his beat in the middle of the rearguard. Our skipper would join in the attack for set-pieces, of course, but rarely came forward in open play. For all his attacking ideals, even Big Jock wouldn't have condoned the anchorman in his defence gallivanting deep into the other team's half and leaving huge gaps behind him. So, I had to keep that in mind that day.'

St Mirren goalkeeper Denis Connaghan, who would be signed by Stein in the immediate aftermath of the humiliating 4-1 League Cup Final from Partick Thistle in 1971, had actually been at Parkhead as a provisional signing, but, due to some confusion over paperwork, he hadn't been offered a contract. The way Connaghan recalled it, he had informed a club official he was going to America for a month to attend his sister's wedding. There were mixed signals and it was erroneously believed the nineteen-year-old prospect was emigrating to the States. The club, therefore, released him from his contract. Undeterred, the beanpole custodian joined Renfrew Juniors, excelled at that level and was swiftly snapped up by St Mirren. As luck would have it, he made his debut for the Paisley outfit that afternoon in the east end of Glasgow.

Connaghan admitted, 'Although I was let go, I was still a Celtic fan. I don't think that ever leaves you. Obviously, I was busy on Saturday afternoons, either with Renfrew or St Mirren, and couldn't get to the games. But I went along for some midweek fixtures when I was free and I was at Parkhead for the European Cup-ties against Vojvodina and Dukla Prague later that season. Ironically, I was playing for the Saints against Dunfermline on the day of Celtic's League Cup Final defeat against Partick Thistle. There were murmurs coming from the fans on the terracings behind my goal throughout the first-half. They were listening to the Hampden game on their transistor radios. I could pick up that Celtic were losing 1-0. And then it was 2-0. Then 3-0. Amazingly, it was 4-0 at the interval. Little did I know at that point, I would receive a phone call the following day to let me know Jock Stein wanted to sign me. It was all done and dusted by Monday afternoon.'

The young Connaghan, though, did not set out to do his boyhood favourites any favours on his senior baptism. He reflected, 'We were expected to get hammered. The previous week we had been thumped 6-1 by Rangers and that opened the way for me to play my first game in the top side. I was actually told by one of the club's management that I would lose goals and not to worry about it. He told me to go out, do my best and just enjoy the occasion. So, I did!'

Joe McBride bulged the net behind the debutant custodian after Bertie Auld had set up the opportunity, but the referee ruled it out, indicating offside against the striker. No-one in the 24,000 crowd was unduly concerned at that stage. Shortly afterwards, Jimmy Johnstone was next to beat Connaghan and, once again, the celebrations were cut short when the match official awarded a free-kick to the visitors. Then Bobby Lennox, with his customary burst of exhilarating pace, got through to drive a shot at goal. The ball clipped the keeper's outstretched leg, spun lazily in the air on its way towards the net before its seemingly-inevitable progress was halted by desperate defender Cameron Murray who headed clear from under the crossbar. Connaghan also contrived to deny McBride, Lennox and Stevie Chalmers on three separate occasions and it was one of football's great puzzles the scoreline remained blank at half-time.

Two minutes after the turnaround, Tommy Gemmell took the opportunity to venture forth and he was right in line, thirty yards out, when a wayward cross broke to him. He strode forward and caught the ball perfectly with his fearsome right foot and there was little Connaghan could do on this occasion as the effort raged past him. The keeper was still in mid-air when the ball crashed behind him into the net. Gemmell said, 'I took a chance going up, but, to be honest, Faither was so inactive he could have taken out a book and a deckchair that day and caught up with some of his reading. St Mirren weren't exactly putting my old mate and me under too much pressure. So, I thought I would go up and see what was happening at the other end of the pitch. Fortunately, the ball fell nicely for me and I just gave it a smack and hoped for the best. Connaghan had been playing exceptionally well and I would get to know later as his team-mate that he was capable of such outstanding performances. I thought that goal would open the floodgates for us that day. Didn't work out that way.'

Unbelievably, the Paisley side equalised only eight minutes after Gemmell's blaster. Frank Treacy, who had scored his side's goals in their 8-2 thrashing in the League Cup, chased a long ball, punted by a defender from deep inside his own half, brought it under control and the pacy forward, basically left unattended, drew Simpson and flicked the ball past the veteran. The sound of silence greeted the goal; the Celtic Park attendees couldn't believe what they had just witnessed. The Saints had been pounded and pulverised for the best part of an hour and now their players were prancing around with undiluted joy.

If the Parkhead patrons found that difficult to fathom, it was nothing to their emotions when the referee saw fit to order off Bobby Murdoch. The midfielder raced over to retrieve the ball as it went out of play. Puzzlingly, the linesman signalled a throw-in to St Mirren when it seemed clear to all in the proximity the award should have gone the way of Celtic. Someone said something untoward and that was enough to see the official frantically wave his flag to attract the attention of the referee. After a quick confab, the whistler summoned Murdoch to come over and then dramatically pointed to the dressing room. I was a friend of Murdoch for many years and, although I accept I may be a shade biased, I never found him to be in the least bit malicious or offensive. I doubted if he would have brought the linesman's parentage into question, but whatever had happened had seen the playmaker immediately banished from taking further part in the proceedings. Celtic were fated not to win their twenty-third successive encounter that day.

During research for this book, the mystery of the Murdoch sending-off was solved - after half-a-century! Tucked away in his 1970 autobiography, 'All The Way With Celtic', was the answer. He revealed, 'The first time I was ever ordered off in my life was in a league match against St Mirren at Celtic Park in November 1966. I was so innocent that it hurt! Things were not going well for Celtic or me on this particular occasion. With the score at 1-1, we were pushing hard for the winner late in the game. The ball went out of play for a throw-in at the Jungle side of the ground and I immediately claimed it was ours. The linesman, however, flagged the other way. I looked at him, shook my head and ran away to take up a defensive position.

'Claims were made by either side as the ball was retrieved. When it was picked up by a St Mirren player, the linesman was seen to have his flag raised. Over went the referee for a chat and his next move was to call me over and ask for my name. I couldn't believe it. I said, "Why are you booking me, ref? I haven't done anything." The referee, Ronnie Henderson, of Dundee, said that I had been accused of swearing at the linesman. He said, "I can only act on what the linesman told me. The game is over as far as you are concerned. You can have an early bath."

'I was off and I hadn't opened my mouth! My heart filled with the injustice of the situation. St Mirren inside-forward Archie Gemmill came over and said to the referee, "You have the wrong man, ref. It wasn't him." But the referee wouldn't change his decision. So, seven minutes from the end, I was off - and I was Celtic's captain for the day, too. Oh, did I feel rough!

'I told our manager that I had not committed any offence whatsoever and that I should never have been booked never mind sent off. He accepted my explanation - particularly when our centre-forward, Joe McBride, owned up, "Bobby's right, boss. It was me who shouted at the lineman."

'Archie Gemmill, the Paisley forward who had been marking me during the match, very sportingly said after it was all over that he was prepared to be my witness when I appeared before the SFA Referee Committee and state that it was a clear case of mistaken identity. After seeing a copy of the referee's report, I sent a letter to the SFA giving my side of the incident and stating that I wanted Gemmill to appear as my witness. But the SFA wouldn't have this at all. I was not allowed any witnesses. I think this is very wrong. When someone is prepared to come forward from an opposition side and say something on your behalf, shouldn't he surely be allowed to do so?

'Anyhow, I appeared before the SFA Referee Committee, which had Morton director Peter Scott in the chair. He asked me for my side of the story and I told him in complete detail. I went outside while they discussed my case and when I was recalled I was told I had been fined thirty pounds and severely censured. It was very obvious they were not too sure of what had gone on and it seemed to me that the compromise was a fine. An innocent man fined. It would break your heart. But this kind of thing is all part and parcel of the game of football.

'I had no hard feelings about Joe McBride. After all, why should he volunteer to be ordered off when the chance was that my case would be dismissed because a genuine and honest mistake had been made? I was quite relieved that I was not suspended. Mind you, maybe I should have had a word with McBride about that thirty quid I had to fork up!'

After the stalemate, Jock Stein was in no mood for hard luck stories. The Celtic manager was raging at the self-centred displays of some of his players who had strayed from his instructions. As he spoke to the Press, Stein made no attempt to disguise his frustration. He said, 'I don't think there is any doubt that some of our forwards' play against St Mirren was plain stupid. Some of them have been warned in the past of the trouble that awaits them if they do not do as they are told in pre-match practice. Yet they persist in going their own way.'

While the Celtic boss actively encouraged improvisation and spontaneity among his players, he didn't subscribe to an individual spending the entire ninety minutes basking in impromptu, unscheduled acts of what he termed unacceptable selfishness. No names were mentioned, no show ponies were revealed, but a fully-fit Jimmy Johnstone, known for his extravagant over-indulgences on the football park, didn't even get near the solitary substitute's spot for the forthcoming games against Partick Thistle and Falkirk. With the wee winger nowhere to be seen, Jim Brogan occupied the No.12 berth against the Maryhill side and Ian Young was called up from the reserves for the trip to Brockville.

Celtic were only ninety minutes away from the second of the quintuplet of trophies that made season 1966/67 the most memorable of all time when Partick Thistle travelled across Glasgow to contest the Glasgow Cup Final. The Parkhead side finished as they had started the tournament - with a 4-0 triumph while Bobby Lennox claimed a hat-trick, as he had done against Rangers in August. Barring Celtic's way to another piece of silverware was goalkeeper George Niven, who had conceded seven goals in one of the Parkhead side's most historic triumphs, the 7-1 League Cup Final win over the Ibrox side in 1957. He must have wondered what lay in store as Stein's team netted four in just over thirty first-half minutes. Stevie Chalmers got the first in twelve minutes and Lennox raced to bang in three in nineteen painful minutes for Niven, who was thirty-seven years of age at the time and in the twilight of his career.

That, thankfully for the veteran custodian, was the end of the scoring. Thistle manager Willie Thornton, a former Rangers player, was wholesome in his praise of his overpowering opponents. He said, 'I have to admit I was most impressed by Celtic's play. I watched them beat Stirling Albion 7-3 last week and they did a first-class job as executioners in that game. They did the same to us.'

It was Joe McBride's turn to take the goalscoring spotlight when Celtic faced Falkirk at the dreaded Brockville on Saturday November 12. Like Airdrie's Broomfield, no-one actually looked forward to attempting to perform on that ground. Bobby Murdoch had the ability to keep a helium-filled beach ball under control during a storm while performing on quicksand, but even the cultured midfielder groaned at the thought of being asked to play at Falkirk. He said, 'If there are two grounds I just hate playing on they are Broomfield and Brockville. I'm never happy on either of these grounds because I invariably develop a bad case of claustrophobia.

'I feel the terracings, stands and crowd are so much on top of me, and so near to the play, that I don't seem to have room to move in, let alone breathe. And as a link player between defence and attack you have got to have land, lots of land, to work in. The funny thing about Brockville is that, while it looks a small, trim, narrow ground, it is actually wider than Hampden Park and most of the other grounds in Scotland. The pitch is actually seventy-seven yards wide. That's two yards wider than Hampden and Celtic Park and five yards wider than Ibrox. I know this will surprise a lot of people, including players.

'Like Broomfield, the terracing walls are right up against you and you get the feeling the fans could reach over and touch you. I should point out right here, I think the majority of the fans at these games are Celtic supporters. Like Rangers, we are never outnumbered by the home support, unless the match is at Aberdeen in midweek, which is just a little too far for the majority of our fans to travel.

'A huge travelling support is always a distinct advantage and those who say the vocal backing Celtic and Rangers get each week is worth a goal of a start may not be all that far wrong. Even so, I never did get rid of the feeling of being hemmed in at Brockville and Broomfield. Though there is a fair bit of space across the field at Brockville, the red shale track really forms the border of the playing surface and one tends to be short with passes to the wing because the track looks so close. If there were another ten yards of turf on either side of the touchline it would make a great psychological difference to midfield players such as myself and give you more confidence in striking the ball firmly in distribution.

'Unfortunately, the proximity of the track, and the terracing, is all against any feeling of extra space on the wings at Brockville. Celtic have come a few croppers on this ground over the years. I recall being in a Celtic team beaten 6-2 there in April 1965. I think the result was more of a surprise to Falkirk than it was to us! I'm glad to say we've come a long way since that Brockville blockbuster.'

Misgivings or not, Murdoch produced another flawless presentation as Jock Stein's men made no mistake in an effortless 3-0 win on the derisible, detested playing surface of their hosts. Joe McBride got a perfect day in motion when he tapped in from close range after the Falkirk keeper fumbled a cross from Bertie Auld in the proximity of his right foot. Just before the interval, the powerful frontman whacked in a second via the penalty spot after a handball had been detected by the referee. It was all over by the sixty-second minute when Bobby Lennox had a shot cleared off the line, it broke to McBride who instinctively forsook personal glory to set up Auld to nail the third.

The victorious team came off the pitch to be informed by a beaming Jock Stein that Rangers had been held to an unexpected 1-1 draw by St Johnstone in Perth. The champions were now three points ahead as they drove relentlessly forward in the defence of their title. There was no midweek rest for six Celtic players who would represent Scotland against Northern Ireland in the Home International Championship at Hampden. Tommy Gemmell, John Clark, Bobby Murdoch, Joe McBride, Stevie Chalmers and Bobby Lennox were in action as the Scots won 2-1 with first-half goals from Murdoch and Lennox. Curiously, Billy Bremner, the Celtic-supporting captain of Leeds United, was the only Anglo-Scot in the line-up that evening with Kilmarnock's Bobby Ferguson in goal and Rangers trio John Greig, Ronnie McKinnon and Willie Henderson also on duty.

Fortunately, all six Celts came through unscathed for the trip to East End Park for the league encounter against Dunfermline three days later. Jimmy Johnstone, after being snubbed by Jock Stein for two games as punishment for his exaggerated excesses in the stalemate against St Mirren, was back on the right wing. The rumbustious meeting against the Fifers emerged as a contender for Game of the Season, a real see-sawing, rattling humdinger that saw Celtic twice behind by two goals and still come back to pick up the points in an implausible 5-4 triumph, with the winning goal being claimed by Joe McBride with a blistering last-minute penalty-kick.

After just over an hour played in the Fife mud, it looked as though Celtic's unbeaten record was about to be dynamited. A determined set of Dunfermline players were winning 4-2 and the visitors were hanging on grimly. Somehow, from somewhere, Stein's men drew courage and unconquerable qualities as they lifted themselves from a veritable swamp and totally transformed the outcome.

Two goals in three minutes saw Willie Cunningham's team, still smarting at their 9-4 aggregate dismissal from the League Cup, put down their marker. Hugh Robertson blasted in the opener in the thirty-first minute and, only moments later, Pat Delaney rifled in a second. Celtic were reeling, two goals adrift for the first time in the campaign.

Bobby Murdoch responded almost immediately after Delaney's effort as he diverted in a cross, but Bert Paton restored his side's two-goal advantage in the thirty-eighth minute. The champions rallied and back-in-favour Jimmy Johnstone nipped in to cut the deficit after keeper Eric Martin had blocked a drive from Bobby Lennox. The 22,000 audience was relieved to hear referee Tiny Wharton's half-time whistle, the shrill giving them the much-needed opportunity to get their breath back. But there was more to come during a tumultuous second-half.

Three minutes into the period, Alex Ferguson banged his team's fourth goal behind Ronnie Simpson and the scoreline remained that way until the sixty-second minute. Bertie Auld, defying the elements and skimming across the skiddy surface, slammed one in via the upright and that goal signalled an almighty effort from Celtic to level matters as they lay siege to Martin's goal. Seven minutes after Auld's effort, McBride ploughed his way through the middle, every sinew straining and his legs pumping as he pulled away from a pack of pursuing defenders, and he finished with a vicious, thumping shot beyond the keeper.

Match official Wharton was already looking at his watch, whistle poised between his lips, when Dunfermline centre-half Roy Barry conceded a blatant penalty-kick. A last-ditch crossball was thrown into the congested area in front of Martin and Barry, for reasons known only to himself, took off in Superman fashion to punch the ball away from the head of the inrushing McBride. The referee had an unobstructed view of the incident and had no hesitation in pointing to the spot. Up to that stage, the teams had shared eight goals in an enthralling spectacle and now, with only a matter of seconds remaining of actual play, Celtic were one kick away from emerging triumphant.

The awesome pressure could have got to McBride as he placed the ball twelve yards from goal. Was there another twist in this remarkable occasion? The striker stepped back, Martin, arms flapping, made himself look as big as possible as he stood on his line, and then McBride came thundering forward. Bang! The ball flew straight and true high into the net and the travelling fans went wild with unrestrained happiness. The Fife players collapsed as one onto the morass of the East End Park pitch. And who could blame them? They had scored eight goals against Celtic in three games and lost them all. Mind you, their opponents didn't help the Fifers' cause by stuffing fourteen goals into their net in rampant reply.

Bertie Auld recollected, 'What a game that was, a real old-fashioned, in-your-face confrontation. You better believe Dunfermline were a right good team back then. I suppose a lot of sides might have folded when they were losing 4-2 after an hour or so. Not this Celtic team; absolutely no chance. Even when we got it back to 4-4 we were looking for the winner. Aye, I suppose a lot of other sides would have seen that as an achievement to get a point in such circumstances, but we never thought along the lines of other players or other teams. We wanted to win. That was our thinking at the kick-off and we had no reason to change our mindset as the clocked ticked down.

'Critics made quite an issue of the late goals we scored that season. I'll let you into a secret; Big Jock trained us for EVERY game going into extra-time. Of course, there would be no added-on half-an-hour in a league game, but we would have been ready for it if that had been the case. In some Cup-ties, you could see opponents just about out of it, on their knees and obviously not relishing the thought of extra-time. It didn't bother us because we had worked all week for two hours of action. That was Big Jock's way of thinking. He didn't see much point in simply preparing his players when there was a Cup-tie coming up and there was the possibility of extra-time. That made no sense to him and, of course, he was quite right. So, we had stamina in reserve when we were playing any game and it was going into the last fifteen or so minutes. We were a strong, extremely fit team. Did anyone ever witness any of our players suffering from cramp back then? I don't remember that ever happening.'

Jock Stein had an interesting take on the breathtaking confrontation. He said, 'In the League Cup Final, our forwards played very badly. It was the defence that saved us and took us to victory on that occasion. So, surely the attack is expected to do a special job in games such as this one? Did you see a single one of our forwards bickering with the defence when the goals were being lost? Did you see any of them losing heart? We're all in this together. We are a team and we won this one as a team.'

A week later, it wasn't quite so frenzied or nerve-shredding against Hearts in the constant drizzle from the heavens at Parkhead. The unfortunate George Miller directed a shot from Bobby Lennox past his own keeper Jim Cruickshank in the twelfth minute, but it wasn't until Joe McBride cannoned a second into the net in the eighty-second minute that Celtic could afford to accept two points were a certainty. McBride zoomed in a penalty-kick in the fading moments to cement a 3-0 victory. Willie Wallace played that afternoon in the maroon of the Edinburgh side, but the next time he performed on the same pitch thirty days later he was wearing the green and white hoops of Celtic. And about to embark upon a truly astounding voyage in the next step of his football career.

Celtic's final game of an eventful November came in the European Cup Second Round first leg against Nantes, the excellent French club renowned for their flamboyant, attacking style. Once again, Jock Stein's outfit had been drawn against a team who had provided several players for their nation's squad for the World Cup Finals in England, most notably Robert Budzynski, a tough, solid and dependable centre-half with the ability to pass the ball out of defence.

There was little doubt, though, of the Celtic player who had caught the imagination of the home support - Joe McBride, the thirty-three goal hitman who had been immediately christened 'Marlon Brando' by the French Press. It was a nickname that baffled even the stocky Celt. Ronnie Simpson recalled, 'The Malakoff Stadium proved to be a smallish ground and the game did not attract a great deal of people with the attendance given as 15,464. In sixteen minutes, we were a goal down. Their full-back, Gabriel De Michele, had attacked down the left wing and pushed through a great ball to Francis Magny. We were caught open and he beat me with his shot, which was low and hard.

'But "Marlon Brando" had us all-square in twenty-four minutes and, in the second-half, Bobby Lennox and Stevie Chalmers also got on the scoring charts. We deservedly won 3-1. The Man of the Match was undoubtedly

Jimmy Johnstone. The French fans rose to him and applauded his trickery. The French newspapers called him "La Puce Volante" - "The Flying Flea" - and that's what he must have seemed to the Nantes defenders as he jinked through their ranks with calculated danger.

'The boss told Jimmy before the game to keep taking the ball up to the full-back and to carry it past him and not to be disheartened if he failed. He was to keep trying to beat him. De Michele did stop him in the earlier parts of the game, but eventually Wee Jimmy had him so bamboozled that everyone was applauding him. Including me! The French team manager, Jose Arribas, did not really give much hope of saving the game at Celtic Park. When you lose a home tie 3-1, you're in dead trouble.'

'Marlon Brando' and 'La Puce Volante' celebrated St Andrew's Day alongside the rest of the Celtic contingent on the banks of the River Loire that evening and prepared for the rigours of a demanding December.

CHAPTER NINE
DECEMBER
HOGMANAY HORROR ON TAYSIDE

"I simply wanted to sign for Celtic and who wouldn't want to play for Big Jock?"

- Willie Wallace,
£30,000 signing from Hearts

It was inevitable Celtic would fire blanks somewhere along the line as they embarked on their 1966/67 crusade. No-one saw it coming, though, at a chilly, windswept Rugby Park on the Saturday afternoon of December 3.

Jock Stein's side went into the encounter against Kilmarnock following a twenty-six goal landslide in seven games the previous month. As the eager Celts lay waste the defences who provided wary and futile opposition, the champions rattled in a total of forty-five strikes in only twelve league outings. Impressive shooting. Unfortunately, Bobby Ferguson, the young Kilmarnock keeper who had just made the step up to international level, was determined not to join the growing list of Aunt Sallies. The twenty-one year old proved to be an impenetrable barrier and Celtic's hopes of kicking off a new month of devastation were thwarted. For the time being, anyway.

In the opening minutes, Ferguson showed a glimpse of what was to follow when he raced from his line to bravely throw himself head-first at Bobby Lennox's feet as the striker prepared to latch on to an expertly-driven through pass from Bertie Auld. Billy McNeill was next to test the redjerseyed custodian with a typical soaring header from a corner-kick, but once again Ferguson was equal to the task. Joe McBride had a go from just inside the box, but the agile No.1 catapulted across his goal to fingertip the ball round the post. Tommy Gemmell joined the procession with a scorching twenty-five yarder and Ferguson matched that effort, too, as he touched the shot over the bar. And so it went on for virtually the entire match.

The keeper was forced to admit defeat late in the game when McNeill sent another header spinning high past his upflung arm, but resourceful defender Andy King raced back to knock the ball off the line. That clearance underlined it was not going to be Celtic's afternoon. However, the players were delighted to hear Rangers had lost 3-2 to Dunfermline at East End Park and the champions' lead at the top of the First Division had actually been increased to four points.

Jock Stein fretted, though, in the aftermath of the scoreless stalemate in Ayrshire. It didn't matter that his players had come up against an inspired opponent in Bobby Ferguson, who was sold to West Ham at the end of the season for £65,000, which, at the time, was a British record transfer fee for a goalkeeper. After parting with £22,000 for Joe McBride some eighteen months earlier, the Celtic manager reckoned it was time the club's cheque book came into operation again. He had been paying particular attention to a forward who had scored two goals in Hearts' 3-2 win over Celtic at Tynecastle earlier that year, January 29, to be precise. Three days after the Rugby Park encounter, the Celtic manager paid £30,000 to the Edinburgh team for Willie Wallace. Ironically, he was twenty-six years old - the same age McBride had been when he had arrived from Motherwell in June 1965.

Wallace recollected, 'I had been in dispute with Hearts and just wanted a transfer. Newcastle United and Stoke City were showing an interest, so it looked as though I would be packing my bags and crossing the border. Then Jock Stein came on the scene and he didn't have to try too hard to sell Celtic to me. As soon as I realised there was a chance of going to Celtic Park and working alongside Big Jock, there was no choice to make. Newcastle United and Stoke City, without any disrespect, had no chance of getting my signature on transfer forms.

'Let's try to clear up a few mysteries that have followed me about for years. I was not, and never had been, a Rangers supporter. The story goes that I was poised to sign for the Ibrox side until Big Jock made his move. There was a tale that the Celtic manager waited until Rangers were away from home and playing in a European tie before he quickly sealed the deal with Hearts. Sounds like a good yarn, but it simply didn't happen that way. I don't know if Rangers were ever interested in me at all. Okay, my whole family were Rangers fans and they would have loved for me to sign for them, but I was overjoyed when I got the opportunity to move to Celtic.

'Yes, some of my family didn't share my enthusiasm for all things Celtic back then. Actually, I admit I did see a lot of Rangers in the Fifties because my Uncle Jim just happened to be President of the Kirkintilloch Rangers Supporters' Club! However, I spent more time watching Falkirk at Brockville which was just up the road from where I lived in Larbert. But I am a Celtic fan now, you can be certain of that. Once you have mixed in that company, you couldn't be anything else. I admit playing in Europe didn't mean an awful lot to me when I joined up at Parkhead. Celtic winning the European Cup five months after I joined would have been a step too far in my imagination. I simply wanted to sign for them and who wouldn't want to play for Big Jock?'

Of course, Celtic's gifted master tactician possessed many talents, but it's fairly certain clairvoyance was not among them. Over the years, the myth has grown that Willie Wallace was bought as a direct replacement for Joe McBride. Not so. McBride had yet to sustain the injury that savagely wrecked his campaign while it was in full flow. Jock Stein's first two signings for the club, in fact, teamed up in attack during Wallace's debut against Partick Thistle eleven days after his arrival. And it was McBride who very thoughtfully set up his new team-mate for his first goal for the club in the same match.

Willie Wallace, whose signing hadn't been registered with UEFA in time to play, took his place in the stand as Celtic prepared to finish the job against Nantes in the second leg of their European Cup encounter in Glasgow on Wednesday December 7. Sitting beside Wallace that evening was Joe McBride, ruled out through injury. At that stage, though, no-one had any reason to be concerned.

Jock Stein promised the supporters his team would attack, despite holding a 3-1 advantage from the first game. Torrential rain cascaded violently before and throughout the match and there was an early scare for the Scottish champions when Nantes' Yugoslavian striker Vladimir Kovacevic sneaked through to alarm Ronnie Simpson. The veteran recalled, 'Their player went on a solo run and beat me with his shot, but the ball hit the post and rebounded clear. He should have scored.'

Jimmy Johnstone, aka 'La Puce Valente', provided the apt reply when he seized upon a Georges Grabowski slip before rifling the ball beyond keeper Andre Castel to put Celtic 4-1 ahead on aggregate in the thirteenth minute. Gerard Georgin equalised with a fine effort that left Simpson helpless. The keeper said, 'It was a great goal from their player with a first-time shot on the drop. At that stage, Nantes were coming back at us and our fans weren't too happy.'

Francis Magny, who had scored in France, had Simpson scrambling, but the veteran managed to grab the spinning ball just as it was about to cross the line. And moments later, the keeper defied the same player with another smart save. Thankfully, Jinky Johnstone sparkled in the drizzle after the turnaround and he skipped through the French rearguard on the right wing to pick out Steve Chalmers with a perfect pass and he nodded in from close range. It was all over a few minutes later when the winger treated the French to a deja vu moment with an identical run and a perfect low cross that was swept in by Bobby Lennox for a mirror image of the first leg score and a 6-2 aggregate triumph. Celtic could now afford to take a breather in the competition with the quarter-final tie against Vojvodina Novi Sad awaiting them in March 1967.

Stevie Chalmers reacted positively to the additional threat of Willie Wallace to his place in the forward line. The whippet-lean, speedy frontman cracked in a hat-trick as Motherwell were downed 4-2 at Parkhead in the following match. Chalmers, who would celebrate his thirty-first birthday sixteen days later on Boxing Day, may have been perceived as the most likely candidate to make way for Wallace. The player who had been at the club for almost eight years after joining from Junior club Ashfield in February 1959 was more than just a shade eager to prove he wasn't quite ready for football's version of the knacker's yard.

Chalmers linked up with the new signing while Joe McBride, with the knee problem beginning to manifest itself, wasn't risked even as a substitute with youngster David Cattenach on the bench. Bang on the half-hour mark, Motherwell's elongated goalkeeper Peter McCloy went down in instalments to push away a low drive from Bertie Auld, a deceptive effort which was arrowing in at his near post. The ball broke loose and Chalmers, with the electric fusion of pace and anticipation, was first on the scene to lash the rebound into the net. Four minutes from the interval, he displayed the same qualities after a shot from Bobby Lennox had cannoned off an upright. McCloy hesitated, his defence was posted AWOL and in raced the Celtic Number 9 to gleefully prod the ball over the line.

Suddenly and unexpectedly, the game exploded into violence when Jimmy Johnstone and Motherwell striker Dixie Deans, a volatile double-act, decided to re-enact their own mini-version of Ali v Liston. It led to an ordering-off for Deans, who, of course, later signed for Celtic and, as you might expect given their history, became a lifelong friend of the club's greatest-ever player. Johnstone escaped censure. Deans, in his autobiography, 'There's Only One Dixie Deans', admitted, 'When I first met Jimmy Johnstone, I wanted to punch his lights out and he wanted to do the same with me. It was the first time I had played at Celtic Park and I was desperate to make the right kind of impact. But we were losing and frustration was perhaps getting the better of me.

'It was a fifty-fifty challenge, but neither of us was prepared to back down. Before you knew it, our fists were flailing at each other. It was the battle of the little big men - I'm five foot seven inches and Jinky was five foot four inches - but I picked the wrong guy to have a square go with. Not because I was feart of the Wee Man. No, because the fisticuffs happened right in front of the old Jungle and some fifteen thousand fans were baying for my blood.'

Five years later, after a £22,000 transfer from Fir Park had propelled Deans along the same career path as Joe McBride, the striker was welcomed to Parkhead by those same supporters. However, back on a December afternoon in 1966, he departed the action to an accompaniment of a cacophony of boos from the patrons of the Jungle who were far from pleased at the treatment of their team's little winger. When the action restarted, Bobby Murdoch unleashed an unsaveable thirty-yarder for the third goal in the sixty-sixth minute. Lapses in defence allowed the Lanarkshire side to haul back two goals before Chalmers made certain with the fourth seven minutes from the end.

There was the welcome sight of Joe McBride leading the attack for the game against Partick Thistle on a frost-covered surface at Parkhead the following week. Willie Wallace and Stevie Chalmers also played in a fearsome three-pronged strike-force with Bobby Lennox backing them up from the left wing. Jock Stein, possibly not as understanding as the match official following last week's fracas on the touchline, decided to leave out Jimmy Johnstone, who still got a place on the bench. Wallace went into the game after being put through the rigours by trainer Neilly Mochan following Stein's orders for extra sessions for his new signing. Apparently, the Celtic gaffer was not enamoured with the player's level of fitness that had apparently satisfied former club Hearts for five years.

The encounter against the Maryhill side was only two minutes old when Wallace scored the first of his 135 goals in his five seasons at the club before his transfer to Crystal Palace in October 1971, surprisingly joined at the London club by a reluctant John Hughes. However, that was far from the thoughts of Celtic's latest recruit as Bertie Auld - 'racing down the right touchline as though being chased by a swarm of bees', according to one colourful newspaper report - slung over a cross to the far post. McBride's timing was superb as he headed the ball across goal and Wallace followed up to nod in from six yards.

Chalmers claimed the second in the fourteenth minute following a corner-kick and the 25,000 fans were cheering again when Wallace blasted in a third ten minutes later. Willie O'Neill thumped over a deep cross from the left, Wallace hit the ball full on the volley and it was a mere white streak as it flew towards its journey's end. One reporter wrote, 'The shot went in like a mortar bomb into the top left-hand corner of the net.' Celtic's goalscoring exploits were certainly inspiring the populous of the Press Box to pen some purple prose. Bobby Murdoch made it 4-0 with an accurate thirty-yarder into the corner, but Arthur Duncan, a pacy outside-left, pulled one back eight minutes before the interval.

Wind and rain whipped up to add to the chill at the start of the second-half, but it didn't prevent McBride adding a fifth eight minutes after the turnaround when he finished off a slick move instigated by Lennox and Wallace. The striker took the salute of the crowd for the thirty-sixth time that season little knowing it would be almost a full year before he would be embraced by those accolades again. Tommy Gibb punished slackness in the home defence to pull one back just after the hour mark, but Chalmers struck again fifteen minutes from time for his fifth goal in two games to make the final score 6-2 in favour of the champions.

'We had scored ten goals it two games and that would have kept most managers happy,' observed Tommy Gemmell. 'But we, as defenders, knew we would be required to put in some extra work in the next few days at Barrowfield. That was our punishment for conceding four goals at the same time and Big Jock was never likely to overlook that statistic. "Every goal comes from a mistake," he would say, "Let's cut out the mistakes and we'll cut out the lost goals." He would often add, "Ach, the training won't do you any harm, anyway." Then he would turn to Bobby Murdoch and Bertie Auld and lecture them about their midfield duties and, after that, he would have a few words for the forwards. Stickler for detail? You don't know the half of it. We were top of the league, in the quarter-finals of the European Cup, had two trophies in the bag and he still wasn't satisfied. Difficult to argue with his outlook, though, when you view the man's record.'

Jock Stein was among the 38,172 crowd at the Vicente Calderon stadium in Madrid on Wednesday December 21 to discover which team Celtic would meet in the European Cup quarter-final. Atletico Madrid and the Yugoslavs of Vojvodina Nov Sad had stalemated 3-3 over their two legs and a third game was required to sort out the winners. The Spaniards won the toss for the tie to be played on home soil and they must have thought they were heading through as they raced into a two-goal lead in six minutes through goals from Adelardo and Enrique Collar. Sylvestre Takac reduced the deficit just before the half-hour mark and Dimi Radovic, later red-carded, levelled in the sixty-fifth minute. Extraordinarily, the Slavs hit the clincher in extra-time with another effort from Takac.

The Celtic team boss had been impressed. 'A very strong, physical team,' he summed up. 'Good in possession with the ability to pick the right passes. Defenders who play the ball and like to bring it forward and dangerous players up front who can score goals. I saw plenty to think about. We can get through, but we will know it will be extremely tough. We will have to be at our best over the two legs, that is absolutely certain.'

Flurries of snow greeted Celtic's visit to ice-bound Pittodrie to face Aberdeen on Christmas Eve. A snell wind whipped in from the north-west and the conditions were hardly conducive to attractive, free-flowing football as players on both sides slithered and skidded unsteadily on a white carpet of frost while twenty-nine thousand hardy souls shivered in the stands and on the terracings. The Dons, unbeaten at home all season, were on the back-foot when Bobby Lennox opened the scoring in the twenty-fifth minute. Bertie Auld skimmed a ball into the heart of enemy territory and centre-half Tommy McMillan slipped as he attempted to cut it out. That was all Lennox needed as he sped onto the pass and smacked the ball away from the advancing Bobby Clark.

Celtic hardly had time to celebrate when it was all-square again five minutes later. Left-back Ally Shewan lofted a high ball into the penalty area, Frank Munro, who had a twenty-two game stint at Parkhead before being released in April 1978, headed across the six-yard line and Harry Melrose was unguarded as he applied the finishing touch. Ronnie Simpson made a valiant attempt to claw the ball to safety, but the power eluded his despairing grasp.

Snowflakes began to decorate the playing surface as the second-half got underway and home keeper Clark, sporting an all-black tracksuit in an attempt to repel the cold, made several good saves. Simpson, at the other end, was earning his keep, too, with some smart stops. Ironically, the closest either side got to scoring the winner came from McBride. Chalmers picked out his frontline partner with a shrewd cross and, as ever, the centre-forward's timing and execution were in sync. He powered a header beyond the searching fingers of the sprawling Clark, but his celebration was cut short when the ball struck the upright and bounced to safety.

How fitting would it have been for Joe McBride to bid his farewell to the campaign with a wonderful winning goal? Fate, alas, had other ideas as the game ended in a 1-1 stalemate.

Celtic were within eighteen minutes of completing the first half of the season with an unbeaten record when they carelessly tossed away a 2-1 advantage to lose 3-2 to Dundee United at Tannadice. Remarkably, the Tayside outfit were the only Scottish team to beat Jock Stein's men during the campaign and, equally as incredible, they triumphed by the same scoreline in Glasgow five months later. And once again they came back from trailing 2-1 midway through the second period. Even the most imaginative purveyor of fiction would have thought twice before conjuring up that ridiculous premise.

Stein and his players would never have known they were on the brink of their first league defeat in nine months - implausibly their last reverse had come in a 1-0 shocker against Stirling Albion at Annfield on February 26 - when they took the lead in the twelfth minute. Tommy Gemmell fired over a low right-wing cross which escaped the grasp of keeper Sandy Davie. The ball ricocheted off the lurking Bobby Lennox and bounced over the line. Finn Dossing levelled ten minutes later and his goal immediately set in motion an on-the-spot inquest among the visiting defenders. Within a minute, though, Celtic were in the lead again. Willie Wallace flashed an angled waist-high drive at goal which took Davie by surprise. Desperately, he tried to push the effort round the post, but only succeeded in nudging it onto the woodwork and the ball rebounded into the net.

As the game edged beyond the seventieth minute, Celtic looked fairly comfortable. John Hughes had been given the go-ahead by Jock Stein to make a surprise comeback after his two-month lay-off following the knee injury sustained in the League Cup Final victory over Rangers. The left-winger, after only two reserve team outings, looked to be easing himself back towards full match fitness. He was up against a wily, experienced opponent in Tommy Millar, the brother of Rangers' Jimmy. The United defender was from the old school who, unlike Tommy Gemmell, preferred to do all his work in his own half of the field and wasn't adverse to clattering into wingers on a regular basis. Hughes was finding it extremely difficult to get into his stride as Millar threw himself into challenges with ferocious gusto.

In the seventy-third minute, United equalised with a bit of a rarity. Ronnie Simpson's cat-like reflexes and keen anticipation made it practically impossible for him to be beaten from a range of around thirty yards. So highly regarded was he among opponents, the Celtic keeper was seldom challenged from such a range. On this occasion, though, Dennis Gillespie, a workmanlike forward, tamed a pass from Billy Hainey, moved the ball a couple of feet in front of him and then let loose a cannonball of a shot that sizzled high over Simpson into the net. It was as spectacular as it was unexpected. Even the home fans in the 25,000 crowd seemed momentarily transfixed before they danced their jigs of joy. Simpson sat in the mud and shook his head in disbelief.

It was an emotion shared with his captain Billy McNeill. 'We all thought Faither was unbeatable by shots from well outside the penalty box. Sometimes the defence might even have been a wee bit slow getting out to deal with the danger twenty-five or thirty yards from goal when we saw a player lining up a shot. We all thought it was a waste of time. But, to be fair, the United player gave that ball a helluva dunt. I only heard a whoosh as it flew over my head. I turned round just in time to see the ball flying past Faither who didn't have a chance. Maybe he conceded two or three goals like that all season and, unfortunately for us, this was one of those times.'

Celtic were still pondering the loss of the goal when United streaked up the field and claimed another two minutes later. A simple long high ball punted forward by centre-half Doug Smith eliminated the entire backline. United forward Ian Mitchell was first to react as Simpson hesitated in coming off his line. Mitchell controlled the ball in an instant, moved in on the exposed keeper, swept to one side and trundled the ball into the empty net. And as the leather sphere leisurely rolled over the line, Celtic's unbeaten sequence was coming to a halt. There would be no happy Hogmanay for strict teetotaller Jock Stein or his players.

At least, though, the Celtic manager could derive some sort of consolation from a glance at the top of the First Division table. After seventeen games, the champions had amassed twenty-nine points, four ahead of Rangers who had played one game fewer. Aberdeen, after seventeen outings, were also on twenty-five points. Stein would have been satisfied with the haul of fifty-eight goals, eight more than the Ibrox team and nineteen ahead of the Dons. However, a frown may have developed with a look at the goals against column. Ronnie Simpson had been asked to pick the ball from his net twenty-two times, seven more than either Billy Ritchie or Norrie Martin at Rangers and one more than Bobby Clark at Aberdeen.

After conceding eight league goals in December, Billy McNeill and Co could look forward to some extra training sessions early in the New Year as life was breathed into 1967, Celtic's year of destiny.

CHAPTER TEN
JANUARY 1967
NEW YEAR, SAME STORY

"Joe McBride will play for us again and that should kill once and for all the stupid rumour he is finished as a player."

- Jock Stein

Winter's unforgiving icy grip, with the attendant obbligato of piercing, shrieking howls and the drifting, persistent snowfalls, forced football in Scotland to a quivering standstill as 1966 frostily crossed over into 1967.

The scheduled Old Firm encounter at Ibrox on January 3 was an early victim of the freeze. The game against Clyde had already met with the same chilly fate. The Celtic players had to wait seven days into the momentous new year before they were required to don their new rubbersoled shoes. The innovative John Hughes, of course, had shown the way the previous January as he tip-toed through the frigid conditions at Celtic Park on his way to ransacking Rangers.

Now, twelve months on, Jock Stein insisted on all his players being kitted with the new shoes from the Adidas manufacturers. An admirable crowd of 37,000 turned out in the frosty east end of Glasgow to welcome their heroes into another year of hope and expectation.

No-one had a clue what lay ahead as the combatants of Celtic and Dundee emerged from the tunnel that chilly afternoon.

Jock Stein's team gave the supporters a bit of a clue by taking a two-goal lead in five minutes before coasting to a 4-0 advantage inside half-an-hour. Ten of the men who would become legends in Lisbon on May 25 that year were on parade; Bertie Auld was the odd man out with a place on the substitute's bench while Charlie Gallagher teamed up with Bobby Murdoch in the middle of the park. John Hughes, after struggling to make an impact in his comeback game against Dundee United on Hogmanay, was rested.

It was Murdoch who pointed Celtic in the direction of a cavalcade of goals in the opening moments when he delivered a vicious cross into the Dundee penalty area. Bobby Wilson, the Dundee right-back, was smack in the line of fire and the ball cannoned off a shin before flying past his static and unprepared goalkeeper, John Arrol. Ninety seconds later, Murdoch picked out Willie Wallace with a forty-yard pass of laser-beam accuracy and the striker killed the ball instantly and, in the same sweeping movement, thundered in a shot from an acute angle that had the keeper admitting defeat again. Jimmy Johnstone administered more punishment on the custodian in the twentieth minute, but, in between the goals, Arrol had made outstanding saves from Stevie Chalmers and Wallace. He had no answer, though, when Johnstone clipped one past him following a clever Gallagher free-kick.

Gallagher, so often Auld's understudy, was gifted with poise and balance and was revelling on the dodgy surface that had only passed an inspection at 8.45 that morning. The delicate inside-forward would never be known as a great goalscorer, but he was the scorer of great goals. And that was ably demonstrated in the twenty-eighth minute when he pulled the ball down, pirouetted and, without even looking up, cracked a shot of awesome power high into the net. By this time, the fans had forgotten about the Arctic temperatures. Celtic eased up after the interval and Kenny Cameron pulled one back for the visitors, but the first game of the 1967 adventure got a fitting last-minute salute when Wallace walloped in the fifth goal.

One impressed national newspaper scribe wrote, 'Someone had to pay for Celtic's defeat at Tannadice on Hogmanay and fate ruled that the team should be Dundee, who were so outclassed that only the brilliance of their goalkeeper John Arrol prevented complete and utter humiliation. Time and time again, Arrol came to his side's rescue with saves bordering on the miraculous as Celtic made light of the treacherous underfoot conditions and bombarded the Dundee goal from practically the first minute to last.'

The Celtic goalscoring spree continued in midweek with Clyde on the receiving end of identical punishment dished out to Dundee. The players of the Shawfield outfit, who would finish an extremely credible third in the First Division upon the completion of the campaign, arrived at Parkhead with the handsome record of picking up win bonuses on their last four sorties outside Rutherglen. Also, Davie White's side had lost only once in their previous eight games. And, for close on an hour, the visitors, including future Celt Harry Hood, showed why they had racked up such an excellent sequence of results. Then the roof caved in on the gallant part-timers.

There was the little evidence of the drama that had yet to unfold when Celtic, as expected, took an early lead in the twelfth minute as Stevie Chalmers accepted a thoughtful through pass from Willie Wallace and launched an unstoppable drive high past Tommy McCulloch, Clyde's highly-respected thirty-two-year-old goalkeeper. Joe Gilroy, however, interrupted proceedings just after the half-hour mark when he slid the equaliser beyond Ronnie Simpson, three years the senior of his opposite number. It remained locked at 1-1 at the interval and beyond.

However, Charlie Gallagher, who scored goals with the regularity of sightings of Halley's Comet, netted his second in successive games to hand the initiative back to the champions. The midfielder nimbly tucked away a low cross from Chalmers in the fifty-fourth minute and the 38,000 crowd had to wait another eighteen minutes before witnessing a spellbinding succession of deadly finishing as Clyde were blown away by a green tempest. Chalmers started the goal parade in the seventy-second minute when McCulloch could only parry a low shot from Jimmy Johnstone. Two minutes later, Tommy Gemmell, from his favourite shooting distance of twenty-five yards, crashed in another as he tested the strength of the rigging and, within sixty seconds, Bobby Lennox headed in the fifth and final goal. Who could have blamed veteran custodian McCulloch for reaching for the smelling salts afterwards?

In glowing terms, one newspaperman noted, 'As if charged by some invisible dynamo, Celtic seemed to play out the last half-hour at a pace even faster than anything that had been set before - and it paid off in no uncertain manner, with three goals in the space of four minutes. That was the end of the match as a contest, but not as an entertainment, for right until the end Celtic kept plugging away for more goals and were denied them only by some resolute defensive play by the stout-hearted Clyde defenders.'

Tommy Gemmell was given a special round of applause from his team-mates and the 19,000 supporters crammed into the confines of Muirton Park as Celtic travelled to Perth to take on St Johnstone on January 14. The cavalier-like full-back was celebrating the occasion of his one hundredth successive first team appearance for the club - and he came close to marking the event by putting the Celtic physiotherapist Bob Rooney's son in hospital. With the game poised at 0-0 and pushing beyond the hour-long evaluation of their opponents, Gemmell, forcing on his forwards as usual, raced on to a ball about thirty yards out and he let loose a mighty effort which appeared to be fizzing towards the top corner of Jim Donaldson's goal. However, defender Benny Rooney, who started his career at Parkhead while his father Bob worked with the backroom team, was either brave or foolhardy - certainly ill-advised - managed to get his head in the way and diverted the ball off target.

One scribe wrote, 'Gemmell almost decapitated Rooney with a shot that hit the centre-half on the brow and sent him to the ground with the ball spinning for yet another corner.'

The Celtic great said, 'What on earth was he thinking? Goalkeepers used to get out the way of my shots and there he was trying to head it clear! Served him right for trying to deny Celtic a goal. He should have known better. Actually, I do recall that moment and I think that shot had goal written all over it until his intervention. He went down as though he had been hit by an invisible cannonball. Thankfully, Benny was made of good stuff and was back on his feet shortly afterwards. And, also, I was grateful that we got the goals afterwards that took the points back to Parkhead.'

Following Rooney's moment of injudicious valour, Jimmy Johnstone sneaked in a left-foot drive for the opening goal in the sixty-third minute and added another six minutes later. There was another two-goal burst late in the game when Stevie Chalmers netted a third in the eighty-sixth minute and Bobby Lennox clipped one over the line only moments afterwards to make the final scoreline an emphatic 4-0 for the league leaders and defending champions. It proved to be a crucial victory for Celtic. On the same day, Rangers beat Dundee United 3-1 at Ibrox to kick off an astonishing twelve-game sequence of league wins, an accomplishment which merely emphasised the tour de force that was Jock Stein's team who were able to meet and overcome such a sustained challenge while retaining their title.

After almost fifty years of working in newspapers, I can vouch for my wonderful city of Glasgow being the world's capital of rumour, innuendo and speculation, malicious or misguided, informed or otherwise. There is always someone 'in the know' with the genuine 'inside info' about this, that and the next thing. God only knows how so many of these tales originate. I've always thought there were too many people with fertile imaginations with too little to occupy their minds or take up their time. Trust me, after so many phone calls over the many years, I have the severely bent ears to prove it.

And so, I am reliably informed, that was the case back in the middle of January 1967 when the whispers began concerning the welfare of Joe McBride, who hadn't been seen in the Celtic first team since Christmas Eve the previous year. Less than a month had elapsed since his enforced absence and that was enough to get the ball rolling. Joe, everyone was reliably informed by the 'insiders', had scored his last goal, his career was over.

Jock Stein was concerned to the extent of getting touch with some of his friends, principally chosen by the team boss, in the national Press. He instructed them to quote him directly as he emphasised, 'Joe McBride will play for us again and that should kill once and for all the stupid rumour that he is finished as a player. The rumour is completely untrue. We are going to prove that when we replay our Second X1 Cup-tie against Hearts. Joe is completely fit now as our supporters will see on Wednesday night.' Celtic edged it 3-2, but the fans who were there to witness the action were not quite as convinced as their club's manager about the merits of the centre-forward. Their doubts were given some substance when McBride was omitted from the team for the reserve fixture at Easter Road three days later after Stein had been informed the pitch was particularly heavy following torrential rainfall in the capital. McBride, for the time being, anyway, came off the radar as the gossips moved onto some other unfortunate victim.

The club's top scorer was, in fact, in the Parkhead stand to witness his Celtic pals squaring up to the Hibs side that had made them work so hard for two points in Edinburgh back in the first week in October. The champions had won that exciting skirmish 5-3 and, in the opening minutes of the return fixture, it looked as though the 41,000 supporters were in for another bumper episode of goalmouth action. Inside the first ten minutes, Willie Wallace and Stevie Chalmers had hit the woodwork and Jimmy O'Rourke had replied for the visitors by blitzing one off Ronnie Simpson's post.

The goal avalanche didn't materialise, though. Celtic won 2-0 fairly comfortably in the end. Wallace had the Parkhead faithful cheering in the twelfth minute when he drove the ball wide of Thomson Allan and Chalmers followed up with the killer second seven minutes before the turnaround. Celtic strangled the game in the second period with their possessional expertise while still maintaining a high level of entertainment. Chalmers' goal was his fourth in three successive league games and he had given the impression he had unhesitatingly picked up the goalscoring gauntlet in the absence of McBride.

The appealing nature of the team's adventurous outlook, moved one newspaper reporter to write, 'To declare that Celtic are the outstanding football side in Scotland is as much a statement of the obvious as to say the best way of remaining alive is to keep breathing. For the critic - be he friendly, alien or neutral - the problem of each passing week rests in how to rephrase former eulogies. On this evidence, Celtic are unlikely to offer him much relief from his difficulty until the season ends.'

January 28 just happens to be the date this author made his debut on the planet. Celtic - and Rangers - supporters may have other reasons to remember this milestone, for both vastly differing reasons. On the face of it, a quiet and unremarkable Saturday was on the cards with both teams taking part in the Scottish Cup against teams from the lower division. Celtic had been drawn against Arbroath at Parkhead and Jock Stein had pondered the wisdom and validity of bringing back Joe McBride against inferior opposition, especially at home. However, he heeded medical advice that informed him the striker still required to rest his problematic knee. McBride was again in the comfy seats to watch the game which was just about over beyond the half-hour mark with the home side coasting along with a three-goal advantage. It would eventually finish at 4-0 and Ronnie Simpson may have even felt a little guilty at accepting his win bonus such was the inactivity around his goalmouth.

Bobby Murdoch sent a twenty-yard rocket screeching high into the net for the first goal in the thirteenth minute and six minutes later Tommy Gemmell demonstrated his shooting power from thirty yards when he torpedoed one into the top corner. Stevie Chalmers applied a typical finish for No 3 and Bertie Auld had a tap-in for the fourth near the end. Everything had gone according to plan for one half of the celebrated Old Firm. However, it wasn't quite the case for the holders of the trophy who had been drawn away from home to play the minnows of Berwick Rangers. It had been billed as a mismatch of colossal proportions. Had it been a boxing contest, no board of control would have issued a licence for the fight to take place in legal circumstances. Or so we were informed.

BERWICK RANGERS 1 RANGERS 0 was the scoreline that sent shock waves through football. The host of BBC Grandstand had to repeat the result a couple of times to astonished viewers such was the unexpectedness and sheer disbelief at the outcome of the game at Shielfield Park. Rangers went into the contest as holders of the trophy content in the knowledge they had never lost in the tournament to a team from a lower division. Also, it had been thirty years since the Ibrox team had vacated the competition at the first hurdle. Sammy Reid was the player behind the sensational result with the only goal in the thirty-second minute. The following day, Reid was back at his job as a gear cutter in a local engineering yard to make up for the time he had been given off to train for the big game.

The story still persists of Rangers captain John Greig asking referee Eddie Thomson to allow another couple of minutes as the game edged towards its conclusion. The match official is alleged to have replied, 'I've already given you four!' The Ibrox stalwart, who later became the club's manager, didn't attempt to play the down the humiliation when he said,

'This is probably the worst result in the history of this club.' Ironically, the Berwick Rangers goalkeeper that fateful afternoon was none other than Jock Wallace, who was player/manager of the tiny club. His take on the score? 'We should have won 3-0,' he said. 'We missed two easier chances than the one Sammy put away.'

Bertie Auld recalled, 'Everyone seemed shocked by that result, but not me. I was convinced Rangers had used up a full season's luck when they beat us in the Scottish Cup replay the previous season.' Tongue in cheek, perhaps? Only the most devilishly mischievous of the Lisbon Lions has the answer to that.

CHAPTER ELEVEN
FEBRUARY
FIGHTING BACK

"This was a Celtic squad not scared of anyone or anything and that allowed us to express ourselves."

- Bertie Auld

The increasing popularity of Celtic - and their exhilarating brand of swashbuckling, entertaining football - could be measured in matchday attendances as figures continued to soar throughout the land. They were the biggest draw in the country and that was exemplified when their league game against Airdrie at Broomfield on Saturday February 4 was a 23,000 all-ticket sell-out.

As ever against crude and graceless opponents, the affair was never far away from developing into a roughhouse. After Jock Stein's side's 3-0 victory, a newspaper reporter observed, 'Airdrie, for the most part, chose to play it tough, paying more attention to the man than to the ball. But with Celtic able and willing to meet them on these terms, no advantage accrued to the home side and the game was less than satisfying as a spectacle. Hughes was a particular target for abuse and, despite persistent provocation, showed remarkable self-restraint.'

Bertie Auld was smack in the middle of the combat zone that afternoon and he said, 'Listen, there had been times in the past when Celtic could get kicked off the park. Our board of directors had almost-puritanical thoughts on the way they believed Celtic players should perform. It was okay for us to be knocked all over the place, but heaven forbid if any Celtic player decided to give some of it back. The directors would tut-tut if they even considered one their players had stood up for himself. If you hurt an opponent who had been kicking lumps out of you all day there was every chance your name would disappear from the team sheet for the next game. Any sort of retribution was absolutely frowned upon.

'Obviously, our opponents knew the score. Every other team was well aware that we had to contain ourselves in fear of a reprisal from upstairs. Sometimes, it was like sending a boxer into the ring with both his hands tied behind his back and telling him to lead with his chin. And, back then, it was just as effective, too. But that all changed when Big Jock returned. Look, we knew we had to entertain, but, first and foremost, we were told to win. Not at all costs, because that was not Celtic's style; never was and never will be. The name Celtic will always be synonymous with fair play. Big Jock was a winner and we were all up for that and, obviously, agreed with the Boss.

'So, we were given a bit more freedom, if you like. Constraints were lifted and attitudes were relaxed. We were never going to win anything by adopting the 'After you, Claude' outlook. In the days before I left the club for Birmingham City, we would get turned over regularly by teams who didn't possess a fraction of our ability. But they set out to stamp - sometimes literally - their authority on a game and there was little we were allowed to do about it. We had guys such as Paddy Crerand who wouldn't tolerate anyone daft enough to give him a hard time, no matter the instructions from above. Paddy was born and brought up in the Gorbals and knew how to look after himself. No-one messed with Paddy. Same went for me. I was just a wee boy from Maryhill, but that was a hard school, too.

'So, it was hardly surprising that Paddy and I were sold within a year or so of each other. Neither of us wanted to go, of course. Also, we could be outspoken and that was frowned upon by the management, as well. So, we were shown the door. After Big Jock took over, we could go to a place like Broomfield and know they would attempt to intimidate us. However, the message was getting across to them that they were wasting their time with any bully boy threats. It may have paid off for our opponents in the past, but those days were gone. And our rivals realised it. I could look around the dressing room and see guys such as Tommy Gemmell, Bobby Murdoch, Billy McNeill, John Clark...I could go through the entire team. Jimmy Johnstone? Frightened of no-one. So, this was a Celtic squad who weren't scared of anyone or anything and that allowed us to express ourselves and play in the manner everyone expected of the team.

'One of Big Jock's favourite sayings was, "Win the battle and you'll win the war". As individuals, we all knew what that meant. Sort out your own personal situation and, if your team-mates do the same, then you've got an excellent chance of winning the game. I never shirked a 50/50 challenge. I could get a dig in and maybe send an opponent spinning on his backside. I would always smile, offer my hand to help him up and say something like, "Come on, son, there's another hour to go." Some of the replies were a bit rude! Almost overnight, our attitude changed and everyone realised Celtic were no-one's pushovers. The message got around fairly swiftly.'

Broomfield, though, was seen as something of a version of soccer's litmus test. Everyone was aware of the zealousness of the Airdrie players who were always keen for opponents to meet the acquaintance of the trackside wall which, unhelpfully for the 'victim', was only a handful of yards from the touchline.

Years later, when Billy McNeill was the Celtic manager first time around, we were discussing the halcyon days of bone-crushing, bruising battles at Broomfield when he was a player. The legendary captain laughed, 'It was a great experience. You know, when I'm buying a player now I look at him and wonder if he could have played against Airdrie at Broomfield on a muddy pitch in winter and stood up to some of their big defenders who thrived on thirty-yard slide tackles. If I thought that he could, then he had a good chance of signing for Celtic!'

On this particular afternoon on a rock-solid surface, there were no traumas lying in wait for the Parkhead side. Keeper Roddie McKenzie fumbled a Willie Wallace shot and that was never advisable with nippy raiders such as Jimmy Johnstone in the vicinity. In a flash, the ball was in the back of the net and Celtic had a twelfth-minute lead. Moments after the interval, Stevie Chalmers turned on the after-burners as he hared through the middle of the home defence before firing beyond McKenzie. In the sixty-ninth minute, the elastic-limbed Irish international keeper thought his luck had changed when he pushed away a penalty-kick from Auld. He was reprieved for only a matter of seconds before the midfielder followed up to skelp the rebound into the net. Three goals scored away from home, none conceded and two points in the bag. It was championship-winning form.

In his usual diligent manner, Jock Stein prepared for the forthcoming European Cup quarter-final ties against Vojvodina Novi Sad the following month by arranging a challenge game against another Yugoslav team, Dinamo Zagreb, on February 7 at Parkhead. The deep-thinking manager promised the fans 'something completely revolutionary' in his team formation against top-class opponents who would end the season with a 2-0 two-legged victory over Leeds United to win the Inter-Cities' Fairs Cup, now, of course, known as the Europa Cup.

The intriguing pledge from Stein was enough to entice 46,000 fans - this author included - to a frosty, foggy east end of Glasgow on a Tuesday evening to witness this new-look Celtic. At first, it was difficult to fathom the experimental line-up, especially with Billy McNeill wearing No.3 on his shorts, Tommy Gemmell with No.8, John Hughes with No.5 and Bertie Auld with No.7. The only player who appeared to have his regular number was Ronnie Simpson. Basically, Stein fielded a team in a 3-4-3 formation with three central defenders in McNeill, Davie Cattenach and John Clark. Gemmell and Hughes were deployed as deep-lying wide players with Bobby Murdoch and Auld in their usual places in the middle. Up front were Willie Wallace, Stevie Chalmers and Bobby Lennox, who was replaced by Jimmy Johnstone after the interval.

The Slavs won 1-0 with a breakaway goal two minutes from the end by their top marksman Slaven Zambata, so, as far as the result was concerned, the plan wasn't an instant success. However, Stein may have been tempted to persist with it had Chalmers, Lennox and Johnstone not been wasteful with excellent opportunities. Gemmell, too, brought out two superb saves from the highly-rated Zlato Skoric with trademark long-range drives. Hughes recalled, 'Jock had all the players at Parkhead four hours before the kick-off that evening to go over his thoughts. He went into fine detail about his newly-devised team pattern and handed roles to me and Big Tommy that ensured we wouldn't get a moment's rest. We would be fetching, running and delivering throughout the ninety minutes. It might have worked in theory, but it didn't in practice. Before the end, the Boss reverted to our usual formation and, ironically, that is when Dinamo scored.'

Stevie Chalmers continued to don the mantle of Celtic's main goalscoring threat when he claimed a second-half hat-trick in the 5-0 trouncing of Ayr United at Somerset Park on February 11. The travelling fans hadn't been too keen to attend the game when they learned the kick-off had been moved forward two hours to one o'clock to accommodate Kilmarnock v Rangers at Rugby Park which was allowed by the authorities to start at the traditional 3pm time.

It still didn't prevent a crowd of 19,000 squeezing into the tiny ground to enjoy another away day and the supporters were treated to a rare Jimmy Johnstone headed goal to open the scoring four minutes from the interval. The diminutive winger found a pocket of space in the crowded penalty area as Tommy Gemmell slung over a peach of a cross and the full-back's close friend applied the finishing touch via his mop of vibrant red curls.

The home side had worked overtime to keep their opponents at bay, but their resistance collapsed in five second-half minutes as Celtic crammed three goals into their net. Chalmers knocked in the second after being set up by Johnstone in the fifty-seventh minute and within seconds John Hughes had battered in another - his first goal since returning from injury. The giant winger set Chalmers free for No.4 and the striker completed his trio with only eight minutes remaining.

The following Saturday offered a bit of a curiosity to the 30,000 fans at Parkhead as Celtic took on Elgin City in the Scottish Cup. The Highlanders had shocked Ayr United on the same day Rangers nosedived at Berwick, but their exploits hadn't convinced the bookmakers they were anything better than a 20,000/1 hope to sample glory at Hampden later in the season. Turf accountants in attendance that afternoon might have been questioning their wisdom with the part-timers holding the champions and trophy favourites to a scoreless stalemate with only two minutes remaining of the first-half.

Jock Stein watched as his players peppered the Elgin City goal and Tommy Gemmell came close to a hat-trick inside the first half-hour. The ball was being blocked and diverted as the anxious visitors valiantly held out. If Mel Gibson had invested in a time machine, he would have recognised there was no need for a casting couch for 'Braveheart' - he had a ready-made cast as the men from the north re-enacted some of the backs-to-the-wall battle scenes that afternoon in Glasgow. However, as the clock ticked down, Celtic, in unshakeable fashion, thumped in three goals. Stevie Chalmers sent a header fizzing into the net in the forty-third minute and, before sixty seconds had elapsed, Bobby Lennox added another. With just moments to go to half-time, Chalmers unselfishly set up Lennox for a third. The poor Highlanders looked utterly devastated as they trudged head down towards the dressing room. So near and yet so far...

They were put out of their misery when John Hughes blasted in a fourth just after the hour mark and Lennox rounded off his hat-trick in the seventieth minute. Willie Wallace went into the history books as the club's first-ever substitute in a Scottish Cup-tie as Jock Stein put him on late in the game for Bobby Murdoch. Wallace announced his introduction by scoring twice to bring the total to seven. The Bravehearts had been undone by William Wallace. There had also been a nice touch before the game when Charlie Gallagher led out the team ahead of skipper Billy McNeill. It was an honour bestowed upon the elegant midfielder after he had been told he had been selected for his first Republic of Ireland cap against Turkey in midweek. Gallagher, a cousin of Paddy Crerand and also born and brought up in the tough Glasgow area of the Gorbals, qualified to play for the Irish through parentage.

The absence of Joe McBride, even from the substitute's bench, was beginning to provoke speculation once again that all was not well behind the scenes at Parkhead. Jock Stein had taken a full complement of players to Seamill for a three-day break before the Scottish Cup-tie and with an eye to the forthcoming European Cup quarter-final against Vojvodina.

McBride missed out on the refresher course at the Ayrshire coast as he was left at Parkhead for intensive training. The Celtic manager, though, maintained his stance that the player would return before the end of the campaign. Stein was famed for his positive thinking, but was also known for his kidology and that presented a conundrum. Just how serious was the injury to Joe McBride? If Big Jock knew, he wasn't telling.

One thing was abundantly clear, though, and that was the mood of Stein following Celtic's next game. After losing 1-0 to Stirling Albion in the compact confines of Annfield Park last season, the manager went ballistic following his team's surrender of a point in a 1-1 draw against the struggling outfit who went into the contest as the third worst team in the First Division and who would remain in that position and just escape relegation at the end of the season. Stein's affability wasn't helped when his team came in a goal adrift at the interval. After dominating for huge chunks of the opening forty-five minutes, Stirling stunned the Parkhead outfit with a goal in the twenty-third minute. George Peebles was allowed far too much freedom on the edge of the box and he wheeled to strike a low drive away from the stretching Ronnie Simpson.

'Big Jock was furious,' said John Hughes. 'I had seen him like that during the interval in a game against St Johnstone at Muirton Park. I had been on the receiving end of a fairly nasty challenge and was left with a gash all the way down my right shin that required immediate attention with stitches obviously needed. "Get that sorted," shouted Jock. "You're going out for the second-half." I knew he was serious. So, too, was I. "I can't play, boss," I told him. "Look at the mess of my leg. The stitches will burst at any time." Clearly, he wasn't happy at my stance. We had Stevie Chalmers as a substitute that day and it was obvious a fully-fit Stevie was a better option than me trying to cope with one leg. But Big Jock certainly didn't like anyone who disagreed with him.'

Ironically, it was Hughes who rescued Celtic on this occasion when he launched a header into the net for the equaliser seven minutes after the turnaround. The champions, though, couldn't carve out a crucial second goal as Stein grew more and more agitated on the touchline. His frustration was multiplied on the terracing among the travelling support as the home side frantically and desperately booted the ball all over the place as they held out grimly for an unlikely draw. It would appear Bobby Murdoch's dread of Broomfield and Brockville had now been matched by his manager's distaste of Annfield. The bulldozers have since removed all three grounds from sight and somewhere above us there just might be two Celtic legends sharing a smile at that thought.

Worryingly, though, Joe McBride, who had played for the reserves in midweek against Dundee, wasn't deemed to be anywhere near fit enough to be named in the squad for Stirling. And the centre-forward would be left at home when Celtic flew out to Yugoslavia and their European Cup quarter-final first leg against Vojvodina the following Wednesday.

Once more the rumour factory sprung into overdrive.

CHAPTER TWELVE
MARCH
MARCHING ON IN EUROPE

"I didn't score a single league goal that season, but the one I got in the European Cup was a wee bit special."

- Billy McNeill

Jock Stein didn't quite get around to instructing the assembled squad of players to dismiss thoughts of conquering Europe, but he left them in absolutely no doubt that the prime target for season 1966/67 was to retain the First Division championship, annexed in some considerable style the previous term for the first time since 1954. Any status earned on foreign fields would be accepted as a bonus; ultimate victory in the European Cup wasn't included in anyone's aspirations.

I interviewed all eight existing European Cup winners when I was writing the book, 'The Lisbon Lions: 40th Anniversary Celebration'. I allotted a chapter to each member of the historic team to give their unique view on events. Billy McNeill's thoughts on Celtic's chances of actually winning the trophy were quite candid. He admitted, 'The European Cup was a trophy that belonged to other teams, glamorous sides from other parts of Europe. Only Real Madrid, six times, Benfica (twice), Inter Milan (twice) and AC Milan (once), had won the most prestigious prize European football had to offer. British football merely had its nosed pressed up against the window, wanting to get in, but being completely ignored.'

I didn't discover one player who admitted to having prior knowledge that the European Cup Final for that particular season would be played in the Portuguese capital of Lisbon.

So, the sharp focus for the campaign was the safe delivery of a second successive title. That being the priority, the Celtic manager would have been reasonably satisfied his team were league leaders going into the month of March. After twenty-four games, it was obviously a straight fight between the Parkhead side and their ancient foes Rangers for the crown.

Celtic had won nineteen, drawn four and lost one to rack up forty-two points. Their persistent challengers from Govan had played the same amount of games and had won eighteen, drawn four and lost two to amass forty points, only two adrift of Stein's team in pole position. Celtic had scored a highly laudable eighty-three goals, eleven more than their pursuers, but had conceded twenty-five, with the Ibrox outfit losing four fewer. There were still ten games remaining, but the two nearest teams to the Old Firm, Aberdeen and Hibs, already knew third top would be their best achievement; both trailed Celtic by ten points.

Jock Stein's team ushered in the month with their European Cup quarter-final first leg against the Yugoslavian champions Vojvodina in a frosty, cheerless and aptly-named Novi Sad. The manager's pre-match talk was about the importance of ball retention against a team who knew how to use the object fairly expertly. Jim Craig was introduced at right-back for his European Cup debut with Tommy Gemmell switching wings and Willie O'Neill dropping out.

With twenty-one minutes to go, Stein would have been satisfied. It was goalless and Ronnie Simpson hadn't been unduly perturbed. And then Gemmell, so often the matchwinner, made a costly mistake. On a difficult, flint-hard surface, the left-back decided to attempt a passback, a movement never encouraged by his boss. Unfortunately, Gemmell's wayward ball fell between Bobby Murdoch and John Clark and that was all the darting Svemir Djordic needed to intercept the pass, square it to Milan Stanic and the winger expertly placed a low drive away from the advancing Simpson.

The legendary Vujadin Boskov, later to manage some of the biggest teams in Europe including Real Madrid, had ordered his side to get a two-goal advantage and his players did their best to comply with his wishes. However, it is to Celtic's spirit and credit that they refused to panic or fold in front of such impressive opposition. The Slavs had to be content with Stanic's solitary effort as the visitors shut up shop with Simpson, Billy McNeill and John Clark repelling some frantic raids for the next twenty minutes.

Gemmell said, 'I didn't make any excuses back then and I'm certainly not going to do so now. However, I underestimated two things that night: the dodgy surface and the pace of a player called Djordic. The pass might have looked like a lost cause to the Slav, but he didn't give it up and his sheer acceleration defied the elements. He got to the ball first, squared it for his team-mate and he thumped it past Faither, who was helpless. I got an earful from my goalkeeper and I put up my hands and said, "Sorry, lads, my fault." I felt dreadful. One slack pass and we were smack in trouble - all our good work had gone for precisely nothing. I knew we would be up against it in Glasgow.'

Bertie Auld recalled, 'Of course, we were all disappointed afterwards in the dressing room. Tommy had made a mistake and he admitted it. However, a team-mate, who shall remain nameless, was so upset he said, "Why did you have to try something fancy? Why not just hoof it up the pitch?" Big Jock heard the comments and immediately rounded on the player. He practically shouted, "Have you forgotten the amount of times Tommy Gemmell has won games for us?" That was typical of the manager, though. He wouldn't have anyone abusing any of his players - unless, of course, it was him!'

Ronnie Simpson paid his tribute to the slick Slavs. 'Vojvodina were undoubtedly the best side we met in the European Cup. They were a disciplined team with a lot of talent and well groomed by Vujadin Boskov, a former international left-half of world class. I thought we paced the game in Novi Sad to perfection and did everything right. Then just as we had the Yugoslav champions on the retreat, we lost a goal - and a daft one at that.

'In sixty-nine minutes, Tommy Gemmell tried to push the ball back to me from a fair distance and didn't get enough on the ball. It ended at Stanic, their outside-left, who was onto it in a flash and fairly romped it past me. John Clark almost got there, but, like most of us, didn't expect Tommy to muff his kick. That changed the pattern of the game a little, giving them fresh heart and we had to be content with a 1-0 defeat, the first time we had lost a leg on our European journey.'

Bobby Murdoch agreed with his keeper about the qualities of the quarter-final opponents. He remembered, 'Vojvodina were the hardest team we met, no argument. Jock Stein had checked them out prior to the first game and had us mentally prepared. He had warned us we would have a hard match and that they moved like a British side. They were a physical team, not unlike ourselves and the Germans. They wouldn't panic, they wouldn't quit. The Boss was right.

'They came at us so fast and furiously in Novi Sad that we were caught out in those early minutes. Their pace and strength surprised us. But we held them, sometimes having to pull eight players back in defence to combat their energetic attacking waves. In our own breakaways, we found they had a magnificent centre-half in Ivica Brzic, who was built like a tank, and a smart keeper in Ilija Pantelic, who was quite the darling of the crowd.

'They were a hard team, who didn't shirk a tackle, but they were fair and, though we took a bit of stick from them in the opening part of the game, I must say I thoroughly enjoyed it. We had paced our game so well that by the interval the Yugoslavs were beginning to feel a bit frustrated. I felt that, tactically, we had played as well as we had ever played in Europe. Then just when they were beginning to sag and we were beginning to show more in attack and take a very tight grip on the game, we lost a silly goal. Tommy Gemmell, under a little pressure on the left, decided to turn and push the ball back to Ronnie Simpson. Unfortunately, Tam didn't hit the ball hard enough. By the time John Clark realised the ball wasn't going to make it, they had scored. Were we sick? And how do you think Tommy Gemmell felt? This inspired the Yugoslavs to pick up their game and so we finished the first leg a goal down.

'The crowd were so excited that they ran on to the field and carried their keeper off the ground. I don't know why they chose Pantelic. They should have carried off their outside-left who was smart enough to take advantage of our one and only boob. When the manager came into the dressing room after the match, he took one look at Tommy Gemmell, who was sitting with his head in his hands, and said, "Get your head up off the floor. You've won games for us. It's not over yet."'

As an interesting postscript, the classy midfielder added, 'Prior to the banquet at the Petrovardin Fortress, which overlooked the River Danube, we saw Inter Milan beat Real Madrid 2-0 on TV in the second leg of their European Cup quarter-final to win 3-0 on aggregate. We figured the great Real Madrid had problems much greater than ours. We were still in the competition!'

Simpson reflected on a meeting with his opposite number at the banquet. 'The Vojvodina keeper, Ilija Pantelic, who was the No.1 in Yugoslavia, sought me out. He told me he was amazed I was still playing in goal at the age of thirty-six. He told me, "If I'm still playing at thirty or thirty-one, I'll consider myself lucky." He made me feel like an old man!'

Pantelic, in fact, had caught the eye of Jock Stein when he watched the third-game play-off against Atletico Madrid. The 6ft 2in Slav looked the perfect sporting specimen, an ideal prototype for a goalkeeper. He was agile, possessed good hands and, generally, controlled his penalty area. The Celtic manager would also have noted he took his team's penalty-kicks and had actually scored from the spot against the Spaniards in Vojvodina's 3-1 win in the first game. There was talk of Stein surreptitiously making enquires about the availability of the shotstopper, but he received no encouragement from the Slavs. Pantelic, though, left Vojvodina for French football in 1969 and finished his career at Paris Saint German. He was thirty-five years old when he decided to hang up his gloves.

On matchdays, Celtic fans arriving early for the best places at which to stand and view the game from the terracing or enclosure would often witness the lone and thoughtful figure of Jock Stein pacing out the playing surface. The management and players would normally arrive at the ground by coach an hour-and-a-half before kick-off and one of the Celtic manager's first tasks was to inspect the pitch. Big Jock, unlike other team bosses, used to irritate the Press by refusing to name a line-up until thirty minutes or so before a game. 'Who would be expected to pay good money to go and see a film if they didn't know who is starring in it?'

the reporters would often point out, with a reasonable amount of logic. They required the team for the Saturday editions of their newspapers, but, of course, their observations meant little to Stein. He never saw the point of making his selection public the day before a game when overnight conditions could see him making sweeping changes. As a gambler, he had no intention of showing his hand to a rival manager, either.

On March 4, only three days after competing on the rock-solid pitch of Novi Sad, the Celtic manager was meticulously scrutinising the conditions of Love Street before putting his eleven together for the game against a St Mirren outfit who had, quite remarkably, taken a point from Parkhead in November, still the only team to manage the achievement at that stage of the season. On the odd occasion, Stein would call upon the services of trainer Neilly Mochan to bring a couple of balls out with him to roll along the top layer. Only when he was totally satisfied, did Stein announce his formation to his players and have the team lines delivered to the match officials, the opposing manager and directors of both clubs. On this particular afternoon, the heavy going meant an unwanted day off for Jimmy Johnstone with John Hughes getting the green light to play on the right wing.

Once again, Stein's scrupulous, diligent eye for the most minute of detail worked in Celtic's favour. Hughes powered through the stamina-sapping Paisley sludge as the champions stormed to a 5-0 victory. Goalkeeper Denis Connaghan, his side's hero in their 1-1 draw in Glasgow, had already given the impression he would be picking up where he left off against his favourite team four months earlier. For half-an-hour, with Hughes running amok on the right touchline, Celtic subjected the Saints defence to a fearful battering without any substantial reward.

In the thirty-first minute, however, Tommy Gemmell embarked on another lung-bursting overlapping expedition on the left wing before bending in an inviting centre. Willie Wallace read the intentions of his team-mate with flawless timing and arrived on the scene at the precise moment to inflict maximum damage and tuck the ball beyond the helpless Connaghan. It remained that way until three minutes after the turnaround when Bobby Lennox doubled the advantage and, within minutes, Hughes repaid his manager for his decision-making, by blasting in the third. With the exhausted Paisley rearguard on the point of collapse, Gemmell zipped in a penalty-kick in the eighty-third minute and Wallace grabbed another in the dying embers of the encounter.

Near the end, Bertie Auld signalled to the bench he couldn't continue after taking a dull one from a frustrated Saints opponent. Remarkably, Big Jock waved him off, but then refused to replace him. Johnstone was on the substitute's bench and eager to get into the thick of things. However, Stein decided, with the team already so far ahead and the points assured, he would not take a chance with his little winger getting injured as the match neared its end. He wanted Johnstone fit and raring to go for the European Cup return against Vojvodina in midweek and, thus, Celtic finished the game with only ten men.

Celtic Park rocked like never before at the dramatic conclusion of the game against the champions of old Yugoslavia. The aggregate score was locked at 1-1 with less than a minute on the clock and a replay in the Dutch city of Rotterdam the following Wednesday the likely outcome. Celtic forced a corner-kick on the right and Charlie Gallagher, taking the place of the injured Bertie Auld, raced over to take it. On a savagely cold evening, the fans could see their breath plume in front of them. No-one complained, though. Collectively, 69,372 individuals came together for one last roar of encouragement. A crescendo of noise enveloped the east end of Glasgow.

Gallagher appraised the situation as bodies jostled for position, elbows visiting opponents' ribs, jerseys being held in desperate grips. Billy McNeill took up his usual post at the edge of the eighteen-yard box. Gallagher shaped to take a short kick, but changed his mind and carefully swung the ball into the middle of the goal. Ilija Pantelic made a move to come off his line. McNeill, surging forward into the throng, was precision itself in his timing. The ball floated in the air as the Celtic captain climbed the highest. There was a thump as it smacked off his forehead. Pantelic looked back in utter anguish, defender Stevan Nesticki tried to perform heroic acrobatics on the line, but it was to no avail. McNeill's header swished straight into the net with glorious meticulousness. Swedish referee Hans Carlsson blew for time-up exactly TWO SECONDS later and Celtic, extraordinarily, were in the European Cup semi-final.

Celebrated London Times sports journalist Geoffrey Green observed, 'The last half-hour produced unbroken heartburn as Celtic thundered forward for the decider. In that space of time, Johnstone, who all through had been a thorn in the side of the Slav's left flank, grew to even higher stature; and on the left wing Hughes, at last, began to use his pace and weight to add a second dangerous sector. The Vojvodina defence suddenly found itself the nut between the crackers. As the minutes unwound, there came great saves from the Slav goalkeeper Pantelic from Gallagher, Hughes, Johnstone, Hughes again, and even Gemmell and Chalmers.

'All were looking at their watches as Gallagher clearly was taking the last corner-kick of the night. Over it came; up went a forest of heads, but there, the tallest of them, was the fair head of McNeill, who nodded the ball home to the top corner. That was victory at the last gasp and Parkhead, and its great swirling concourse, took wings.'

Celtic had levelled the tie just before the hour mark when Tommy Gemmell made amends for his first leg loss of concentration that may have cost so dear. He used John Hughes as decoy as he dashed down the left wing and pitched over an inviting cross. Pantelic sprang from his line, but the courageous Stevie Chalmers was even faster off the mark and he got there just ahead of the keeper to knock the ball into the gaping net.

The hero of the hour, Billy McNeill, recalled, 'I didn't score a single league goal that season, but the one in the European Cup was a wee bit special, even if I do say so myself. I couldn't have timed it better. I know Big Jock and all the lads rated Vojvodina as by far the best team we met that year, including Inter Milan. The Yugoslavs were superb technically, but were also fairly adept in possibly the not-so-finer points in the game. There was also some memorable mind-games going off the pitch between the Boss and their manager Vujadin Boskov.

'Even before the first game, Big Jock clearly wasn't impressed by Boskov's pre-match prediction. The Slav boss stated emphatically he believed Vojvodina would be victorious by "at least two goals". Jock thought, "Oh, really? We'll see about that." When they won by a solitary effort from Stanic, Boskov came out again and declared he hadn't been too impressed by Celtic and his team would win again in Glasgow. Now if

Boskov was trying to get Jock fired up for the return he couldn't have done a better job. The Big Man spoke to the Yugoslav Press and went on record as saying, "Vojvodina are a very good team, but we are better and we will win in Glasgow." It was sheer bravado because we all realised just how difficult the Slavs would be in the return leg.

'Boskov and his players turned up at Celtic Park the night before the game and they wanted a work-out on the pitch under the floodlights. It was normal practice for teams to go through this routine as it made a lot of sense for them to get a feel for the conditions they are going to encounter twenty-four hours later.

'The Vojvodina boss wasn't best pleased, then, when Big Jock gave him the news neither he nor his players would be placing a foot on the pitch at Celtic Park. "Sorry, there's been too much rain in Glasgow recently," Jock informed him. "We can't take the chance of the pitch cutting up." He did have a point, but Boskov was far from convinced. He made all sorts of protestations; he would take it up with the Celtic chairman, he threatened. Jock waved it away in his usual fashion. "You can train at Barrowfield and I'll make sure the lights are switched on. Off you go."

'To say the Slavs were not amused would be putting it rather mildly. They were fizzing, but, at least, Boskov and his boys got the drift that Jock Stein was, indeed, the man in charge at Celtic. As far as football matters went, there was no higher power. Vojvodina, though, were determined to have the last word during the game in Glasgow. As I said, they were an extremely talented and resilient outfit and they weren't slow to hand out a wee bit of punishment every now and then. We had to endure close to an hour of frustration before we got our own back when Stevie Chalmers made it 1-1 on aggregate after a typically unselfish run and cross from the left by Tommy Gemmell.

'I have been told the referee blew for time-up two seconds after the restart following my goal. Now that is a late, late goal. We won a corner-kick on the right and I'll always recall Big Jock waving us all up for one last assault on their goal. Charlie Gallagher, who had a sublime touch, raced over to take it. Actually, I think Charlie was about to take a short one, but a Slav defender raced to cut it off and Charlie changed his mind. Thank God!

'Charlie was left with no option but to put the ball into the mix. There was the usual barging and jostling as I made my way forward. The Slavs had marked me very well at set-pieces and I hadn't really had a sniff at goal. On this occasion, though, my timing was just absolutely spot-on. Charlie swung it in, I kept my run going, the ball hung in the air, I got a good leap, made superb contact and the next thing I saw was the effort soaring high into the net. Pantelic had strayed a bit from his line and they had a defender on the goal-line who did a fair impersonation of a goalkeeper as he leapt up with his left arm to try to keep the ball out. He was wasting his time - that was a goal all the way as soon as it came off my napper.

'Vojvodina went crazy when the referee awarded the goal. They were convinced I had fouled Pantelic. I can hold my hands up all these years down the line and tell the world I didn't even touch their goalkeeper. I was nowhere near him, as a matter of fact. However, you might ask Stevie Chalmers if he had blocked Pantelic! He may have taken a half-yard step in front of the big goalie when he was leaving his line in an effort to cut out the cross. So what? It was all part of the game back then as it still is today. Believe me, the Slavs weren't slow in getting in front of me any time I came forward. But, thanks to Charlie's deadball accuracy, there was nothing anyone could do to prevent me from making contact on that occasion and managing to do some damage.

'I knew it was late in the game, but, honestly, I had no idea that it was quite as late as that. As I ran back to take my position in the heart of the defence, I shouted over at John Clark, "Keep concentrating, Luggy. We're not going to lose a goal now." Luggy just looked at me and said, "What are you talking about, Caesar? The game's finished. It's over and we're through." Seconds later it was, indeed, well and truly over and our great adventure was still on track.

'I remember the Vojvodina players cracking up as they kicked off and the ref blew for time-up. Actually, one of their own players raced into the melee and started shoving his team-mates all over the place to get them to calm down. He was a big lad, too, and, thankfully, they did as they were told. It could have been very interesting going up the tunnel that evening. That tunnel could tell a tale or two, that's for sure. These were the days before TV cameras seemed to spring up everywhere and sometimes there could be some "sorting-out" done in the darkness of that tight, little area that led to the dressing rooms. Not that I ever got involved myself, you understand!'

Stevie Chalmers recollected, 'Scoring the most historic goal in Celtic's history in Lisbon is something I will always treasure, but I would like to think I also played my part in beating Vojvodina in the quarter-final. And I am not talking about my goal that made it 1-1 on aggregate and set up the grand finale for Big Billy to head in the last-minute winner. Our skipper was accused of fouling their goalkeeper Ilija Pantelic, but I can now confess he didn't come close to touching him - because I did!

'It wasn't a foul, though, I hasten to add. It was something that happened all the time in penalty boxes and I was blocked off a few times myself. However, on this occasion, I took a wee step in front of the keeper as he left his line in order to cut out Charlie Gallagher's right-wing corner-kick. It was only a half-yard or so, but it managed to put Pantelic off his stride. He couldn't get anywhere near the swirling ball and Big Billy, as he did so often, got his head to Charlie's cross to bullet an effort high into the net. Celtic Park erupted! The Yugoslavs were pointing fingers at everyone. They shouted at the referee, but he was having none of it. The goal was good and he pointed to the centre circle.'

Chalmers was another convinced of the qualities of dangerous foes. He added, 'Yes, like all the other Lisbon Lions, I really rated Vojvodina. You know I couldn't name any of their outfield players although Pantelic was gathering a bit of a reputation throughout Europe as being a top goalkeeper. He was class alright although, to be fair, he wasn't exactly overworked in the opening game when they won 1-0. It was an entirely different story in Glasgow, though, as you might expect. The atmosphere at Celtic Park was electrifying that night. The fans were in great voice and they did become our twelfth man.

'Again, I was fortunate enough to score and it was all down to Big Tommy belting down that left wing. Both Tommy and Jim Craig would run all day up and down their wings. Tommy, on the left, swung in an inviting cross and I tried to get between the goalkeeper and a defender. It was one of those crossballs that just needed a touch to knock it over the line. Pantelic threw himself at it, but got caught up with his own defender - nothing to do with me this time, honest! - and the ball dropped right in front of me. I couldn't miss and I just fired it over the line. That set up the big finish and Billy duly provided us with our semi-final passport - with a little assistance from yours truly.'

Bobby Lennox said, 'People often ask me what was my favourite goal in that European Cup run. Well, it wasn't one of mine! As it happens, I only scored two, in both legs of our 6-2 aggregate win over Nantes in the Second Round. Neither, I have to say, was particularly spectacular. However, Big Billy's winner against Vojvodina was something special altogether. Naturally, I was overjoyed for all the obvious reasons, but I was also doubly pleased because we had stuck two past their goalkeeper, Ilija Pantelic.

'I would like to believe I am a fairly easy-going type of bloke, but I really hated that guy. I know making a comment like that is way out of character for me, so please let me explain why I disliked the Vojvodina No.1 so much. In the first leg in Yugoslavia, I made a challenge for a 50/50 ball as I was quite entitled to do. I did it every week in Scottish football and no-one complained. Pantelic didn't like being disturbed, though. I slid in, my momentum took me forward and the goalkeeper collapsed on top of me as he collected the ball.

'It certainly wasn't a foul, but Pantelic wasn't too happy. He got to his feet and motioned to help me get up, too. It was all very sporting, but if anyone had bothered to take a closer look they would have seen the Slav had a handful of my hair as he 'helped' me back up off the ground. I've got a sense of humour, but that was no laughing matter. We were also fairly satisfied with the first leg result although, of course, it's never ideal to lose by any margin in Europe against first-rate opposition. However, as we travelled back, we were all convinced we would overturn their one-goal advantage. Me? I just wanted to stick one or two behind a certain Mr. Pantelic to welcome him to Glasgow in no uncertain fashion. Alas, I didn't get my wish, but we still beat them and that was the main objective all along.

'However, if you see footage of our first goal by Stevie Chalmers have a look at what I'm getting up to. I'm right in the goalkeeper's face and giving it "Yahoo!". Normally, I would run to the goalscorer to offer my congrats and give him a pat on the head, but I just couldn't help myself for making a beeline to their crestfallen keeper and letting him know exactly how I felt. I'm sorry, I had to do it. If I was happy then, you can imagine my feeling of sheer elation a minute from time when Big Billy sauntered forward in that manner of his and got his head to Charlie Gallagher's beautifully-flighted right-wing corner-kick. My friend Pantelic was caught in no-man's land as the ball soared high into the net. I kept away from him that time, I didn't want to push my luck! He was a big guy, after all, and his side had just been sent reeling out of Europe. I must say in his favour, though, we shook hands at the end of the game and he wished me all the best for the rest of the competition. I appreciated that.'

Jim Craig, who had missed the earlier rounds against Zurich and Nantes, reflected, 'The guy who gave me most bother was Vojvodina's Milan Stanic, who got their goal in the first leg in Novi Sad. He was skilful and tricky, but I remembered Big Jock's words. He said, "Lean on him and see if he has a heart that size of a pea". So, dutifully, I "leaned" on Stanic at one point. Lo and behold, he suddenly thought it was a better idea to go and play somewhere else on the field. Problem solved. Vojvodina were a fabulous team, though. They played in a typical, controlled Eastern European fashion and were superb at keeping possession. You can run for miles with the ball at your feet, but it's not so easy when you are chasing around trying to get it back. That can be exhausting and the Slavs put a lot of emphasis on retaining possession. We may have lost the first game 1-0, but we weren't disheartened. Simply put, we believed we could overturn their advantage in Glasgow. And so it proved, but we did leave it a bit late, didn't we?

'I thought we played well that night and, unfortunately for yours truly, I was next to Big Jock in the dug-out on the right touchline throughout a dramatic second-half that was fraught with anxiety. All I could hear above the din of almost 70,000 fans was "Cairney, do this" or "Cairney, do that". It wasn't easy playing right-back when Big Jock was in full flow. I used to look round every now and again and shout, "Why don't you have a go at Bobby Murdoch or Wee Jinky?" Luckily for them, they were probably out of earshot and were spared the verbal volleys from the manager. Big Jock would also yell at you to pass on instructions. Aye, right! I simply concentrated on my own game - that was enough to be going on with.'

Bobby Murdoch said, 'We were told during the preparation for the match that we had not to panic if we didn't score early. We had to be patient. The game ran ninety minutes and we would just have to wait until we got our chances. We knew it would be a fight. Vojvodina were a big, powerful side and, unlike our previous European Cup opponents, they had something to hold onto. They didn't have to come at us. We had to go at them and get the goals.

'At the interval, we still hadn't scored. And neither had they. We had gone at them hard from the whistle and pushed them from every angle, but we couldn't break them down. Into the second-half, we were beginning to despair a little. Then came a break down the left from Tommy Gemmell, so desperate to make up for his slip the previous week. Tam hit the ball hard across goal and Panetlic came out to meet it, let it slip onto his shoulder and the ball dropped to the ground. This was the kind of chance Stevie Chalmers lapped up. He was on to it like a hawk and hammered the ball into the net. Vojvodina were a different side now. Earlier, they had been deliberately slowing the pace of the game with their keeper bouncing the ball about and taking a long time to kick it out. Their centre-half was also regularly knocking the ball back to his keeper when he could have found a man upfield.

'Celtic were pushing hard now with the crowd whipping us on. Seventy minutes...eighty minutes...eighty-five minutes...and we were beginning to think of a play-off in Rotterdam. An extra match we didn't want as we were involved in so many games at home. Then in the final minute of the game, we got a corner-kick on the right hand side of the field. Charlie Gallagher ran out to take the kick and obviously meant to take a short one, when Jimmy Johnstone ran out with him. Dimitri Radovic, the Yugoslav full-back, raced out when he saw Charlie's intentions.

'As always, Billy McNeill moved up to the edge of the Vojvodina penalty area. Smartly, Charlie decided on a long kick. Over it came and there to meet it was the head of Billy McNeill to hammer the ball high into the Vojvodina net. What a goal! What a winner! The Slavs were beaten, they just couldn't come back after that. There wasn't time. I've never seen the Boss so excited. He didn't want to wait for the final whistle. He wanted to race onto the pitch there and then and smother us in congratulations. The crowd scenes were indescribable. We had made it by seconds.'

Even veteran Ronnie Simpson was almost swept off his feet by the euphoric wave hurtling around the ground at the end. He said, 'Celtic Park was a mad-house with me as mad as a hatter. Afterwards, I remember what the Boss had told us at half-time. "Get a grip of the middle of the field. You're giving Vojvodina too much space to work in. I want you to stay in constant attack." It worked.' Pictures in the Press the following day showed the thirty-six-year-old goalkeeper swinging from his crossbar like an overgrown kid. 'I couldn't help myself,' he said by way of explanation.

The record books will show that the earliest big-hitting Tommy Gemmell ever scored a goal was in the twenty-eighth second. Unhappily, there was no cause for celebration because the landmark strike came against Celtic. The maverick left-back somehow contrived to slice a clearance beyond Ronnie Simpson to hand Queen's Park a goal of a start in the Scottish Cup quarter-final at Parkhead a mere three days after the jubilation of the European triumph.

The breezy individual can look back now on the effort that silenced the large majority of the 43,000 Parkhead crowd for all the wrong reasons and smile. 'Sean Connery, old 007 himself, was introduced to the players before the game and then we all went out to get some photographs taken at the trackside before the kick-off. We all knew James Bond had a 'licence to kill', so I thought I would award myself a 'licence to thrill' and help our amateur opponents to make a game of it.

'Aye, that will be right! Faither gave me an earful and I knew I had to atone as swiftly as possible. Thankfully, I got that chance only six minutes later when we were awarded a penalty-kick. Even then, the ball hit the underside of the bar before flying into the net. Now, if I had missed the spot-kick questions might have been asked.'

With the unintentional assistance of the extrovert defender, the Hampden side had become the third team to score three goals against Celtic at home that season at that stage, matching Dunfermline's haul in the League Cup in September and Stirling Albion's tally in the league in November. The Fifers conceded six and the Annfield side were hit for seven. Queen's Park did marginally better and lost five. Stevie Chalmers put the Cup favourites ahead in the twenty-third minute, but the valiant opponents stunned the home support again eight minutes later when Niall Hopper equalised. A two-goal salvo before half-time from Willie Wallace and Bobby Murdoch made it 4-2, but the Spiders outrageously claimed a third forty seconds after the interval with Hopper again on target. It was left to the ever-willing Bobby Lennox to see off the impudent Mount Florida outfit with a fifth goal six minutes from the end.

The drama didn't conclude with Lennox's strike, unfortunately. Jimmy Johnstone got himself involved in an unseemly brawl with defender Miller Hay and both combatants were fortunate to remain on the pitch with an extremely lenient referee Jim Callaghan content to brandish only yellow cards, possibly taking into account the game had merely seconds to go until he blew for time-up. Johnstone's misbehaviour didn't escape the notice of chairman Bob Kelly or his unimpressed boardroom members watching the action from the directors' box. Jock Stein may have changed their outmoded attitude towards vigorous tackling, but he was helpless to save his wee winger from punishment on this occasion.

Gemmell recalled, 'We all realised Jinky had a temper - must have had something to do with red hair - and he just lost the plot against the Queen's Park player. As I recall, it hadn't been a particularly dirty game. Something, however, caused my wee pal to blow a fuse. The incident happened over at the Jungle down at the corner flag, so I didn't get a good view. But I have to say it did look as though Jinky had demonstrated the well-known art of what is quaintly known as 'The Glasgow Kiss'. Or, put another way, he stuck the heid on him. I think Jinky got a punch in the face in retribution, but we all thought that was the end of it at the final whistle. We could have guessed something was wrong when Big Jock told Jinky to remain behind after we had all changed, cleaned up and prepared to leave. The grim look on the manager's face told us the Wee Man was in trouble.'

The Celtic directors hastily convened a meeting in the boardroom and, after short deliberation, Johnstone was informed the club would not tolerate such unacceptable misbehaviour by one of their players and he would be suspended forthwith for a week. The player might have considered himself fortunate. Before the influence of Stein, the board might have been persuaded to lobby for public flogging to be reintroduced. Johnstone was forced to pull out of the Scottish League squad that was due to play their English counterparts - dodging a 3-0 defeat while doing so - and the league game a week later against Dunfermline. The old Celtic board, though, weren't so engulfed in morals as to prevent Johnstone training every day with the first team.

Jock Stein handed Johnstone's No.7 shorts to John Hughes, but, sending out mixed signals to Dunfermline, he ordered Yogi to hug the left touchline. Once again, the ploy worked with the sturdy raider spending an enjoyable afternoon terrorising the Fife club's right-back Willie Callaghan. In only three minutes, Stevie Chalmers took off on a spectacular horizontal dive to get his head to a Willie Wallace left-wing cross and divert the ball past his former team-mate Bent Martin low at his left-hand post. Alex Ferguson levelled matters in the nineteenth minute, but Tommy Gemmell sent an eruption of a penalty-kick high past Martin to restore the lead. Wallace nodded in the third before half-time and Ferguson, with the praiseworthy attribute of never giving up, handed his side faint hope with a second goal three minutes from the end.

Celtic, though, refused to surrender a third and the points were in the bag. Just as well because Rangers beat Ayr United 4-1 at Somerset Park on the same afternoon to go top of the table on the slenderest of goal average margins. However, the champions had a game in hand and no-one at Parkhead was pushing the panic button, but their age-old foes were refusing to give them any breathing space in a fairly anxious race for the title. It had all the indications of going all the way to the wire.

A crowd of 41,000 was in attendance to take in the encounter against Dunfermline and, incredibly, it meant the champions had been watched by over one million spectators at Celtic Park that season.

Following the triumph, one national newspaper reporter informed his readers, 'The more I see of Celtic these days, the stronger becomes the impression that the strain of chasing domestic and European honours is having its effect. Certainly, against Queen's Park the previous week and again on this occasion, when they played their fiftieth match of the season, their defence was not all it might have been.' The correspondent went on to reflect, 'Having said that, I must hasten to add that Celtic were far ahead in technique and thoroughly deserved to record their fourth victory of the season over the Fife club.'

The Ibrox side's occupation of the pinnacle was short-lived as Celtic played on the following Monday evening and they only required a reasonable degree of competency to overwhelm a feeble Falkirk team 5-0 at Parkhead. A lot of the talk before the game was centred on the European Cup semi-final draw which had paired Celtic with the champions of Czechoslovakia, Dukla Prague. Not a lot was known of the Czech Army team apart from the fact their most notable personality was cultured midfielder Josef Masopust, who had been named European Footballer of the Year in 1962. At the age of thirty-six, though, some observers, in football parlance, thought he was now 'in bus pass territory'.

Jock Stein immediately delved into the Czechoslovakian fixture list to see if he could find a suitable date to watch Dukla; the Celtic manager detested going in 'blind' against opponents. It was obvious, however, Celtic had a major obstacle to overcome if they were to prove worthy of a place in the European Cup Final in Lisbon on May 25 where their opponents would be either the contrasting duo of Inter Milan or CSKA Sofia, who were drawn in the other semi-final. Big Jock was a man who explored and investigated rivals with a ferocious need to know.

He had already discussed the Dutch upstarts of Ajax with his good friend Bill Shankly, the manager of Liverpool. The Amsterdam team, largely unknown outwith their borders, had decimated the Anfield side 5-1 in the first leg of their second round European Cup-tie in Holland. They had galloped into an unassailable four-goal interval lead and the English champions' only response was a last-kick-of-the-ball counter from Chris Lawler. Unusually dismissive of opponents, Shankly claimed the result was a 'complete fluke' and Liverpool would turn it around in the return on Merseyside. Ajax twice led before the game settled at 2-2 and the Dutch progressed on an overwhelming 7-3 aggregate. A young player by the name of Johan Cruyff had scored three goals over the tie. Stein, with his natural curiosity, quizzed his friend on the merits of the stylish Amsterdammers.

Shankly assured Stein Ajax had deserved their victory, he had no complaints and admitted he had witnessed something completely new in the construction of a team's tactics. Of course, the system later became known as 'Total Football', but, in the sixties, this was a brand new concept and it was highly unusual to witness outfield players who were naturally comfortable in every position within the structure of the team. 'John' - as Shankly persistently called the Celtic manager - was told Ajax had the players and strategy to turn football on its head and win the European Cup that season. The Liverpool boss was not known for his wild speculation or outrageous predictions. Stein took everything he said on board and decided to travel to an Ajax game at some point in the near future. However, Dukla Prague, skilful and methodical, derailed Cruyff and Co at the next stage of the competition. The Czechs achieved a 1-1 draw at the old De Meer stadium, with a capacity of 19,000, and edged a tight affair 2-1 in Prague. Without watching them live, Stein realised they were a team of some pedigree and quality.

Before that appetising double-header against the Czechs, though, there was the urgent requirement of another two points against Falkirk that would catapult Celtic back into pole position in the defence of their First Division title. Jimmy Johnstone, suitably chastised, was back in his familiar position at outside-right with John Hughes still wide on the opposite flank. The Brockville side resisted the champions' varied assaults until the twenty-fifth minute when Johnstone plonked a pass in front of Stevie Chalmers. His first shot was blocked, but he latched onto the rebound and fired home from close range. The canny, calculating Bertie Auld doubled the advantage before half-time with an ingenious lob from the edge of the box that sailed high into the net.

The goal of the game, though, belonged to Hughes, in the sixty-sixth minute, when he decided to go on one of his trademark solo runs with a net-bursting twenty-yarder to complete his impromptu act of defence-shredding ability. Falkirk's lumbering centre-half Doug Ballie welcomed Johnstone back to the fold by flattening him a minute later and Tommy Gemmell flashed in the inevitable spot-kick. Chalmers collected the fifth shortly afterwards. After a solid night's work, Celtic were top of the league by two points, with a total of forty-eight from twenty-seven games.

Almost unnoticed in the midst of the frantic football action, Joe McBride's season had come to a halt. The centre-forward had been forced to admit he would not be in action until the new campaign got underway following a cartilage operation at Killearn Hospital in Stirlingshire. Jock Stein expressed sympathy for the player and at the same time had a sideswipe at the rumour-mongers who insisted McBride's career was over. He said, 'The specialists have advised Joe to give his knee complete rest over his period of recuperation. Of course, Celtic will miss him and what he gives this team, but we want him back to full strength and we accept the decision of the surgeons. However, Joe has proved over and over again he can deal with challenges and we look forward to him taking up where he left off in the new season. He has got a lot more goals to score for Celtic Football Club.'

The blow, of course, had been lightened by the arrival of Willie Wallace and that was highlighted on a wintry Saturday afternoon in Edinburgh on March 25 when the versatile international returned to face his former Hearts team-mates at Tynecastle. A crowd of 25,000 was in place by the time of the kick-off and there had been talk of Wallace being given a hostile reception from the home supporters after his supposed 'defection' to Celtic. If that talk was expected to mess with the player's head it was a waste of someone's time. Wallace simply responded with, 'I'm a Celtic player now, we're top of the league and that's where we want to stay. I'll do everything I can to guarantee a win. It doesn't matter that it's Hearts or anyone else, two points are our priority.'

Wallace was as good as his word as he notched a clever second goal direct from a free-kick in Celtic's 3-0 victory in the freezing capital. Bertie Auld claimed the opener three minutes from the break when goalkeeper Jim Cruickshank could only beat away a Jimmy Johnstone cross to the edge of the penalty box. The midfielder, poised like a cobra, waited for the ball to drop before volleying a sweet left-foot drive into the exposed net. Just after the hour mark, Wallace's bones were rattled by former team-mate Chris Shevlane, a hard-working right-back who would join up at Parkhead in the summer on a surprise free transfer. Wallace placed the ball about twenty-five yards out and foxed his old friend Cruickshank with a deliberate low shot into the corner. The keeper didn't even move. With five minutes remaining, Tommy Gemmell was given the opportunity to put the result beyond doubt when Celtic were awarded a penalty-kick.

The left-back looked aghast when his effort was saved, but referee Archie Webster immediately ordered a retake, presumably for Cruickshank moving before the kick was taken. Gemmell accepted the opportunity to make amends and bulged the net on this occasion.

The games were coming thick and fast as the final tape to the campaign beckoned. Celtic now had to face Partick Thistle on Monday night and a remarkable crowd of 30,000, sensing something wonderful was in the air, packed into trim Firhill to catch the latest thrilling instalment. Bobby Murdoch had hirpled out of the game against Hearts with an ankle injury and hadn't recovered in time for the game in Maryhill. Willie Wallace took over his right-sided midfield role and looked as though he had played there all his career. And he threw in a goal, too, in a 4-1 victory that was anything as comfortable as the scoreline suggested. Thistle made life extremely difficult for their visitors that evening in Glasgow's west end.

Bertie Auld wasn't risked, either, as Jock Stein paired Wallace with Charlie Gallagher in midfield, the first time the duo had performed alongside each other. It worked a treat. But Jimmy Johnstone was the Celtic player who picked up the gauntlet in the inexorable, exacting and, ultimately, exciting trek towards two points. The little outside-right turned in a mazy, mesmerising display to defy the conditions of the uneven, bumpy surface. He was up against a doughty, indomitable defender in George Muir, who, in Scottish football circles, was known euphemistically as a 'stuffy, wee full-back'. In plainer terms, the Thistle player wouldn't think twice about attempting to launch an opponent somewhere near Great Western Road. It was a 'tactic' that wasn't designed to win any accolades from aficionados of football or international recognition, but it was effective; some outside-rights of the era were terrified to trespass into Thistle's half such was the fear Muir struck into their heart. If that was the case with Celtic's little maestro, his disguise was perfect. Johnstone tore Muir and Thistle to shreds and set up the opening three goals.

The first came straight off the Barrowfield training ground and would have had Stein purring with delight in the dug-out. Johnstone lined up to take a right-wing corner-kick and Billy McNeill, as usual, sauntered to the edge of enemy territory to add his aerial threat to proceedings. Tommy Gemmell lined up on the left-hand side of the penalty area waiting for knock-outs and rebounds that he would despatch back from whence they came on a regular basis. However, Jinky signalled to his best pal Bobby Lennox to take up a position outside the congested six-yard area. Lennox, unhindered, retreated about twelve yards and Johnstone picked him out with a perfect execution and the striker did it justice with a supreme volley that saw the ball tear past George Niven for the crucial breakthrough goal just four minutes from the interval. Fittingly, it justified its acclaim as Celtic's one hundredth league goal of the season.

At half-time, Stein warned his troops to maintain their concentration. Thistle, he knew, were dangerous on the break and they possessed a sharp frontman in Johnny Flanagan, a tricky, will-o'-the-wisp striker who had been linked with Celtic in the past. Big Jock admired Flanagan, but didn't rate him as highly as Lennox and he didn't see that he could play both in the same forward line. As luck would have it, it was Flanagan who piled the pressure on the Parkhead side that evening with the equalising goal seven minutes after the turnaround. Once again, the former winger utilised his acceleration to race onto a through pass and, unexpectedly, hit a shot on the run before Ronnie Simpson could set himself. Flanagan's searing twenty-five yard effort flashed past the perplexed Celtic keeper and crashed into the net via the upright.

Johnstone answered the SOS. He teased and tormented Muir as he came in from the right, jinking one way and going another. Muir was helplessly beaten and wing-half Tommy Gibb attempted to close down the void without success. Johnstone curled a cross impeccably onto Stevie Chalmers' head and Niven was picking the ball out of the net for a second time in the fifty-ninth minute. Eight minutes later, Wallace, from another accurate right-wing corner-kick from Johnstone, hit a first-timer that skidded on the slippery surface and eluded the desperate dive of the veteran keeper. Chalmers made certain with another header following an excellent left-wing delivery from Gemmell.

The enterprising left-back never tired of extolling the virtues of his team-mate and close friend Johnstone. 'God only knows how many times I've been asked to name my most dangerous opponent. It's an answer in two parts - on the field in competition, George Best; in training, Jimmy Johnstone. I faced Bestie a few times at club and country level and he was a magnificent player; tricky, two-footed, good in the air and, forget those slender looks, as hard as nails. Jinky? What can I say? I looked at him during games and just thanked my lucky stars I was in the same team. I could see him right in the mood before some matches and I knew some poor left-back was going to get the runaround from the Wee Man. What was it Liverpool defender Emlyn Hughes said after a Scotland v England game? "I came off the pitch with twisted blood," was his great quote. More than a few must have felt the exact same condition after Jinky went to work on them.

'I faced Jinky every day in training, of course, and you hoped he wasn't in one of those moods to continually thrust the ball through your legs and run around you shouting "Goodbye!" as he did so. Trust me, it wasn't funny after awhile. I would say to him, "Do that again, you wee so-and-so, and I'll kick you up the backside." He never responded to threats. Unfortunately, If anything, it spurred him on to do it again and again. Every now and again Big Jock would look over and shout, "Right, Jinky, that's enough of that. We're here to train - get on with it." On those occasions, you were thankful the manager was in the vicinity to put an end to that morning's torture. There was no badness in Jinky and he wasn't attempting to show you up or anything like that. He just had this tremendous sense of mischief and fun although I have to admit there were times when I wondered about his particular sense of humour. Especially when I was on the receiving end.'

CHAPTER THIRTEEN

APRIL

CZECHMATE AND LISBON, HERE WE COME!

"Everything just went so well on my European Cup debut. I couldn't have scripted it better myself."

- Willie Wallace,
Two-goal debutant against Dukla Prague

Jock Stein was only too aware of the date as the Celtic coach transported his players from Seamill to Hampden for the Scottish Cup semi-final against Clyde on April 1, traditionally known, of course, as 'April Fool's Day'. It was a potential banana skin against part-time opponents who went into the encounter as 5/1 rank outsiders.

Davie White, the bold and aspiring thirty-three-year-old Clyde manager, was earning deserved acclaim for what he was achieving at the prudent Shawfield outfit. He made no brash or outrageous boasts before the match and merely announced he hoped his team would do enough to make their supporters proud. He wasn't quite in the same class as Stein in the kidology stakes, but he had a fair stab at it, anyway. White, who spent his entire nine-year playing career at the homely Rutherglen club, was asked if he had anything special lined up for his team as they prepared for the big game. Producing the underdog card, he replied, 'Well, if I could get all the players off their work at the same time that would be great.'

Stein, the master in the specialised art of deception, might even have smiled at the bluff by the ambitious young pretender. The shrewd Celtic manager would have been well primed about the form of Clyde during their 1-0 league win over Dunfermline at Shawfield the previous month. He wouldn't have forgotten their 5-1 trouncing of a fine Hibs team in November. Nor would he have overlooked a 1-0 victory over full-time Morton at tricky Cappielow in an earlier round of the Scottish Cup.

There was more than just a 'let's-forget-about-the-ball-and-get-on-with-the-game' approach from his last-four opponents. One newspaper scribe had watched in obvious awe at White's assembled bunch of butchers, bakers and candlestick-makers and wrote, 'Clyde move the ball out of defence into attack with the grace and accuracy of a conjurer opening his scarves to reveal a dove.' Nobody's fools, then.

Jock Stein wasn't buying into the notion that the game was already a foregone conclusion. Emphasising that outlook was the fact the Celtic medical staff had worked all week in an effort to have Bobby Murdoch one hundred per cent fit to play after missing the Partick Thistle game with the ankle injury sustained the previous Saturday against Hearts. The broad-shouldered midfielder with the svelte touch underwent two x-rays before Stein reluctantly ruled him out and once again played Willie Wallace in the right-hand side of his midfield twosome. On this occasion, he would be partnered by Bertie Auld with Charlie Gallagher dropping onto the substitute's bench.

Drizzle greeted Billy McNeill and Harry Glasgow, the respective captains, as they led their teams out of the tunnel, across the red ash running track and onto the drenched pitch. The infuriating Hampden Swirl was once more making its annoying presence known. This was to be Celtic's seventeenth domestic Cup-tie of the season, including the League and Glasgow Cups, and Stein's team had won the lot. Clyde, with combination of true grit, exceptional organisation and generous fortune, were ninety minutes away from ending the sequence. The encounter finished all-square without either keeper being invited to retrieve the ball from his net.

And, yet, Celtic claimed with validity for a penalty-kick four minutes from time; the proverbial stonewaller that was witnessed by everyone in the 56,704 crowd with the curious exception of the only man who mattered, referee John Gordon. The match official was no stranger to controversy and, in 1978, was banned by the Scottish Football Association after receiving gifts to the value of £1,000 from AC Milan before a UEFA Cup second leg tie which the Italians won 3-0 against Levski Sofia following a 1-1 draw in Bulgaria. The suspension was just twelve years too late for the frustrated Celtic contingent congregated around the vicinity of Mount Florida that afternoon.

Photographs in the following day's newspapers showed incontrovertible proof that Clyde defender Davie Soutar had used an elbow to divert a goalscoring shot from Jimmy Johnstone off the line. Remarkably, Gordon waved play on to utter disbelief of the Celtic players and obvious relief of their Clyde counterparts. It would be trite to imply the part-timers did not deserve something following their superhuman efforts, but it is difficult to ignore the fact that luck intervened on sporadic occasions to keep them interested in the national competition. Billy McNeill twice powered headers beyond Tommy McCulloch and resolute defender Glasgow cleared the first and, moments later, John McHugh performed another last-ditch rescue from under the crossbar.

One watching scribe observed, 'To be truthful, it was a dour battle, fought without marked inspiration by either side. The general standard of passing and finishing was deplorably low and, although there was perhaps more excitement in the second-half during which Clyde were facing into a troublesome wind, it was fleeting and, as often than not, completely unproductive. It is perhaps indicative of the afternoon's trend of events that all the players who passed muster were in defence. Billy McNeill, as well as being a masterful centre-half, was the game's most effective attacker, even if he did confine his efforts in that sphere to corner-kicks.'

The reporter continued, 'Such was the ineffectiveness of the forwards that it was not until thirty-one minutes had elapsed that either goalkeeper had to make a save of any consequence and, even then, it was by a defender, Tommy Gemmell, who brought out the best in Tommy McCulloch with a tremendous shot from twenty yards which looked netbound all the way until the goalkeeper miraculously turned the ball over the crossbar one-handed.'

Jock Stein left immediately after the game to catch a plane bound for Czechoslovakia to watch European Cup semi-final opponents Dukla Prague. He admitted, 'Yes, it's disappointing not to finish the tie and we had the chances that would have gone in on another day. An extra fixture at this stage of the season is something we could do without, but we are still in the tournament and we will just have to win the replay.'

The second game would have to be played again on the following Wednesday which would give the Celtic manager, scheduled to return from the Czechoslovakian capital on Monday, forty-eight hours to prepare his players for another Hampden tilt. His mood was heightened somewhat when he was informed Rangers had lost 1-0 to Dunfermline at Ibrox and Celtic were now two points ahead at the top of the table with a game in hand and only five matches left to play. The Parkhead side were now massive favourites to achieve their second successive championship.

In front of a crowd of 55,138 in the replay, Celtic were two goals ahead by the twenty-second minute, courtesy of efforts from Bobby Lennox and Bertie Auld, and had as good as booked their third successive Scottish Cup Final berth during Jock Stein's reign and their fifth in seven years. Willie Wallace again lined up in the No.4 shorts, but, on this occasion, was hardly a direct replacement for Bobby Murdoch. Stein gave that position to Charlie Gallagher with Auld playing beside him on the left. By the time Davie White had cottoned on, his team were heading for the exit.

The opening goal arrived as early as the second minute when Stevie Chalmers had a shot blocked and Lennox swooped on the rebound. And Auld, displaying his usual quick thinking, claimed the second after Chalmers had nodded the ball into his path. The midfielder flummoxed his marker Stan Anderson with a swift shuffle of his feet and a change of direction before belting an effort high past Tommy McCulloch. Jimmy Johnstone had looked out of sorts and it was no surprise he was replaced by John Hughes just before the hour mark. It was later discovered the winger had been suffering flu symptoms and he wasn't even considered for inclusion to the squad for the game against Motherwell three days later as Celtic travelled to Fir Park, the scene of the previous season's joyous title celebrations.

The players may have had their focus somewhat blurred with the European Cup semi-final first leg against Dukla Prague at Parkhead due the following Wednesday, but they failed to spark on this occasion. It was a fairly dismal confrontation and the nearest Celtic came to breaking the deadlock in the first-half was a trademark header from Billy McNeill that was knocked off the line by Davie Whiteford with his goalkeeper, Peter McCloy, out of position and in distress. Charlie Gallagher limped out of proceedings at half-time and was replaced by Jim Brogan, whose forte was more destructive than constructive, but it didn't prevent the champions from winning 2-0 to keep their place at the pinnacle of the First Division with four games remaining and a match in hand.

The barrier-breaking goal arrived just before the hour mark when Bertie Auld crossed for Willie Wallace to strike an awesome volley wide of McCloy. Tommy Gemmell made certain in the seventieth minute with another blistering penalty-kick. It was a vital win to put Jock Stein's team on fifty-four points while the best Rangers could have managed was a total of fifty-eight. Celtic also had the distinct edge on goal average, with one hundred and five strikes compared to the Ibrox side's ninety-eight while Ronnie Simpson had conceded twenty-eight as opposed to their twenty-seven.

On a crisp, still Wednesday evening of April 12, Celtic moved within an hour-and-a-half of a place in the European Cup Final. Jock Stein's pre-match requirement was stark: a two-goal advantage to take to Czechoslovakia. The players responded and Dukla Prague were dismissed 3-1 in front of 74,406 excited supporters who were beginning to believe their team just might be in with a chance of conquering Europe. The thought would have been disregarded as a combination of irrational, unreasonable and absurd only eight months beforehand.

Willie Wallace went some way to replay his £30,000 transfer fee with two splendid goals in his debut appearance in Europe's premier trophy. Jimmy Johnstone, a source of inspiration on this occasion, claimed the other. But the encounter kicked off in controversial fashion when Stevie Chalmers had a goal disallowed. Tommy Gemmell flighted an inviting ball downfield, Wallace got a touch to Chalmers, he slipped it to Johnstone coming in from the right and the little winger chipped it back for Chalmers to nod in at the near post. The referee ruled Johnstone's foot was dangerously high while collecting the ball and cancelled the effort.

Dukla, it must be pointed out, were no dummies on an evening that was perfect for football. Josef Masopust would never be invited to blow out the candles on a thirtieth birthday cake again, but he was looking very comfortable in his team's engine room as he dictated the flow of the game with masterly poise. In the gangly Stanislav Strunc he had a willing accomplice in making life a trifle uneasy for the Celtic defence. Ronnie Simpson had to look lively on two occasions before he actually set in motion the game's opening goal in the twenty-eighth minute.

The keeper, who normally initiated attacks with throw-outs, mainly to Bobby Murdoch and Bertie Auld, elected to launch a clearance down the middle. Chalmers got a flick and it fell for Auld who teed it up for Wallace. His shot deflected off a defender into the path of Johnstone and he gleefully lifted it over the head of the outrushing Ivo Viktor, another internationally-acclaimed goalkeeper. However, that effort was nullified on the stroke of half-time when the Celtic central defence got into a real muddle on their own eighteen-yard line. Strunc pounced and stroked the ball away from Simpson. Celtic Park was struck dumb.

Simpson remembered, 'Masopust created the opening with a through pass to Nedorost. The inside-left slipped and looked as though he had handled the ball, but he managed to flick it to Strunc, the tall, ungainly outside-right, who fairly crashed it where I didn't want it to go.'

Tommy Gemmell said, 'In the dressing room, we got the usual pep talk from Big Jock and, rather obviously, conceding a goal just before the interval is horrible timing. But you can't come off the pitch feeling sorry for yourself. You must not dwell on it; you have to concentrate fully on what is still to come. "Just play like you did in the first-half and you'll win," urged the Boss. Actually, we were already thinking along those lines, anyway. I know I was.'

Just before the hour mark, the left-back punted the ball forward and Wallace was running free of the Czech defence to get a wonderful touch off the outside of his right boot to send the ball soaring into the net for the second goal. Five minutes later, a desperate Ladislav Novak pawed away a high ball from Bobby Murdoch and received a booking for his goalkeeping tendencies. It didn't get any better when Bertie Auld stepped up to take the resultant free-kick. He dithered a bit to unsettle the defensive wall and then touched the ball sideways to Wallace who bulleted an unstoppable first-time drive past Viktor. The ball was stretching the netting before he even had the opportunity to twitch a muscle.

With twenty-five minutes still to go, the Czech champions were on the verge of collapse and surrender. They were there for the taking as Celtic rolled forward in numbers, the fans urging them on for more goals. Chalmers slashed one past the post, Wallace wasn't far off target with another and Murdoch sent a left-foot belter just over the crossbar. Wallace even knocked one against the face of the bar from a Chalmers cross. Masopust the maestro had disappeared under the onslaught, but he and his team-mates held out until the end and Celtic had to be content with a 3-1 advantage to take to Prague.

Willie Wallace said, 'There has always been the suggestion I should have taken my European bow in the quarter-final ties against Vojvodina. I have heard that, although I was registered to play in the domestic competitions, someone had been a little late in getting the forms to UEFA to allow me to play in the European tournament. I signed for Celtic on December 10 1966 and the first leg against the Yugoslavians was on March 1 1967. That's a fair period between signing and that game and, to be completely honest, I don't know how long you had to be registered back then to allow you to play in Europe.

'I am not complaining, though. You never know what might have happened if I had played against Vojvodina - maybe we wouldn't have got through! As it was, I was more than delighted to play against Dukla Prague in the following round. I had been sitting alongside the injured Joe McBride in the stand at Celtic Park to witness that astounding quarter-final against the Slavs and I thought, "Wispy, this is the place for you!" I wanted a slice of that, believe me. I know the other lads would all say the same thing, but the atmosphere generated by our support during those European occasions was just breathtaking. Quite staggering, really.

'I was well up for the Dukla game. I had anticipated it for weeks and just hoped I would get the go-ahead from Big Jock to play. You never took anything for granted with the Boss because that would have been a huge mistake. But everything just went so well for me on my European Cup debut. I couldn't have scripted it better myself. A 3-1 victory and two goals from me. Okay, it would have been nice to have claimed a hat-trick, but I wasn't grumbling. I came close, you know. I actually hit the crossbar near the end. Big Jock had told us beforehand, "Get a two-goal advantage and I'm sure we'll get through." My first goal came just before the hour mark when Big Tommy launched one downfield. It might have been a clearance, but he has always assured me it was an inch-perfect pass! Anyway, suddenly I had a bit of freedom in the Dukla penalty area, and managed to flick the ball with the outside of my foot and it carried past their keeper.

'About five minutes or so later, Celtic Park just went crazy when I scored again. It was all down to the cunning antics of Bertie Auld. He stepped up to take a free-kick, paused and looked as though he was about to recentre it. I knew what was coming next, though. Bertie merely slipped the ball to the side and I was coming in behind him to hit it first time. The ball flew through their defensive wall and was in the net before Ivo Viktor could move. It looked like an impromptu bit of skill from Wee Bertie, but, take my word for it, that little bit of trickery came straight off the training ground. We practised that move every day.

'It was an idea from Big Jock who was always looking at ways of developing free-kicks and corner-kicks. He continually urged us to put variety into deadball situations and Wee Bertie seized the moment against Dukla Prague. The Czechs were startled. They began pointing at Stevie Chalmers and claiming offside. Stevie had followed my shot into the net, but there was no way he had been off. It was just his speed getting round the back of the wall that got him into that position. When I connected with the ball, I can assure everyone that Stevie was well onside.'

Jimmy Johnstone took a knock against the Czechs and was forced to withdraw from the Scotland team that was due to play world champions England at Wembley the following Saturday. Stevie Chalmers, as first reserve, expected to get his team-mate's No.7 jersey, but new international manager Bobby Brown had been so impressed by Wallace's two-goal salvo against Dukla that he was brought in and immediately given the right-wing role.

Ronnie Simpson's wonderful fairy tale continued as the Scots triumphed 3-2 in front of a crowd of 99,063. There might have been some English fans in attendance, but they were rarely seen and certainly not heard. Brown, the first-ever full-time manager appointed by the Scottish Football Association, awarded the Celtic keeper his first international cap at the age of thirty-six - fifteen years after playing at Wembley and helping Newcastle United to a 1-0 English FA Cup victory over Arsenal. A relatively unknown forward who had failed to make the grade at Chelsea, Jim McCalliog, at the age of twenty, became the first Sheffield Wednesday player to be capped by Scotland in forty-seven years.

Bobby Lennox and Tommy Gemmell completed the Parkhead quartet for football's piece de resistance. The defender recalled, 'You could have written Bobby Brown's pre-match tactics on the back of a stamp and still have had space left over. In short, there weren't any. Of course, I was used to Jock Stein meticulously planning for all our games. It didn't matter if it was Real Madrid or Raith Rovers, you knew exactly what you had to do when you went on the pitch against your opponents.

'To be fair to Bobby Brown, if we didn't already know what were about to face at Wembley that day we must have been living on the moon for a year or so. We got England rammed down our throats constantly after they won the World Cup. According to the scribes across the border, we were wasting our time even turning up for the game. Apparently, it would have been easier to nail jelly to a wall than to believe we would win. It was a foregone conclusion.

'The bookmakers rated us as 7/1 against and, as we all know, these guys rarely got it wrong. They might just have lowered those odds had they been in the Scottish dressing room that day. I sensed a real 'we'll-show-'em' attitude from my team-mates. Absolutely no disrespect to Bobby Brown, but we didn't really need a manager that wonderful afternoon. The atmosphere was electric. We were in London to do the business and shut up the English once and for all. We didn't need anyone to stoke the fires in our belly for this one. There was no point in any motivational speaking. In fact, there was no point in tactics. Every single Scot in that dressing room was puffed up and ready to go long before the kick-off. We all knew what we had to do. I do admit the adrenalin was pumping a wee bit fiercer than normal.

'They had gone nineteen games unbeaten until they came up against us that afternoon. No doubt they were confident of extending that run against a bunch of no-hopers. Didn't quite work out that way, did it? The Celtic players were getting used to creating a sensation or two that season.'

Willie Wallace revealed he was more than just a little surprised to receive the telephone call to tell him to pick up his boots and join the international players just two days before the Wembley extravaganza. 'Amazed? You could say that. I hardly had time to draw breath. It was unfortunate for Jinky, but it opened the door to me and presented me with a truly memorable occasion. I was playing through the middle at Celtic, but I was asked to take Jinky's place on the right against England. That might have seemed strange to some, but, in fact, I had played outside-right on a few occasions for Hearts before moving to Parkhead.

'Happily, I was involved in our first goal when I fired in a low shot from the right side of the penalty area. Gordon Banks went down and got a hand to it, but couldn't hold the attempt. He spilled it and that was all Denis Law needed to swoop and put the ball away. Denis's reflexes in the box were like lightning. Make a mistake when this lad was around and you would be punished. He was incredible. Banks must have had that sinking feeling as soon as the ball bounced from his grasp. It came back to Denis at a fair pace, but he didn't even break stride as he walloped it into the net.'

England's world-class keeper Banks recalled, 'The Scots really had themselves stoked up for that match and we knew they were ready to run through brick walls for victory. As far as Scotland were concerned, this was the World Cup Final. Denis Law scored their first goal from a rebound after I had pushed out a shot from Willie Wallace. Twelve minutes from the end, Bobby Lennox, who had been giving George Cohen a lot of problems on their left wing, made it 2-0. Jack Charlton pulled a goal back almost immediately and then I let in a bad goal from Jim McCalliog. I committed the cardinal sin of not guarding my near post properly as I came out to meet him after he had evaded two half-hearted tackles. Geoff Hurst made it 3-2 and we nearly scrambled an equaliser in one of the most dramatic finishes to an England v. Scotland match.'

Remarkably, there had been opposition from some quarters to Ronnie Simpson getting the No.1 position in front of Bobby Ferguson, who was on the verge of leaving Kilmarnock for West Ham for a record £65,000 fee for a keeper in the summer. Bobby Brown, a former Rangers goalie, stuck firmly to his guns about the decision to bring in the thirtysomething Celt.

He said, 'I knew Scotland had a problem in that position. I had witnessed it first-hand on several occasions. I thought it was time for a change and not for one moment did I ever think Ronnie Simpson would let us down. He was a reliable, safe pair of hands. He also had experience of the Wembley pitch after having played there twice for Newcastle United in the early Fifties, so the ground would hold no surprises for him. To my mind, he was the most consistent goalkeeper around at the time and it was hardly a risk putting him in against England. I didn't care what age he was; I was only ever interested in ability. Anyway, he must have been doing something right if Jock Stein picked him for Celtic week in, week out.'

Afterwards, in the jubilant Wembley dressing room, Gemmell recalled, 'Faither was genuinely upset that England had managed to score two goals in the last six minutes or so. That underlined the perfectionist in our goalie. We had just had a very famous victory over the reigning world champions, but, clearly, he hadn't wanted to concede any goals. Some people are never happy!'

A wicked, wet and windy Wednesday evening in the grey east end of Glasgow provided the unlikely back drop for a heroes' welcome for Celtic's four Wembley victors, Ronnie Simpson, Tommy Gemmell, Willie Wallace and Bobby Lennox. Throughout a blustery day in the city, the rain had been incessant while ferocious gusts of piercing wind did little to assist the entertainment factor. Aberdeen, for their part, showed little intention of providing anything by way of enjoyment for the 33,000 paying customers as their team boss Eddie Turnbull, no-one's idea of a favourite uncle and a well-known antagonist of Jock Stein, set out ruthlessly to stop his opponents from playing. It had been billed as the dress rehearsal for the Scottish Cup Final at Hampden in twenty days' time and the Pittodrie chief, clearly, wasn't going to risk his team getting turned over.

If it was the Dons manager's sole intention to ruin the game as a spectacle, he succeeded spectacularly. It was a non-starter as his players, with the exception of lone striker Jim Storrie, displayed an unfathomable aversion to crossing into the Celtic half of the field, especially after a nondescript opening forty-five minutes. So, there was no surprise that the game ended goalless and provoked the terse response from the Celtic boss of, 'Well, at least, we're a point nearer the title.' He refused to elaborate.

A newspaper reporter noted that play throughout had been 'scrappy and inconclusive' and there had been a severe lack of 'directness, thrust and accuracy'. Under the headline of 'Celtic held to draw in featureless game', he added, 'From the restart, it was obvious Aberdeen would be content to settle for a draw. They set up a defence calculated to keep Celtic out and succeeded without undue strain. Altogether it was a frustrating occasion for the home supporters, who cannot yet be certain that their favourites will clinch the championship. Having played the same number of games as Rangers, thirty-one, Celtic are three points ahead of their nearest challengers, whom they have still to meet at Ibrox, having also to play Dundee United and Kilmarnock at Parkhead.'

On April 25, Celtic proved they, too, could put up the shutters when they cemented their place in that season's European Cup Final with an uncustomary withdrawn performance against Dukla Prague in the Czechoslovakian capital city. The unsung hero was Stevie Chalmers, who spent a punishing ninety minutes being pummelled by a frustrated defence who couldn't risk taking their eye of the eager Celtic attacker.

Chalmers remembered, 'That was the one and only time I was banned from entering my own team's half of the field. Big Jock laid it on the line, "Keep busy, Stevie. Let them know you're out there." Thanks, boss! I was never afraid to put myself about and, as I recall, a few players bumped into my elbows that afternoon. It's a man's game, after all. I just kept going for the entire game and the Dukla back lot weren't pleased. It was one of the hardest shifts I ever put in, but we were ninety minutes away from the European Cup Final and if that doesn't give you momentum then nothing will.

'Obviously, Dukla wanted to give me a hard time. They tried to get me to retreat back into my own half beside my team-mates, but I was having none of that. I had a job to do and that was to get about their defence and keep them stretched. Not the most glamorous role in the team, I'm sure you'll agree, but one that was vital in that game. The Czechs were a very good team and they liked to build from the back. They used their captain Josef Masopust a lot, passing the ball through the midfield. So, that's where I came in. I was asked to harry them, chase them and make sure they didn't get the opportunity to dwell on the ball.

'If that's what Big Jock wanted, then that's what Big Jock would get. I was desperate to stay in his first team. But Dukla did pin us back by their attacking play. They had scored that vital away goal and they must have thought a 2-0 win against us was within their scope. They may even have been heartened to know we had thrown away a three-goal advantage in Budapest against MTK in a European Cup-Winners' Cup semi-final only three years earlier. But this was a different Celtic team with an entirely different attitude.

'So, if Dukla believed they were about to face a collection of players who would collapse under pressure, then they were to be sorely disappointed. They may even have noted that we had also lost in our previous away game, the 1-0 defeat in Yugoslavia against Vojvodina. But we were learning all the time and we put our experience to a good use in Prague.

'Ironically, Big Jock actually looked a bit disappointed at the end of that match. Sure, he was delighted that Celtic had become the first British club to reach the Final of the European Cup. However, he realised we hadn't done it in our normal fashion. The flair, the attacking ambition, the adventure weren't in evidence and those facets of our play were very important to him. Afterwards, he gathered us around him in the dressing room and said, "We will never play like that again. I will never ask you to play all-out defence again." If we were defending in games after that, it was because we were being pushed back and never because it was a pre-arranged tactic.'

Billy McNeill, in commanding form throughout the tie, recalled, 'What a game Stevie had in Prague. We felt a bit sorry for him. At one stage, late in the second-half, he got into a bit of bother and suddenly he was surrounded by about four of their players. We were too far away to lend him some support. Thankfully, the referee sorted it out!'

Bobby Lennox added, 'Big Jock had come up with a strategy that was foreign to all of us and we were going to make sure the backdoor was bolted firmly shut. My pal, Wee Jinky, just about played the entire game standing beside Jim Craig at right-back. I spent an awful lot of my ninety minutes keeping Big Tommy company over on the left. That's not exactly how it was planned. Dukla, a fine team, pinned us back for lengthy periods of that game. They took control in front of their own fans and they made a real contest of it.

'They made it hectic for all of us and we were forced to defend to the very end. The only guy who wasn't given any defensive duties that day was Stevie Chalmers. I remember Big Jock telling him, "Chase everything." And, you know, he did. From start to finish, Stevie put himself about all over the place. The Czech defenders must have hated the sight of him. He never gave them a moment's rest. He was a one-man forward line. Somehow, it seemed so fitting that Stevie should get the winning goal against Inter Milan. He earned it with his exhausting stint in Prague.'

Ronnie Simpson didn't remember being too flustered during the encounter. 'The Dukla Prague coach Bohumil Musil admitted he had been very impressed by our performance in the first leg. However, he stressed his team of soldiers still had a chance in front of their own fans in the return. We didn't try to be smart in Prague and set out to contain the Czechs. Just before we went out on to the pitch, for one of the most important games in our careers, Jock Stein told us, "Right, we've done our job. Now let's see what Dukla can do." He reassured us that he was convinced they couldn't raise their game enough to upset us. He was right again.

'They had a couple of shots which went close, but nothing more. They appeared to lack the speed required to beat our defence and we calmly settled for 0-0. The Boss was delighted. He even bought champagne for the Press and I got a half-bottle to myself - all over my suit when somebody opened a bottle behind me. But who cared? "We're on our way to Lisbon, we shall not be moved!" we sang until our throats were dry.'

John Clark observed, 'The Juliska Stadium has a nice ring to it, hasn't it? That was Dukla's ground and it was anything but pleasant. It was a foreboding, grey old place that could have done with a lick of paint. It looked as though the construction outfit who were putting it together got fed up halfway through and went home. The atmosphere wasn't helped when it looked as though the entire Czechoslovakian Army was there, too. It could have been a terrifying experience, but, being only ninety minutes away from the European Cup Final, we were prepared for anything.

'Jock, of course, went against all his principles and philosophies that day to play defensively and those poor Czech fans never saw the real Celtic on that occasion. They must have been more than just a bit bemused when they saw us perform against Inter Milan; surely they didn't believe they were witnessing the same players or the same team.

'I think even wee Jimmy Johnstone was given defensive duties against Dukla. Can you imagine the Wee Man as cover at right-back? Me, neither, but that's where he played for the entire game. We were helped, too, with the presence and reassurance of the experienced Ronnie Simpson behind us. His was the fairytale to end all fairytales and he wasn't going to allow anyone to take it away from him. He talked us through that game as only he could. When the Czechs got through and, thankfully that wasn't too often, Ronnie was there to pull off the save.

'The Dukla players were gracious in defeat, but I do remember Masopust being a bit grumpy. He had played in a World Cup Final in 1962 and now, in his mid-thirties, he must have been looking forward to an appearance in a European Cup Final. Sorry, Josef, we were in no mood to be denied our place in Lisbon.'

Now for the little matter of the Scottish Cup Final.

CHAPTER FOURTEEN
APRIL
BIG JOCK'S HAMPDEN MASTERPLAN

"I'm happy to keep the ball out of my net by any means necessary. If it hits my backside, knees or elbows and bounces to safety you won't hear me complaining."

- Ronnie Simpson

Welcoming sunshine greeted Billy McNeill and Harry Melrose as they led out their Celtic and Aberdeen teams for the Scottish Cup Final at Hampden on Saturday April 29 1967. Jock Stein had shackled the players in order to grind out a safe result in midweek in Prague and promised never to again adopt rigid, soul-destroying, safety-first tactics.

'He was as good as his word,' recalled Bertie Auld. 'He must have agonised over ordering us to suffocate the game as we did against Dukla. But this was a different day, a trophy was there to be won and Big Jock was only too happy to tell us we would be reverting to the style that had earned us so much applause among neutral observers. You should have seen the smiles on some of my pals' faces. Wee Jinky wasn't really cut out to be an auxiliary right-back and Stevie Chalmers looked delighted to hear there would be some colleagues beside him to keep him company in the Aberdeen half. There was an extra bounce in every Celtic player's step that afternoon. And that of the Boss, too, I hasten to add.'

A crowd of 126,102 was in place, but there was no sign of Stein's sparring partner Eddie Turnbull, known simply throughout the footballing fraternity as Ned. The gruff Dons manager, with the voracious appetite for upsetting people, had been an adversary of Stein dating back to their playing days. Twelve years before this Cup Final, Celtic, skippered by Stein, had unexpectedly beaten Hibs, with Turnbull in the team, 2-0 to lift the Coronation Cup. The Easter Road side, with their 'Famous Five' forward line of Smith, Johnstone, Reilly, Turnbull and Ormond, were expected to stroll off with the silverware against a side which finished a poor eighth in a sixteen-team league. Stein, though, was absolutely resolute in nullifying the main goal threat of Lawrie Reilly while goalkeeper Johnny Bonnar produced the performance of a lifetime to take the one-off trophy to the east end of Glasgow with goals from Neilly Mochan and Jimmy Walsh.

Turnbull, obviously, wasn't the type to forgive and forget. However, he was taken ill on the morning of the Scottish Cup Final and doctors persuaded him to stay away from the south side of Glasgow. It's doubtful if the presence of the brusque Pittodrie gaffer would have changed the outcome of the game. Stein had meticulously plotted a surprise for his arch nemesis; Jimmy Johnstone was instructed to take up a place just off the centre with Stevie Chalmers pushed wide on the right and Willie Wallace leading the attack. It worked a treat.

Wallace scored the goals - one in each half only seven minutes' worth of playing time apart - in the 2-0 triumph while Johnstone skipped and cavorted throughout his ninety minutes of freedom and Chalmers rolled back the years with a tireless, selfless, stamina-sapping exhibition on the touchline. Thirty-six-year-old Ronnie Simpson, picking up his first Scottish Cup medal to place alongside the two FA Cup honours he won with Newcastle United in 1952 and 1955, was unbeatable on the rare occasions the Dons broke through. Jim Craig, Wallace and Johnstone also lifted their first Scottish Cup medals on a thoroughly pleasurable and satisfying afternoon for those of a Celtic persuasion at the national stadium. All eleven players would go on to even greater heights in Portugal in twenty-six days' time.

The opening goal arrived in the forty-second minute and, surprisingly, it came from a raid on the left. Up until then, Celtic's best work had been done on the opposite flank with Johnstone bamboozling Tommy

McMillan, in the middle of the opposition's rearguard, and Chalmers doing likewise to left-back Ally Shewan. Bertie Auld switched play with his educated left foot and placed a diagonal pass into the tracks of Bobby Lennox, coming in from the left. Dons skipper Melrose, who had scored for Dunfermline against Celtic in the 1965 Cup Final but still finished on the losing team, was never going to win any first prizes for his tackling ability or his pace. Lennox whipped away from the midfielder, sized up the situation in the penalty box and, with Bobby Clark lured to his near post, zipped over a cross which Wallace, on the six-yard line, first-timed into the vacuum that was left exposed by the rashness of the keeper.

Four minutes into the second-half, Johnstone, perpetual motion itself, chased what could have been a lost cause to the bye-line before hooking over an inviting cross to Wallace, acknowledged by many at Parkhead as one of the finest strikers of the ball, and he didn't disappoint with a half-volley from eight yards that ripped high past the motionless Clark. The organisers could have placed the green and white ribbons on the trophy there and then. Lennox came within inches of a third goal when he burst into the box from the left and sizzled in a vicious drive that gave the Dons keeper no chance, but, unfortunately, his elevation was just out and the ball carried mere inches over the bar.

At the other end, Simpson made athletic diving saves from Jimmy Wilson and Jim Storrie and, with only three minutes remaining, showed his extrovert goalkeeping qualities when it looked as though Aberdeen would surely collect at least a consolation goal. Jens Petersen, the Dons' Danish defender, had been thrown into attack in a vain attempt to unsettle Billy McNeill and John Clark. With time running out, he found himself isolated with an open goal after Wilson had played a ball in from the right. He stabbed an effort towards the vacant net and Simpson, who had been at the opposite post, ran along his goal-line to boot the ball away at the last moment. It wasn't the sort of save that would figure in any goalkeeping manual, but that would have meant little to the remarkable veteran.

He would often say, 'Who remembers how you keep the ball out of the net? In years to come, someone will look at the result and see Celtic have had another shut-out and that's all that matters. I'm happy to keep the ball out of my net by any means necessary. If it hits my backside, my knees or my elbows and bounces to safety you won't hear me complaining. It's my job and I'll do whatever it takes to make sure I've got a clean sheet and our opponents have a duck egg.'

Of course, Simpson's story was the most romantic among the Celtic players, the football fable to beat them all. Celtic's version of Peter Pan might have expected to finish the 1966/67 season playing for Berwick Rangers in the old Scottish Second Division where they finished tenth in a league of twenty. Instead, as the history books show, he picked up a European Cup medal, played his first game for the Scotland international side and was voted the Football Writers' Player of the Year. Take into consideration the fact he also won medals in the league, the Scottish Cup, the League Cup and the Glasgow Cup. Not bad for someone whose next birthday would see him turn thirty-seven.

Yet things could have been so vastly different for Simpson, who was adored by his Celtic colleagues. Jock Stein had dropped him from the Hibs first team with Willie Wilson taking over the No.1 spot. His Easter Road career looked as good as obliterated and Berwick Rangers were searching for a new goalkeeper. They turned their attention to Simpson and they were confident of landing the experienced professional. Hibs would hardly have proved difficult to deal with as far as the transfer fee was concerned. That was when fate stepped in to so rudely interrupt Berwick Rangers' progress in their pursuit of Simpson. Celtic, too, were in the market for another keeper. John Fallon was the man in possession, but they did not have reliable cover. The unpredictable Frank Haffey, who had conceded nine goals to England at Wembley in 1961, had just been sold to Swindon Town for £8,000 in 1964. That opened the door for Simpson and he decided 'it was worth a chance.'

However, he couldn't have been best pleased when he was told, a year later in March 1965, that Jock Stein was about to take over as manager of Celtic. After hearing the news about the impending arrival of Stein, Simpson is reported to have gone straight home and informed his wife that she should get ready to pack. 'We're on the move again, Rosemary,' he was alleged to have said. Stein had sold Simpson to Celtic for a transfer fee described by the the-then Celtic boss Jimmy McGrory as being in the region of 'sweeties'. Most assuredly, glory, medals and international honours did not figure in the wildest dreams of Simpson at that stage of his career.

There had been talk of a fall-out between the player and Stein nearing the end of his days at Hibs. Neither Simpson nor the manager was ever eager to talk about any friction between the pair. Luckily for Celtic, if there had been any ill-feeling between two strong characters, it never surfaced in their six years together in Glasgow. Naturally, their finest moment came in the Portuguese capital against Inter Milan and, quite remarkably, that historic game came almost twenty-two years after Simpson had made his debut for Queen's Park.

Remember, too, this was the goalkeeper who had represented Great Britain four times as an amateur and played twice in the 1948 Olympic Games. He had, of course, also earned two English FA Cup medals with Newcastle United in the fifties. Those not-inconsiderable achievements might have been more than enough for most individuals. Simpson had also served Third Lanark in his distinguished career before eventually landing at Celtic.

Billy McNeill was a fully paid-up member of the Ronnie Simpson Fan Club. 'Faither was quite magnificent, as simple as that. You always felt safe when he was behind you. He talked you through a game and must have been exhausted even though he might have had very little to do. Being a Celtic keeper back then was either the best job in football - or the worst. Because we had the ball in our opponents' half most of the time, Ronnie would be virtually unemployed. I know some keepers much prefer to be in the thick of it. Obviously, if you are busy it helps you keep your eye in. You're on the go all the time and that is no bad thing.

'In Ronnie's case it was all about concentration. And, my goodness, did he possess that much-needed commodity in plentiful supplies. He could have been asked to do nothing for eighty-nine minutes and then produce a wonder save right at the end. It really was a gift and he put every ounce of his vast experience to a good use.'

Tommy Gemmell recalled, 'Ronnie's presence in goal undoubtedly had a calming effect on our back four, including me. He always looked in charge although, of course, he was not the most imposing of figures. Big

Jock had a thing about goalkeepers and I'm not too sure he trusted any of them. They were a necessary evil in a team where all the other performers used their feet. Maybe Big Jock had played in front of a few accident-prone keepers during his time as a centre-half and that had a bearing on his thinking later in life. Critics have often said spotting a goalkeeper was Jock's Achilles Heel and they may have had a point - certainly he brought plenty to the club during his time there, but Ronnie made the position his own.'

John Clark said, 'Ronnie Simpson received everything he deserved in football. It would have been a travesty if his career had just drifted away into oblivion; another of football's forgotten performers. Of course, that came so close to being the situation before he joined up at Celtic Park. We all know of his qualities and he was a genuinely funny man. He could be every bit as droll as the great Chic Murray, a fairly unique Scottish comedian in his day. There was no chance of anyone getting big-headed when Faither was around. His one-liners would soon put someone in their place if he thought they needed it.

'Like Big Billy mentions, Ronnie was a real treasure to play in front of simply because of his steady stream of advice throughout the ninety minutes. I hadn't encountered that before and it did make life that little bit easier. He would spot someone making a run and let you know right away. "Luggy, watch your left" or "Luggy, jockey him, keep him on his right." It was all appreciated and he was spot-on every time.'

Ronnie Simpson was only one win away from picking up his second First Division title-winning medal after his Scottish Cup Final shut-out against Aberdeen. But sometimes even the most romantic of football legends do not always go according to plan.

CHAPTER FIFTEEN
MAY
SINGING IN THE RAIN

"We knew the next game was against Rangers and we fancied winning the title at Ibrox."

- Tommy Gemmell

The Celtic support rolled up in their numbers getting ready to test their larynxes to the limit as they prepared for another raucous silverware celebration.

On Wednesday May 3, four days after the 2-0 victory over Aberdeen, the Scottish Cup was paraded at Parkhead in front of 44,000 fans, a following who fully expected to see their favourites crowned Scottish First Division champions for the second successive season. Dundee United, the only Scottish team to have beaten them back on Hogmanay, were the opposition, so revenge would indeed be a dish best served cold after a wait of four months.

To underline the achievement of Jock Stein's team requiring a solitary point to clinch the crown, you only have to look at the condition of Scottish football as a whole at the time. Despite their extraordinary Scottish Cup defeat at Berwick in January, Rangers had quickly stabilised and had actually won through to the European Cup-Winners' Cup Final where they would meet and lose 1-0 to Bayern Munich in Nuremberg a week after Celtic were due to play in the European Cup Final in Lisbon.

Adding weight to the strength and competitiveness of the top flight was the accomplishment of Kilmarnock in reaching the UEFA Cup semi-final where they lost to 4-2 on aggregate to a Dinamo Zagreb side which went on to beat Leeds United 2-0 in the two-legged Final. The Slavs had knocked out Dunfermline earlier on the away goals rule after the tie had finished level at 4-4. In the same tournament, Dundee United humbled the mighty Barcelona 4-1 on aggregate, winning home and away, before losing 3-1 to Juventus.

Without argument, football at the upper echelons in Scotland was in an extremely healthy state and it took an exceptional manager with a special set of footballers to impose their superiority. Step forward, Jock Stein and his Celtic players.

However, their Tannadice opponents at Parkhead that evening were clearly not there to just make up the numbers. Playing an offensive team such as Celtic fitted seamlessly into their hit-on-the-break strategy. And they proved it for the second time that campaign; Celtic suffering once more as they fell for soccer's classic sucker-punch in an uncharacteristic anti-climax. They had gone into the game in the realisation they had not lost a league game at home since April 17 1965 when they went down 2-1 to Partick Thistle, although it would be fair to assume the players on that particular Saturday might have been concentrating on the Scottish Cup Final against Dunfermline the following week.

Stein made some cosmetic changes against the Tayside opponents with Stevie Chalmers getting a well-earned rest from the starting line-up following his exertions against Dukla Prague and Aberdeen. However, even at the age of thirty-one, the sprightly forward was still on call as a substitute. Bertie Auld was given the night off and watched the game from the stand while his dad Joe took up residence with his pals immediately opposite in the Jungle. Charlie Gallagher and John Hughes got the nod from Big Jock to start the contest.

And everything looked to be going according to plan when Celtic were awarded a penalty-kick in the twenty-fifth minute after Bobby Lennox had been sent tumbling in the box. Tommy Gemmell fairly thrashed his effort wide of goalie Sandy Davie. It remained that way with the champions-elect strangely failing to ignite, despite the desperate and vocal exhortations from the terracings. The Tannadice men kept their powder dry until the fifty-fourth minute when, unusually, Billy McNeill and John Clark went walkabout and Billy Hainey got in behind the central defenders, drew Ronnie Simpson from his line, rounded the exposed keeper and stroked the ball unerringly into the vacant net. A hush greeted the goal.

However, the fans found their collective voice seven minutes later when Willie Wallace restored Celtic's advantage. Centre-half Doug Smith and keeper Davie made a terrible mess of attempting to deal with a hanging cross into the box and the ever-alert Wallace seized on the loose ball to roll it home with ease. That was the signal for mass celebrating among the fans, but, astonishingly, United came back again to equalise. In the sixty-eighth minute, the home defence didn't deal with a routine corner-kick and Dennis Gillsepie, who had scored at Tannadice in December, was allowed to run in uninterrupted to send a header flying past Simpson.

Once more, an unanticipated cloud of trepidation materialised over the ground. The supporters knew, though, that a point would still be good enough to win the title. Three minutes after Gillespie's effort, Jackie Graham sneaked through to snatch a third for a United side who were refusing to follow the script. Celtic lost 3-2 for the second time to the same opponents and still required a point to make sure the flag would be flying over Parkhead at the start of the new season.

Tommy Gemmell had in interesting spin on the situation. 'Ach, we weren't too bothered. We knew the next game was against Rangers on the Saturday and we fancied winning the title at Ibrox. So, it wasn't all bad. Mind you, I don't think Big Jock shared my train of thought.'

Even before the United setback, the Celtic manager had been far from happy with the Scotland boss Bobby Brown and the Scottish Football Association selectors. Stein frowned after NINE players were brought into the international squad for a non-event friendly against the USSR at Hampden, scheduled for Wednesday May 10. Ronnie Simpson, Jim Craig, Tommy Gemmell, Bobby Murdoch, Billy McNeill, John Clark, Jimmy Johnstone, Willie Wallace and Bobby Lennox were all called up and that left Stevie Chalmers and Bertie Auld wondering if their aftershave had let them down.

Big Jock didn't see the funny side. 'We're trying to win the European Cup for Celtic and also Scotland as a nation. My players need a rest, the last thing they require is an extra fixture during this month. Yes, it's a compliment, I suppose, and my players have done well enough to be wanted to represent their country, but the timing is not good for us.'

Later in the evening, Stein and his players discovered who they would play for the right to be acclaimed the best team in Europe. Inter Milan and CSKA Sofia, two teams of contrasting pedigree but with the shared belief that dull defence was the foundation for success, had drawn 1-1 on aggregate in their semi-final. The Italians won the toss for the play-off to be staged in Italy and Renato Cappellini, who would have an interesting brush with Jim Craig later in the month, settled the outcome. The centre-forward headed the only goal of the game in the thirteenth minute and that allowed Helenio Herrera's team to happily retreat into their defensive shell for the remaining seventy-seven minutes. It wasn't enthralling or entertaining, but it was effective.

And the super-cool Herrera, immaculately-coiffured and expensively-dressed, took his front row seat at storm-lashed Ibrox Stadium on Saturday May 6 as Celtic set out to make history by lifting the championship at the ground of their greatest rivals. The bloated grey skies over Glasgow had burst from early morning and the torrential rain poured down vigorously, practically in rivulets, creating havoc with the electrics throughout the city and bringing the underground to a virtual standstill. Even the attendance was shy of the 90,000 anticipated with 78,000 fans in the stadium in time for kick-off. Various travel services had been severely curtailed during the freakish monsoon conditions. The Ibrox playing surface very swiftly resembled a quagmire. However, the underfoot swamp failed to prevent the players from both teams from serving up breathtaking entertainment with little Jimmy Johnstone taking top billing in a fascinating 2-2 draw where Celtic were a mere nine minutes away from their first league win in Govan in nine years.

Tommy Gemmell recalled, 'Jinky was immense that day. What made the achievement even more remarkable was the fact the entire game was played in a downpour. The heavens opened and I'm fairly sure I saw a bloke in a large ark packed with animals floating past at one point! Jinky, though, was in his element. He should have disappeared in the mud, but he decided to turn it on. His shirt was drenched and sodden and falling off his shoulders, his boots were just about submerged in the glaur, but nothing was going to deter him taking centre stage. Up against him that afternoon was Davie Provan, who was a tall, rangy guy.

'Helenio Herrera must have noted that the Rangers player was being torn apart by Jinky. Inside, outside, through his legs - it didn't matter to the Wee Man. He was in the mood and he was unstoppable. The Inter Milan boss would have been wincing through the ninety minutes as he witnessed all this unfolding before his very eyes. Herrera was known as "The Magician" in Italy and I bet he wished he could somehow make the Wee Man disappear.

'If he had arrived in Glasgow believing Jimmy Johnstone was merely a run-of-the-mill outside-right, then he got on his Milan-bound flight with different ideas. Jinky capped a wonderful display - easily one of the best I have ever seen by an individual player anywhere - with a soaring left-foot shot into the roof of the net from about twenty-five yards. Norrie Martin was in the Rangers goal that afternoon and he took off in determined fashion, but there was no way he was going to prevent that effort from rattling the rigging. By the way, I did say left foot. A lot of folk thought that was the one Jinky used for merely standing on, but, take it from someone who used to get tied in knots attempting to stop him in training, he could use both feet with equal ability.'

After his usual careful deliberation before any game, but particularly against Rangers, Jock Stein fielded the team he would choose to represent Celtic in the dramatically-changed circumstances of Lisbon later that month. He was resolute in his determination to clinch the club's second successive championship at Ibrox.

Stein's family were staunch Protestants from Burnbank and his father George was a fervent Rangers supporter. The family hoped Jock, a useful centre-half or left-half, would one day sign for the Ibrox side. That was the wish of his father. His son should play in the blue-red-and-white of

Junior side Blantyre Vics before swapping it for the blue-red-and-white of Rangers. Jock, though, displayed an exceptional independent streak early in life. He was not rebellious and never displayed the slightest bit of curiosity concerning the religious divides of a small mining community, but, later in life, Jock Stein never made the slightest attempt to disguise the fact he thoroughly enjoyed beating Rangers.

In his usual forthright manner, Bertie Auld told me in 'Celtic: The Awakening', 'Publicly, Big Jock would inform everyone that a meeting with Rangers was just another game. Privately, the players all knew just how much he enjoyed putting one over our old rivals. I would go as far as to say he detested Rangers. I don't think that is too strong a word. He really disliked them.

'We all knew his background, we realised where his roots lay, but we also saw him after a win over Rangers. You would have needed plastic surgery to get the smile off his face. We could beat any other team 2-0, 3-0, 4-0, you name it and we could still get a rollicking when we turned up for training on Monday. If he had seen something that upset him, irrespective of the winning margin, he would give us pelters. However, we could play awful, get a lucky goal and beat Rangers and we never heard a thing; not a murmur. Lose, though, and life wasn't worth living.

'He rarely, if ever, talked about the sectarian divide. He was a Protestant managing a club with Catholic origins and he had Protestant players such as Ronnie Simpson, Willie Wallace, Tommy Gemmell and myself playing for him. Religion didn't come into it as far as he and Celtic were concerned. It did across the Clyde, though. For long enough Rangers would not sign a Catholic. It was well-known that they were put off signing a young player who would go on to become world class because of his name, Danny McGrain. If only they had known.

'Jock used to insist if there were two players of equal ability and one was a Catholic and one was a Protestant, he would sign the latter. He would say, "Well, Rangers can't sign the Catholic, can they?" Sadly, that was the case back then. Jock found it extremely distasteful. In truth, though, he was only interested in a guy's playing ability and not the school he had gone to. Maybe that fired him up just that little bit more for games against Rangers.'

John Fallon knew what it was like to be on the receiving end of Stein's ire after underperforming in an Old Firm game. The goalkeeper, who had been a late replacement for Ronnie Simpson, lost two extremely soft goals in a 2-2 draw on January 2 1968, the second just one minute from time. 'I must admit it was a howler,' said Fallon. 'After the game, Big Jock looked as though he wanted to strangle me.'

So, the Celtic manager would have been far removed from best pleased when Rangers scored their first goal against Celtic that season after their 4-0 trouncing in the Glasgow Cup, the 2-0 loss in the league at Parkhead and the 1-0 defeat in the League Cup Final at Hampden. At least, Ronnie Simpson wouldn't be in the direct line of fire from Stein; there was little the veteran could do to repel Sandy Jardine's right-foot twenty-yard thunderbolt as it crashed behind him, abruptly shaking loose a cascade of raindrops from the net at the same time.

The Ibrox players must have thought the strike had presented them with a half-time lead as it arrived in the forty-first minute. However, Celtic, displaying the qualities expected of genuine champions, equalised within sixty seconds. Bobby Lennox squeezed a low drive away from the sprawling Norrie Martin and then groaned in dismay as the ball collided with the far post. His disappointment dissipated in a heartbeat as Johnstone, lurking with intent and reacting more swiftly than the Rangers defence, plonked the rebound into the net.

In the seventy-fourth minute, Celtic's miniature sorcerer conjured up an inspirational virtuoso moment that was immediately seared into the memory banks of anyone fortune enough to witness his generous gift of the extraordinary. The slight winger, after gliding on to a right-wing throw-in from Stevie Chalmers, somehow dredged himself across the soaking marsh with Rangers defender Davie Provan quite content to pass him inside onto his 'weaker' left foot. From somewhere within that slight frame, Johnstone found the reserves of strength to take a touch and then heave an utterly unstoppable shell high past Martin into the keeper's top right-hand corner of his net. He was immediately submerged by his delighted team-mates as the home defenders argued among themselves. They had just been in the presence of genius and had no need to attempt to apportion blame. Johnstone, swinging his arms like a happy schoolboy, trotted over to his outside-right berth as Rangers prepared to recentre the ball.

With time running out, Willie Henderson cut inside to drill a low shot across Simpson towards the far corner. The mud-spattered custodian got down to it in a flash, but, unhappily though, he couldn't keep hold of the greasy ball and it squirmed loose into the tracks of Roger Hynd, a muscle-bound wing-half converted to centre-forward for this game, and he couldn't fail to miss from four yards. Nine minutes later, referee Willie Syme, a match official who would never receive a Christmas card from Jock Stein, blew for time-up. Sportingly, John Greig, the despondent Rangers captain, was the first to congratulate Johnstone with Provan next in line. At least, they realised they had faced an irresistible force that damp day in Govan.

'It was a strange sensation to win the league championship at Ibrox,' recalled Gemmell. 'Obviously, our supporters were showing their delight and, like Fir Park the previous season, we had made to make absolutely sure away from our own stadium. But I also remember the Rangers fans cheering well after the final whistle. No, they weren't applauding us, but I think they were more than a little relieved they hadn't seen their team turned over again. Besides, it was also the Ibrox side's last domestic game of the season before they prepared for their Cup-Winners' Cup Final against Bayern Munich. So, we had both sets of Old Firm fans happy at full-time - that had to be a first!'

There was no rest for the victorious and four days later six of the Celtic players who performed at energy-draining Ibrox were taking their place in the Scotland line-up to face the USSR at Hampden, the nation's first international since beating England at Wembley almost a month beforehand. Bobby Brown selected Ronnie Simpson, Tommy Gemmell, Billy McNeill, John Clark, Jimmy Johnstone and Bobby Lennox to start the game while Willie Wallace replaced Manchester United maverick Denis Law at half-time. Sunderland's Jim Baxter, who was captain for the night, Eddie McCreadie (Chelsea), Frank McLintock (Arsenal) and Jim McCalliog (Sheffied Wednesday) made up the remainder of the team.

A crowd of almost 53,500 turned out to see the visitors win 2-0 during a fairly lukewarm encounter with both goals scored in the opening half. It was evident it was no easy task to keep Gemmell out of the headlines even on tepid occasions such as this one. The rampaging full-back scored only two goals while representing his country on a mere eighteen occasions. One was a penalty-kick in an 8-0 runaway World Cup qualifying victory over Cyprus in 1969 - and the other was for the USSR.

Gemmell's gaffe arrived in the sixteenth minute and, years later in his book 'All The Best', he told me, 'I scored over sixty goals for Celtic - not all of them penalty-kicks, I hasten to add - and that's not bad going for a left-back. However, while I was playing for Scotland, I only netted two. Embarrassingly, one of them was in my own net! And, even worse, it was against my old mate Ronnie Simpson. Honestly, you don't need comedy scriptwriters in football. We're all masters of improvisation. So, how did it come about? Sadly, I can't even blame the conditions at Hampden on that sunny Wednesday evening.

'Our opponents didn't need a helping hand with players such as Albert Shesternev - known as "Big Al" during the World Cup Finals in England the previous year - Josif Sabo, Valerij Veronin, Igor Chislenko and Eduard Malofeyev in the team. They also had one of the greatest goalkeepers of all time gracing Glasgow that night, the legendary Lev Yashin, known as the Black Octopus. He was the first goalie to wear an all-black kit that so many others copied in the sixties. Octopus? Well, he seemed to have more arms than was considered the norm. Yashin was at the veteran stage at that time and it must have been a rare occasion when my old mate Ronnie wasn't the oldest man on the pitch. Ronnie was thirty-six years old and his Soviet counterpart was a year his senior.

'Well, how did my mishap occur? Good question. I blame Ronnie! There were only sixteen minutes gone when I was tidying things up at the back. The game had started off at a genteel pace and maybe I was a bit slow to get into the flow. Anyway, without even looking over my shoulder, I turned to flick a high pass back to our keeper. Imagine my horror, then, when I heard a howl from the Hampden terracings and I swiftly looked round. Ronnie, for whatever reason, had wandered onto his eighteen-yard line. I turned to see our keeper scampering back trying to catch the ball as it sailed serenely into our net.

Wallace in Wonderland ...ecstatic Celtic fans hail Willie Wallace at the final whistle in Lisbon. The player, bought from Hearts by Jock Stein during the season, scored a double on his European Cup debut in the 3-1 win over Dukla Prague in the semi-final first leg in Glasgow.

C-H-A-R-G-E! The Celtic supporters can't contain their joy as they spill onto the pitch in the realisation their favourites have just made history by beating Inter Milan to become European Masters.

Support act...the fans congratulate John Fallon (extreme left), the substitute goalkeeper who was Ronnie Simpson's back-up all the way through the glorious campaign.

Paradise postponed ...triumphant captain Billy McNeill, aided by assistant manager Sean Fallon, attempts to get through the celebrating throng on his way to collecting the European Cup.

The Big Man ...Jock Stein is almost engulfed as police clear a path for the legendary manager to make his way to the Celtic dressing room minutes after the final whistle.

On a wing and a prayer ...the victorious Celts prepare for the flight home. **Top:** Matchwinner Stevie Chalmers, Jim Craig, Bertie Auld, Bobby Lennox *(partly obscured)*, masseur Jimmy Steele, Billy McNeill, Tommy Gemmell, Willie Wallace, Bobby Murdoch and John Hughes.

Hail the conquering hero ...Jock Stein, his mission accomplished, acknowledges the cheers of the fans as the team arrive back in Scotland.

Paradise ...Jock Stein *(right)* and deputy manager Sean Fallon *(second left)* join the players on the victory parade around Celtic Park only twenty-four hours after becoming the first British club to conquer Europe.

The man who almost wrecked a dream ...Sandro Mazzola, scorer of Inter Milan's early penalty goal, holds a Celtic shirt many years later. Sportingly, the cultured footballer admitted the better team won in Lisbon on May 25 1967.

READ ABOUT CELTIC HEROES PAST AND PRESENT
EVERY DAY ON **WWW.CELTICQUICKNEWS.CO.UK**

'I looked at Ronnie and said, "For fuck's sake, why didn't you give me a shout? Why weren't you on your line, you old bastard?" That, you should know, was a term of endearment. Ronnie was always good at returning fire. "Why the hell didn't you look where you were putting the ball?" Thankfully, the goalie could get his point across, but he was never a big curser. Mind you, he might not have been too delighted when I said, "Faither? You should be known as Grandfaither after that goal!"

'It didn't get any better when Fedor Medved netted another just before the interval and that's the way the scoreline finished. We had beaten England 3-2 at Wembley the previous month and, quite possibly, we had gone well into overtime indulging that success. I also had to face the wrath, not only of Ronnie, but also another five of my Celtic colleagues who had figured in the game - Billy McNeill, John Clark, Jimmy Johnstone, Bobby Lennox and Willie Wallace. We all had better fortune, I seem to remember, in a club game that was played in Portugal fifteen days later.

'At the end of the match, there was the usual scrum of newspaper reporters waiting to talk to the players. They selected me for the main question. They chorused, "What on earth were you thinking about at the own goal?" I had to think fast. I answered, "I looked up and saw an old guy coming out of goal and I thought it was Lev Yashin, so I decided to lob him." I don't think anyone bought into that.

'My other goal while representing my country was hardly memorable, but, at least, it was for Scotland! There is a good story about it, too. We were strolling to a 7-0 World Cup qualifying rout over Cyprus when we were awarded a penalty-kick with only fourteen minutes to go. Colin Stein, the Rangers striker, was on fire at Hampden that May afternoon in 1969. He had rattled in four goals in the space of thirty-nine minutes and was doing his utmost to beat Denis Law's Scottish international record. The Lawman had scored foursomes in games against Northern Ireland in 1962 and Norway a year later. The bold Colin wanted to go one better and grabbed the ball as soon as the referee pointed to the spot. It was natural enough for an in-form hitman to want to take the award. In fact, the penalty was given at what was commonly known as the Rangers End of the national stadium and the fans in there behind that goal were chanting for their Ibrox hero to have a go.

'No chance! I was the designated penalty-taker for the team and the onus was on me. Colin could plead all he liked, I was taking that spot-kick. A Celtic player allowing a Rangers player overtake a legend like The Lawman? Sorry, Colin, it was never going to happen. I put the ball on the spot and I did what I always did. I smashed it as hard as I could in the direction of the goal and hoped for the best. It flew into the net and that completed the scoring. Colin looked a bit miffed at the end. The Cypriot keeper's name was Michalaikis Alkiviadis and someone should tell him he was in legendary company. He became only the second goalkeeper, along with the icon that was Ronnie Simpson, I scored against in an international. That would have been something to tell his grandkids!'

Bill Anderson was the referee who brought the league season to a jubilant finale at Parkhead when Celtic beat Kilmarnock 2-0 on Monday May 15 - coincidentally the same match official who had activated the glorious campaign against Manchester United on August 6 the previous year. Helenio Herrera took the precaution of sending a platoon of spies to the game and they must have been more than a tad perplexed to see someone by the name of John Cushley playing at centre-half and another unknown in John Fallon performing in goal. Jock Stein was up to his old tricks and he even fielded skipper Billy McNeill wearing No.8. The Celtic players, with a second successive crown safely deposited in the Parkhead trophy room, were warned by their manager against turning in a self-congratulatory performance against Kilmarnock. 'Time enough for all that stuff at the end of the season,' he barked at the conclusion of his pre-match team talk.

Cushley, with West Ham manager Ron Greenwood, a friend of Stein, watching from the stand, played his one and only game for Celtic in their campaign of splendid triumph as they eased to victory with goals in each half from Bobby Lennox and Willie Wallace in front of 21,000 fans. A month later, the dependable Cushley, an uncomplaining understudy for McNeill, joined the London side for £25,000. Coincidentally, he would team up with goalkeeper Bobby Ferguson, who was also making his last appearance for Kilmarnock before his £65,000 switch to Upton Park. The goalie, who had lost his international place to the redoubtable Ronnie Simpson, had no chance when Lennox ran onto a Wallace lob to thump in the first goal in the twenty-fifth minute and it was an identical story midway through the second-half when Wallace controlled a Bobby Murdoch lobbed pass with his back to goal, pivoted and then blasted in an unstoppable effort.

All that was left was for the Celtic players to hoist a reluctant Jock Stein onto their shoulders and parade him in front of the delighted support. And then the thoughts turned to Lisbon.

CHAPTER SIXTEEN
MAY
HAIL! HAIL! THE CONQUERORS ARE HERE!

"It was only when I felt the magnificent three-foot-high trophy in my hands that the full impact of the moment came home to me - Celtic were the European champions!"

- Billy McNeill

The angels smiled down from the heavens on the day Celtic conquered Europe. A noble Billy McNeill, the handsome Celtic captain with the sun highlighting his blond hair, emphasising his physique, with his pristine green-and-white hooped shirt positively shimmering in the glow, held aloft the European Cup as he commanded the rostrum of the Estadio Nacional looking for all the world like Apollo ascending Mount Olympus.

Inter Milan, the team who had dominated European and world football for two of the past three years, had been vanquished. Their defensive tradition dismantled, their suffocating tactics blown away, their masterly reputation devastated. Celtic, refreshingly entertaining, had put sparkle and gaiety back into the beautiful game.

Years later, Billy McNeill, a genuine club legend, reflected, 'To my mind, the greatest thing about our European Cup victory is that we did it in the Celtic manner. We always wanted to play with flair, adventure and style. We were determined for people to remember us for our attacking philosophy. I would like to think we managed that in Lisbon. It was a breakthrough for British football. It was marvellous for Scottish football. However, the main thing for everyone connected with the club, the manager, his assistants, the players and tea ladies, it was truly wonderful for Celtic Football Club.'

Proud ambassador McNeill expanded on his memories. 'I've never had a tougher job than accepting the European Cup. It was the most stirring and exciting moment of my life. But I had to steel myself for it. I had just crossed the safety line into our dressing room at Lisbon after being swamped by the congratulations of our fans. My back ached with all the slapping. My jersey had been torn off as a souvenir. Now I had to go out and face them all again to collect the trophy.

'I put on a fresh jersey and, with assistant manager Sean Fallon and Ronnie Simpson giving me moral and physical support, I set off. The trophy was to be presented at the far side of the ground. It seemed there was just one way to get there - through the throng and right across the pitch. By the time we had made ten yards, Ronnie had got lost. Sean was on my left and around me was a posse of police. But the back-slapping, handshaking and general chaos never let up.

'We came to an obstacle - the six-foot-wide moat around the pitch. It was supposed to keep the fans on the terracing. Or, put another way, off the pitch. Some hope! Somehow, I made it to the other side. From there it was up the steps to the rostrum. The presentation was made by the President of Portugal, Americo Tomaz. And it was only when I felt the magnificent three-foot-high trophy in my hands that the full impact of the moment came home to me - Celtic were European champions!

'I have to admit in the emotion of it all everything is a bit blurred. Also, I still had to get back to the dressing room. It was a bit easier than the first journey. This time we were led outside the stadium, hustled into a police car and whipped, siren wailing, through the crowds to the dressing room entrance. We had a bit of a job getting away from the policeman. It appeared he was determined to have his photograph taken with us and the trophy. But Sean and I eventually disentangled ourselves, dived for the dressing room and got through the scrum unscathed - except for the fact I had lost my jersey again!

It was only then that I got the chance to sit down and soak up the satisfaction of being captain of the Celtic team which had just won the European Cup.'

The club's onfield leader and inspiration, along with many of his fellow triumphant team-mates, reckoned the victory over the feared Italians was one of the easiest games of the campaign. He said, 'Certainly, I had more difficult encounters in domestic games that season. Neither John Clark nor I were under any threat against Inter because the other guys in the middle and up front were doing their jobs so well. My biggest problem that day was whether to pass it out of defence to Bobby Murdoch or Bertie Auld. I would gather the ball and suddenly there was a shout in unison, "Give it to me, Caesar!" I would look up and there was Bobby and Bertie urging me to pass the ball to them and let them get on with it.

'Before the game, Big Jock was fairly strict with the players at our luxurious hotel in Estoril. We relaxed, played cards, read books and generally just took it easy. There was a magnificent pool at the hotel and Big Jock would only allow us thirty minutes to go for a swim. He would point to the sun in the clear blue sky and say, "That is your enemy, remember that. It will sap your energy. Be careful what you do."

'It may seem a strange observation to make, but Inter Milan scoring so early with Sandro Mazzola's penalty-kick was one of the best things that could have happened to us. It was their natural style to try to hold onto anything they had. They had a goal to protect and they seemed quite content to filter into their own half and do their best to keep us out. Although I was a central defender, it was not the way I was brought up to play football. It certainly wasn't the Celtic way. Our supporters wouldn't have tolerated that and, in any case, we all knew the fans deserved better. I said it then, I'll say it now and I'll say it again - those guys on the terracings were absolutely brilliant; they were our twelfth man. We never, ever took them for granted.

'We were invited to take the game to the Italians and it was an invite we so readily accepted. We really should have been in front by half-time, but their goalkeeper, Giuliano Sarti, was quite outstanding. When we got in at the interval, we couldn't wait to get out to restart the second-half. The penalty-kick decision really inspired us. We were all rattling on about the injustice of it and there was no way we were going to be beaten by a dodgy refereeing decision.

'Jim Craig, won't thank me for this, but, having watched the incident several thousand times, I now think the referee called it right. Back then, though, we were all united in believing the match official had done us no favours whatsoever. I know Cairney will still argue that it was never a spot-kick, but let's just say it certainly acted as a catalyst for us to get out there and turn them over.

'I recall it was actually quite calm in our dressing room at half-time. There were no histrionics. Big Jock simply insisted, "Keep doing what you're doing and we'll be okay." He did make one telling observation, though, when he asked our wide men to think about pulling the ball back closer to the edge of the penalty box because Inter were crowding into the six-yard area as they tried to protect their goalkeeper. When you look again at our first goal, you'll see how good that advice was. Cairney was calmness personified when he came racing into the box onto Bobby Murdoch's pass. His cutback for Tommy Gemmell was just right and Tommy simply belted one of his specials high into the net. Sarti had no chance. Eleven Sartis would have had no chance!

'Stevie Chalmers duly knocked in the winner with about five minutes to go and Inter Milan were out of it. They were a beaten team. If, by some chance, they had equalised, then the game would have gone into extra-time. Believe me, those guys didn't want to endure another half-hour of what they had already been through.'

Tommy Gemmell invited me to his comfortable abode in Dunblane while I was putting this book together. Quite by chance, one of the Sky sports channels was showing a thirty-minute feature of great European teams and the focus in this programme was on the Lisbon Lions. My notepad was instantly discarded and, thanks to the generous hospitality of my host, replaced by an accommodating large glass of cold white wine. I knew from the offset this would be a tough book to write! The legendary Celt and I settled down in front of his TV set to wonder at some of the magic for the umpteenth time over the past forty-nine years.

I sneaked a look at my big friend as his sixty-third minute shot flew high into the net for the equaliser. Gemmell smiled and said, 'Aye, it wasn't a bad wee goal, was it?' I'm sure I detected a small tear in his eye as he added, 'You know, I still get a tingle every time I see that goal. I'll never tire of watching that moment.'

This is an extract of a chapter devoted to the player which appeared in the 'Lisbon Lions: 40th Anniversary Celebration' book. It was 2007 and he travelled back in time to recollect, 'As we prepared for Lisbon, Big Jock took me aside and told me, "You'll get the freedom of the left wing. That Italian Domenghini won't chase back - he doesn't know how to tackle. I know what his game is all about. He'll want to do his tricks and flicks at the other end of the pitch. The hard work will be left to the guys behind him. You're going to enjoy this game."

'Sure enough, Big Jock, as usual, was absolutely spot on. Domenghini was a seasoned and gifted Italian international and, yes, he was exceptionally dangerous going forward, but he didn't want to know about defending. When I received the ball I never had to look over my shoulder. I knew he would simply be standing there, hands on hips, waiting for one of his colleagues to get the ball off me and feed it forward to him.

'He was a bit precious, as they say in football. Porcelain, even. Around my part of the world we would have labelled him a lazy beggar! He may have possessed bundles of skill, but he would never have been in any Celtic team managed by Jock Stein, that's for sure. So, certain in the knowledge that I would be unhindered throughout the ninety minutes, I launched into as many assaults on the Inter Milan defence as was possible before complete and utter exhaustion would have set in.

'In domestic games, it had become a bit of a habit for rival teams to mark me. I suppose I should take it as the extreme compliment, but it was a pain in the backside. It was difficult enough being a defender, so when you got the opportunity to get forward you wanted some freedom. Once I got a bit of a reputation, though, I suddenly found these sorties being blocked. Wingers were being asked to defend first and attack only if they got the opportunity. That's why I thoroughly enjoyed Lisbon. I could join the attack safe in the knowledge that Domenghini would not be tracking me and, basically, making a nuisance of himself.

'If you watch that goal again, keep your eye on the Inter Milan No.6, Armando Picchi, who charges out from defence as Jim Craig passes the ball inside for me. Picchi, who was the Inter captain, comes at me at pace, but, for whatever reason, he hesitates and turns his back just as I am about to pull the trigger. I have to admit that if he had kept his momentum going then there would have been every chance he might have blocked my effort. If he had come out with his foot up or to the side he might have made contact with my shot. Maybe he was thinking of his manhood, marriage prospects or whatever, but, thankfully, he had a swift change of mind and got out of the way.

'As I recall, I was screaming at Cairney to put the ball in front of me. I was timing my run and I didn't care one whit if Domenghini was with me or not. Nobody or nothing was going to get in my way. At last, Cairney put the pass in - perfectly weighted, may I say - and, well, the rest is history. Wonderful, wonderful history. Just before I pulled the trigger, I noticed that Picchi was in their keeper's line of vision and Sarti would not have got a great view of the shot until it was too late.

'He still made a spectacular effort to keep it out, though. I'll give him that. Actually, I thought then - and I still do now - that my shot was a goal all the way. It was destined to hit the net. You instinctively know these things. I belted it right on the money. It was a sweet strike alright and, of course, I had been fortunate enough over the years to knock in a few from distance. Most of the times you know there is nothing the goalkeeper is going to do to keep it out.

'I have to say, though, that Giuliano Sarti had looked unbeatable that day. He was immense throughout and sometimes you start to believe it is just not going to be your day. We hit him with everything, but he thwarted us time and time again. He patrolled his area with so much confidence and composure. He looked pompous and even a wee bit arrogant.

'It took us until the sixty-third minute to get that goal and, yes, as legend has it, I did swear at the gaffer shortly afterwards. He was yelling from the touchline, "Keep it tight - we'll get them in extra-time."

'I looked over and shouted back, "Fuck off, Boss, it's 85 degrees out here and we're going to finish it here and now." Thankfully, that's what happened and Big Jock never once mentioned our little bout of touchline verbal's afterwards! I said I thought Sarti was arrogant, but I had to take that back when I met him at a Lisbon Lions function in the Eighties. He was flown over as a special guest for the evening and he turned out to be a charming individual and he had the good grace to concede that we deserved to win. He told me, "Your victory was a triumph for sport." It takes a big man to make such an admission and we all greatly appreciated it. But, by God, did he make us work hard to achieve it.'

Veteran goalkeeper Ronnie Simpson recalled the countdown to the historic game. 'After lunch at 1pm, we were packed off to bed for two hours. I was sharing a room with John Fallon, who slept soundly. My normal practice is to doze off and read in between times and for some time I have got into the habit of reading a golf magazine. It gets my mind completely away from football as I am very interested in the sport, being a 4-handicap player at Dalmahoy. Neilly Mochan, our trainer, got us up around 3pm when we had a wash and a shave and then reported for our spot of loosening-up work.

'The hotel guests watched us jog around and exercise and most of them took photographs. We then had steaks, which we had taken with us from Glasgow, and then boarded the bus. The six-mile journey shouldn't have taken us any more than twenty minutes, but before very long we were trapped in the middle of the heavy traffic heading for the game. We had no sooner taken our seats in the bus than the songs began - Bertie Auld, John Clark, Jimmy Johnstone and Tommy Gemmell are the boys who usually get us going. They were all in fine voice. We got the full repertoire about four times before we finally sighted the stadium. We were late.

'Surprisingly, we got no police escort or outrider to take our bus to the stadium. Our bus driver had to fight his way through the traffic. When he realised he was making little headway and that the minutes were ticking by, he pulled the bus off the main drag and tried to get to the stadium by another route. He was promptly told he couldn't go that way and the bus had to reverse back into the main stream of traffic.

'We were all getting a bit keyed up now and our manager was trying to impress on the chap who had been attached to us an interpreter the importance of being at the ground well before the 5.30pm kick-off. Someone even shouted at a policeman on a motor cycle asking for assistance to get through the traffic. But the policeman remained where he was. At last we got to the stadium, through the sole efforts of the bus driver, just before 5pm. As it turned out, it was probably a good thing, as it gave us less time to think about the game in the dressing room. Players, like any other group of people, are not robots. They all have their idiosyncrasies and their own thoughts on how best to prepare themselves mentally for a game.

'Some of our boys like to walk over the ground before a game. Some, like myself, don't like to see the ground until we run out for the game itself. And before every game, I have a cold shower, whether the weather is cold or hot. It is a habit I developed during my years with Newcastle United where some of the players there told me it was the best thing to tone you up for a game. It's a tip I accepted and found does me a lot of good. On occasion, Billy McNeill also takes a cold shower prior to a game.

'The dressing room accommodation was unusual. It was like two small rooms joined by a passageway in which there were showers and baths. It meant that the team had to be split, so the manager decided that the defenders - goalkeeper to left-half - should dress in one section with the forwards and reserve keeper John Fallon in the other. The doors of each room were firmly closed and no-one was allowed in. Our manager saw to that.

'Inter Milan? I didn't see them when I arrived at the stadium and I just couldn't have cared less about them. The atmosphere was really building up now as we got ourselves stripped for action. I can honestly say that the players weren't in the least bit worried about Inter Milan. We all seemed to sense that we were going to do something in this game. We got the impression that we were going to be allowed one chance and that was it. The boys were eager to get started. They were ready. The last words of Jock Stein were, "This is your one chance. Let's try and take it." I've never seen Billy McNeill or John Clark so excited.

'We wanted to make sure of victory for Celtic and Scotland - that was what we were playing for. Not the bonus. We didn't even know what the bonus was and at that stage none of us cared. We would have played for nothing. This is one occasion no player in his right mind would want to miss. We, at Celtic Park, are never told what our bonus will be before any game. All I can say is that the bonuses are very generous and that our bonus for winning the European Cup was bigger than expected. I think this was because of the manner with which we won. Had we lost, we would still have been paid a huge bonus. My first Cup-winning bonus with Newcastle United was twenty-five pounds. The European Cup bonus was a few quid more than this! It was paid exactly one week later.'

Jim Craig was involved in a key moment only seven minutes into the game. He recalled, 'I didn't go overboard in my protestations when the referee awarded Inter Milan a penalty-kick after my tackle on Renato Cappellini. What would have been the point? The referee was hardly likely to change his decision once he had pointed to the spot. Let me say here and now, though, that it was never a penalty-kick. Absolutely no way. It doesn't matter now, of course, but I still hold the belief that the referee got it totally wrong.

'Folk have said I tackled with the wrong foot. Others have said I should have tried to play the Inter Milan centre-forward offside. Everyone is welcome to his or her opinion, but I am as convinced as I was back then that it was no penalty-kick. Cappellini was a big bloke, but he went down like a sack of tatties when I challenged him. Of course, he was looking for a penalty and the referee didn't disappoint him. He couldn't wait to point to the spot. I've lost count of the times I have replayed that incident in my mind and I always come to the same conclusion - the referee made a bad call.

'You could say that I helped to make a game of it! How would the remaining eighty-three minutes have panned out if Inter Milan hadn't got that penalty-kick? Who knows? But it certainly handed the impetus to Celtic and we knew exactly what we had to do in an effort to turn things around. I think we achieved our goal fairly well. One interested spectator that day at the Estadio Nacional was my Dad. He was a manager in the furniture department of Glasgow South's Co-op and, as a result of this, he worked on a Saturday and could only get to midweek matches. However, he really floored me by saying that he did not want to go to Lisbon.

'I couldn't believe my ears and asked him why. He was quite honest about it. He said he thought Inter Milan would be too strong for us and he did not want to go over there and see us being beaten. I accepted that, but, just in case he changed his mind, I held a ticket for him and booked a seat on the plane. As the days passed, I worked hard on Dad, but he only changed his mind at the last minute. However, I had the ticket and the seat all ready, so off he went on the great adventure.

'Dad couldn't have been too happy when I was involved in the penalty incident, that's for sure. I had been assured that Cappellini was, in fact, all left foot, so when he ran in on goal from the right hand side, I assumed that at some point he would want to put the ball to his stronger foot. I decided that I would block any attempt to do so, but when the challenge came, he went down rather like an ageing actor and I believe the referee was completely conned by it. A question I am often asked is, "What does a player think about in a time like that?" Well, in my case, I can assure you that my thoughts were with my Dad up in his seat. I had spent time persuading him to come over against his better judgement and now he had to sit through it all.

'Dad told me afterwards, "I didn't think it was a penalty-kick, to be quite honest, because the Italian player wasn't going towards goal and I think he had over-run the ball. Probably, the referee was as nervous as the players and over-reacted. What worried me more was that it might be the only goal of the game and my son would get the blame for the defeat. In retrospect, it probably helped a lot because the Italians just fell back into defence and Celtic were allowed to take control."

'Actually, I still laugh at the recollection of Big Jock at half-time. Of course, we were all disappointed to be 1-0 down, despite bossing the first-half after that goal. I wasn't too enamoured by the fact that I had been adjudged to have given away the penalty-kick. Jock came over, threw an arm around me and said, "Don't worry, Cairney, that was never a penalty. Never in a million years. Don't worry. Don't blame yourself. Put it behind you. Show them what you can do in the second-half."

'At the end of the game, though, Big Jock sidled up to me and said, "What on earth were you thinking about at the penalty? What a stupid challenge. You almost cost us the European Cup with that daft tackle." That was so typical of Big Jock, though. He knew the right buttons to push at the right time. That was part of his make-up and I suppose that's what made him so special. He could have taken me apart at half-time, but that would hardly have done my morale or confidence any good. He waited until that silverware was heading for the Celtic Park trophy cabinet before he told me what he really thought. I still don't believe it was a penalty, though. And, at least, I had the satisfaction of laying on the equalising goal for Tommy Gemmell.

'In fact, if you are going to talk about penalties, can I mention the one we didn't get when their excellent goalkeeper Guiliano Sarti hauled down Willie Wallace in the second-half? Sarti actually grabbed Wispy's leg and pulled him to the ground as he was about to roll the ball into a gaping and inviting net. It was like something out of a wrestling match, but, on this occasion, the referee was not impressed and waved play on. Yes, it was an injustice, but it simply made us all the more determined to win that match. Nothing was going to prevent us. Nothing or no-one.'

Ronnie Simpson recalled the spot-kick scenario like this, 'Sandro Mazzola sent a magnificent ball through our defence, past Billy McNeill and John Clark, and right into the path of the running Renato Cappellini. The centre-forward was well inside the box and lining up his shot when Jim Craig came across and tackled him from Cappellini's left side. Down went the Italian as he went over Craig's right leg. A blast of the referee's whistle and I realised he had awarded a penalty-kick. I just couldn't believe it. The tackle had seemed fair enough to me. But a penalty it was, despite protests.

'I decided immediately that I would dive to my left when the kick was taken. Mazzola was the Inter expert and he made a good job of it. He hit it to my right-hand corner, while I threw myself to the left. I guessed wrongly and Celtic were a goal down. I did feel, however, that even had I dived to my right I would not have stopped it as the ball hadn't left the ground and had entered my net a few inches from the post. In other words, a perfect penalty-kick. Craig was very unhappy about all this and said so at the interval. But he was quickly silenced by the rest of the boys who said, "Forget it." I thought that Craig had done exceedingly well to come across and get in his tackle. He was unlucky, that was all.'

Craig added, 'I've often been asked who I thought was Celtic's Man of the Match in Lisbon. Wee Jinky? Bertie Auld? Bobby Murdoch? Modestly, I believe the two full-backs, myself and Big Tommy, did rather well. Seriously, though, it was all down to team work. We had some smashing individuals, but Lisbon on May 25 1967 was a time and place for all of us to stand up and be counted. No-one shirked his responsibility and we won as a team.

'It would have been wonderful for the players to have been awarded the European Cup and been allowed to take a lap of honour, not just for the fans present in Lisbon, but for the many thousands watching on television throughout Europe. The presentation of our medals was also anti-climactic, to say the least. At the banquet following the game an official came up and placed two containers of medals on our table. We more or less helped ourselves to them. It was a rather strange end to such a fantastic, unforgettable day. But, hey, we were the champions of Europe and, at the end of the day, that was all that mattered.'

John Clark didn't have far to look for inspiration before taking the field that day. The Celtic sweeper possessed an encyclopaedic knowledge of world football and a memory bank to go with it. He recalled the x-certificate performance against MTK Budapest in second leg of the European Cup-Winners' Cup semi-final in Hungary as a motivational tool - if, indeed, one was required.

He said, 'It took utter humiliation in Hungary to make absolutely certain there was going to be a lot of partying in Portugal when we lined up to face Inter Milan. As we prepared for the game, I couldn't help but cast my mind back to Budapest three years earlier when we blew the opportunity of playing in the Cup-Winners' Cup Final. We arrived for the second leg on April 29 1964 with a handsome three-goal advantage from the first semi-final at Celtic Park. Stevie Chalmers, with two, and Jimmy Johnstone had scored against MTK Budapest and we believed - stupidly, not arrogantly - we held an unassailable lead over our opponents. How wrong we were!

'The history books will show the Hungarians won 4-0 and every single Celtic player was totally embarrassed. Devastated is probably a better word. We had thrown away a massive advantage and we had no-one to blame but ourselves. The pitch was okay. The referee was fine. We were awful, naive in the extreme. We were lucky there wasn't the live coverage on television of European football that we have today. A few us might have thought it would be preferable to spend the rest of our lives in the Hungarian capital rather than come home and face the wrath of our raging support after an appalling, wretched display.

'Back then, though, all the TV audience in Scotland saw were some flickering black-and-white images that lasted only a matter of minutes. There were no panels of so-called experts pouring over our every error, highlighting a blunder here and a clanger there. Believe me, this was one for those connoisseurs of calamity. MTK played well enough, but we should never have lost 4-0. Tommy Gemmell, Billy McNeill, Jimmy Johnstone, Bobby Murdoch, Stevie Chalmers and I played that night. I say 'played', but I'm using the term loosely. We were all on the pitch, but we hardly performed. Remarkably, all six of us would be in the side three years later that conquered Europe.'

Willie Wallace also revealed the part Inter Milan's left-back Giacinto Facchetti, a genuine sportsman, unwittingly played in the lead-up to Tommy Gemmell's wonder strike. He said, 'I am glad to say I had a hand, quite literally, in big Tommy's equaliser. I took the shy that moved the ball around the field before it finished behind the redoubtable Sarti. I recall I was going to throw it into the penalty box, but their giant defender Facchetti blocked my view. Big Jock used to hammer it into us to play the ball into the opposing team's box because you couldn't be offside at a throw-in. If you had a guy, for instance, standing right on the bye-line your opponents would be forced to cover him because he would be onside.

'By that reckoning, their defence would fall back and that would give someone else the opportunity to be played onside if there was a flick on or a rebound. So, in effect, I should have pitched the ball into the mix. But Facchetti prevented that and I actually threw it back to Big Tommy. I thought, if nothing else, it would be better for us to keep possession. And from that came our leveller.'

For reasons of accuracy, I put a stopwatch on the precise moment Wallace took the shy to the exact second the ball bulged the net behind Sarti. Here is how I wrote it in the Lisbon Lions book.

'Thirty-one seconds. One throw-in. Six passes. A thundering shot. That's all it took for Celtic to turn football on its head on that magical, memorable, exhilarating day in Lisbon on May 25 1967.

'For over an hour the marauding green-and-white legions had battered away at the Inter Milan goal without success. Goalkeeper Giuliano Sarti had been seen as a possible weak link in the Inter Milan defensive armoury which was otherwise festooned with seasoned internationals. But his was an extraordinary act of defiance that day; an impressive one-man barricade standing in the way of Celtic and destiny. He repelled raid after raid with one of the most astonishing goalkeeping performances ever witnessed.

'Bertie Auld, sensing a rare opening, clipped the crossbar with a cunning left-foot effort while running at speed. Shots and headers rained down on the black-clad No.1 who dealt with everything with an annoying assurance. Jock Stein ventured to the touchline, his massive left paw pointing the way for his troops. "Keep going," he urged. "Keep moving forward."

'Sixty-one minutes. Still Sarti and Inter were standing firm. Sixty-two minutes. Still nothing doing. Sixty-three minutes. Celtic had a shy thirty yards from the bye-line on the left. Willie Wallace, confronted with the daunting frame of Giacinto Facchetti, was looking for a team-mate in a good position. Facchetti held his ground. Wallace shaped to throw it and changed his mind. Gemmell loomed into view to offer an option. The ball duly dropped at his right foot. He switched it across the park to Jim Craig on the right.

'Craig rolled it inside for Bobby Murdoch who was crowded out on the edge of the box and the ball was retrieved by Jimmy Johnstone, on the left. He touched it back to John Clark who thrust it foward again to Murdoch, this time in the old inside-left channel thirty yards from goal. The Italians, methodical as ever, refused to be put off their stride. They regrouped, covered, picked up a man, shut down space. Celtic continued to show commendable patience as they passed the ball around.

'Murdoch slipped a simple pass in front of the galloping Craig. He controlled the ball as he gathered momentum heading for the danger zone. Another touch - three in all - before he squared it across to Gemmell. There was no break in his stride as he reached the eighteen-yard box with precision timing before clubbing the ball high past Sarti. The unbeatable was beaten at last. Hallelujah!

'Thirty-one seconds. A throw-in. Six passes. One thundering shot. That's all it took.'

Stevie Chalmers has always been the first to admit his matchwinner wasn't quite in the same category as Gemmell's cracker. He recollected, 'I might be the guy who got the winning goal, but, believe me, being involved all the way through and playing in every game is something that will live with me forever. Okay, how did I feel when I netted against Inter Milan with only five or six minutes to go? Exhausted! Cramp was coming on, but that evaporated as soon as that ball hit the back of the net. Okay, it may not have been as spectacular as Big Tommy's effort, but, for me, it was special because it was part of a routine we worked on day in, day out at training at Barrowfield.

'Big Jock would get myself, Joe McBride, Willie Wallace, Bobby Lennox and John Hughes to line up around the six-yard line and he would get Big Tommy, Bobby Murdoch, Bertie Auld, Jim Craig and Charlie Gallagher to hammer over crosses from the left and, after that, the right. Then he would vary the routine with Big Tommy playing the ball back from the line to, say, Bobby to hit the ball diagonally across the face of the goal. He would then do the same on the right with Cairney laying the ball back for someone to hit a similar effort into the penalty box. This would go on for hours until you knew off by heart where you were expected to be in the penalty box whenever a move was developing. It was no fluke, believe me, that I was standing where I was when Big Tommy pulled the ball back to Bobby to thump in his shot from the edge of the box.

'People have said they thought Bobby's effort might have found the net without my help, but Bobby himself would have told anyone his shot was heading for a shy! I simply sidefooted the ball past Giuliano Sarti, Inter's superb goalkeeper, and the European Cup was heading for the east end of Glasgow. You'll see pictures of Sarti appealing for offside - well, he would, wouldn't he? - but there was no way I was off. I was well onside when I got my touch to the ball. Big Jock always hammered into us the importance of being aware of where you were in the opposition's box. He didn't want a move breaking down because of a lapse of concentration on anyone's part.'

Bobby Lennox, present-day golfing partner of Chalmers - 'A couple of bandidos,' according to Gemmell - reckoned his mate did the Inter Milan players a massive favour with his winning goal. He reasoned, 'Really, the Italians, if they had any puff left, should have overtaken any Celtic player in the race to congratulate Stevie.

'If that game had gone to an extra thirty minutes we would have hammered them, believe me. I am utterly convinced we would have notched up a scoreline that would have embarrassed the Italians. They were out on their feet nearing the end of that game. They were shattered after chasing shadows for eighty-five minutes and they didn't look as though they were up for some of the same in a bout of extra-time. It would only have been a matter of time before we scored again and the way we were playing that day I don't think we would have known how to take our foot off the gas. We wouldn't have had the inclination, either. We would just have kept on going, no matter what the score might have been.

'Their goal had led a somewhat charmed life although, to be fair, their keeper, Giuliano Sarti, should have got some sort of individual medal for his bravery as he kept the scoreline respectable. But even he would have capitulated in the event of another half-hour. He simply couldn't have replicated his efforts in the regulation time. So, when Stevie sidefooted that one in from six yards, it put Inter Milan out of their misery. That is not meant to sound big-headed or arrogant. Anyone who knows me will tell you that is certainly not my style. I'm just stating a fact. The Italians were on the verge of collapse. Meltdown was minutes away. I think the stretcher-bearers might have been working overtime during any extra-time period.'

Bertie Auld admitted he had been disappointed he hadn't been given the opportunity to pit my wits against Inter Milan's world-renowned Luis

Suarez. He said, 'Injury forced him out of their team and, immediately in the aftermath of our triumph, the Italians pointed out they would have picked up the trophy again if their much-vaunted Spanish midfielder had been playing. Believe me, that is utter nonsense. Suarez? They could have fielded Superman and they wouldn't have prevented us from winning that day!

'The Italians, as ever, were just a bit too quick to delve into that well-thumbed tome, "The Big Book of Football Excuses", although, to be fair, their manager, Helenio Herrera, and a few of their players were just as swift to congratulate us. They knew they had been outplayed, outfought and outwitted.

'But I really would have loved to have squared up to Suarez. I was on the left-hand side of the Celtic midfield and his favoured position was on the right of the Inter midline. It would have been very intriguing to see how we got on, to say the least. These days you can get live pictures of players and watch them in action at the flick of a button thanks to satellite television. Back then, of course, that was not the case. You rarely saw up-to-date film of foreign players and you had to take what your boss told you about so-and-so's strengths and weaknesses. They were all a bit mythical back then and you had to accept someone's else's word about their ability. Of course, you could catch up with reports in the newspapers, but there was nothing quite like matching up with the guy in the flesh. Genuinely, I welcomed that opportunity in Suarez's case.

'Suarez was one of the first football superstars. We all took a sharp intake of breath when we were told Inter Milan had paid a mind-boggling £214,000 to sign the player from Barcelona in 1961. That was massive money all those years ago; easily the world record transfer. Look at the Celtic team that took the field at the Estadio Nacional six years later - it cost a total of £42,000, a mere fraction of what Suarez had signed for. We were also informed the Spaniard had negotiated a signing-on fee of £60,000 for himself. I didn't think there had been that much money printed. The player was said to be picking up around £7,000-per-year in wages. Okay, I know an average player in the Scotland's top flight can now command a figure like that on a weekly basis, but back in the Sixties that was massive dough. If I've got my sums right, the Celtic players were lifting something in the region of £1,300 in those heady financial days.

'So, can anyone blame a wee chap from Maryhill for wanting to go toe-to-toe with this bloke? I would have loved it. I would have thrived on it. Apparently, Suarez was said to be suffering from a thigh strain in the run-in to Lisbon, but we did hear other suggestions that, at thirty-two, he might not have fancied playing against Celtic. He would have known about our high energy levels. He would have heard about our fitness and our willingness to go flat out for ninety minutes. He was a cultured playmaker, of course, but this might not have been a setting for him to show those skills. I'm not say he chickened out, but what I will say is that it did not matter one jot whether or not he was on the field of play on Thursday May 25 1967 - we would have still won the European Cup.

'Think about this, too. Suarez was not known for enjoying defensive duties. He did all his playing facing the opponents' goal from middle to front. Would he have chased Tommy Gemmell into corners? Would he have made runs to block off Bobby Lennox? Would he have trailed all over the place alongside yours truly? I doubt it. His replacement was a guy called Mauro Bicicli and he was actually more of a defensively-minded player and, naturally enough, Inter needed those sort of performers the way the game developed. Maybe, then, we might have won a bit more comfortably than 2-1 if Suarez had turned out.

'I was also disappointed to read about the Italians saying they had struggled for a replacement. They were having a laugh, weren't they? Inter Milan with their many millions, the most expensively-structured line-up in the world could not find a suitable player to take over from Suarez? A team that had won the European Cup in two out of the previous three years and had also lifted the World Club Championship twice over the same period? Pull the other one!'

Auld continued his observations, 'I hit their crossbar with a run and shot as we swept down on them looking for a first-half equaliser. I've often been asked if I intended a cross because the ball took a strange swerve and ended up heading for goal. Take it from me, that was an attempt at goal. I put a little bend on the ball as I moved into their box and I thought my attempt looked good. Well, it would have had to be better than good to beat their keeper Sarti who was unbelievable. However, the woodwork got in the way of me and glory and the ball bounced to safety. Thankfully,

Tommy and Stevie had better fortune later on.

'But let's look at that Celtic line-up. We weren't exactly a cosmopolitan bunch in 1967. For a start, we were all born within thirty miles of Celtic Park with myself, Ronnie Simpson, Jim Craig, and Stevie Chalmers being allowed to boast that we were, indeed, true Glaswegians! The others came from places such as Bellshill, Bothwell, Craigneuk, Uddingston, Kirkintilloch and, in Bobby Lennox's case, Saltcoats. I always thought that was just a place people went for their holidays; I had no idea people actually lived there. Anyway, the Glaswegians among the lads used to kid the others on about being hicks from the sticks. Big Billy, from Bellshill, was often fond of saying, "Don't ask me, I'm just a lad from the country, you better ask Bertie." But we were one big happy bunch, you can believe that. There is genuine camaraderie among us and nothing will ever split that up.

'What was so special about the team? Well, the word team gives you a clue. We may have had some excellent individuals such as Jimmy Johnstone, Tommy Gemmell and Bobby Murdoch, but we all fitted into a structure. We trusted each other and that was so important. It was comforting to go out on the field on matchday and know you had so many good players around you. Take Ronnie Simpson, for a start. How reliable was he? You instinctively knew he would do a good job. He may not have looked like your typical goalkeeper, but, to me, there was none better. He may have been on the small side, but Ronnie always insisted he was close to 6ft. He must have been using a different measuring tape from anyone else in the world, that's all I can say! But he was a brilliant shotstopper and was extremely agile.

'Do you know, of the team that faced Inter Milan, only Ronnie and myself had played football outside Scotland? Amazing. Ronnie, of course, won two FA Cup medals with Newcastle United while I had my stint at Birmingham City before I returned to Paradise. Jim Craig, Tommy Gemmell, Bobby Murdoch, Billy McNeill, Jimmy Johnstone, Stevie Chalmers and Bobby Lennox had all been brought up through the ranks at Celtic Park, although I believe Luggy may have been on the books at my old club Birmingham City very briefly. Willie Wallace, of course, arrived from Hearts. And Big Jock had never managed outside Glasgow,

Edinburgh and Fife. See what I mean about hardly being cosmopolitan!

'I've already said the Boss was the man who deserved all the credit for what Celtic achieved and quite rightly so. He was way ahead of all the other managers of that era with his thinking and planning. He would develop wee things in training and opponents and supporters alike might have thought we were improvising on the pitch during a match, but, believe me, we had gone over these things meticulously in training at Barrowfield. He was a great believer in the old adage, "Fail to prepare, then prepare to fail."'

Auld added, 'I missed out on only one game during Celtic's run to Lisbon - the dramatic last-gasp 2-0 victory over Vojvodina - after failing a late fitness test. Even I was left gasping for air at our truly wonderful support. I swear Celtic Park was rocking that night. Of course, I would have loved for nothing more than to be out there contributing, but the next best thing was watching the action and roaring on the lads. What a game that was. Honestly, the hairs still stand on end at the recollection. It was one helluva exciting rollercoaster ride of emotions. Everything that is good in football was on show that cold, grey, but truly unforgettable, evening in the east end of Glasgow.

'I was witnessing two football teams at the peak of their powers and it was all spellbinding stuff. Celtic would surge forward in wave after wave of attacks, but the Slavs were an extremely accomplished unit and they looked fairly comfortable as they soaked up awesome pressure while always looking for the out-ball to turn defence very quickly into attack. They were a very polished side with a very good manager in Vujadin Boskov. Charlie Gallagher took my place in midfield that night and let me tell you something about Charlie - he would have been a first team regular in any other team in the land outside Celtic.'

Matchwinner Stevie Chalmers concluded, 'Lisbon was made all the sweeter because I had been at the club eight years before then, signing from Junior club Ashfield on February 6 1959, and there was absolutely no way I could have ever believed Celtic would one day conquer Europe. After putting pen to paper, I made my debut just a month later, an instantly forgettable 2-1 defeat from Airdrie at Celtic Park. Possibly not surprisingly, that was my only league appearance of that particular campaign.

'After Lisbon, I came home to spend my bonus money. To be honest, I can't remember too much about my so-called spending spree. My wife, Sadie, would have got something, of course, and I probably spent the rest on things around the house. Not exactly Flash Harry, eh? But winning the European Cup was not all about money. It was about football and putting Celtic's name on the European map. We managed that and, of course, Big Jock was smiling afterwards because we did it in the Celtic manner.

'Ach, I suppose we weren't a bad side.'

CHAPTER SEVENTEEN
MAY
THE SACRIFICE OF A SHOWMAN

*"The Italians were starin' doon at us and we're grinnin' back
up at 'em wi' oor great gumsy grins. We must have looked like
something oot o' the circus."*

- Jimmy Johnstone

It took the rest of the newly-crowned Lisbon Lions a fair bit of time
amidst the euphoric aftermath to convince Jimmy Johnstone he hadn't let
the team down. The little winger figured he hadn't played to potential as
Inter Milan were swept aside.

There can be little doubt that the man who was daubed Mickey by Jock
Stein after the famous Walt Disney cartoon mouse, but known as Jinky
to his team-mates, was a complex character who continually sought
reassurances - even minutes after being part of a historic Celtic team that
had just claimed the glittering European Cup.

Bobby Murdoch, in his 1970 memoirs, gave an interesting insight into the
psyche of his good friend. He said, 'Probably the most controversial player
we've had at Celtic Park since I established myself in the first team is little
Jimmy Johnstone. For a wee fellow, Jimmy has had a fairly fiery career, to
put it mildly. Controversy and problems are never far away.

'Yet you won't find a bigger worrier anywhere than Jimmy Johnstone.
We came into the Celtic team during the same season and played on the
right-wing together. Because of this, I have got to know him really well

and I really do understand him. As a footballer, I rate him as one of the best I have ever seen anywhere. He is positively brilliant on the ball, yet in those early days when we were both trying to create an impression with our rather immature standard of play, Wee Jimmy just wouldn't believe he was any good.

'He had no faith whatsoever in his own ability and I used to shout myself hoarse telling him that he could take the full-back any time he wanted. He had to be encouraged all the time. I was almost a private coach to the Wee Man, shouting stuff like, "The full-back is scared stiff of you, Jimmy" or "You can take him any time you like" or "You've got this team worried sick". And so on for ninety minutes. He had to be kidded and coaxed all the way.

'In the years since, however, he became steadily more confident and now demands the ball from all of us. It is always his plan to make a fool of the full-back so that he will lose his composure and panic into mistakes. When he is on form there are times I almost feel sorry for the opponent. Jimmy, though he now owns a restaurant and pub and drives a Jaguar, still feels insecure. He still takes all his problems on the field with him and there are times when his concentration isn't what it should be. He's the kind of person who has to see hard cash in his hand before he believes that he is really as well off as people say he is.

'There's always a bit of fire in a red-head, of course, and Jimmy is no exception. He takes it very badly when he has one of those days when nothing goes right for him. A lot of his trouble on the field has simply come about because he has lost patience with himself and has taken it out on an opponent. He has no hatred for any player, it is just that he blows up so easily when things are going against him.'

Former Celtic manager and player Davie Hay, now a distinguished and worthy ambassador of the club, was closer to Jinky than most and accepted he was the Wee Man's unofficial off-the-park 'minder'. He said, 'Jinky possessed a self-destruct button. He could be a complex personality if he perceived there was an injustice being done to him. It could be real or imagined, but you could always detect that Jinky was fretting about something.'

Many years after Lisbon, Jimmy Johnstone, in a reflective moment, said, 'I'm proud that I was part of the greatest club in the world. To be the first British team to win the European Cup, but more so to be part of the greatest Celtic team ever. That's something else, isn't it?

'Picture it, though. Who were we? We were nobodies, just a bunch of guys. Here we were in Lisbon, playing against the mighty Inter Milan. If you remember, they had won the European Cup and the World Championship twice in three years. Big Jock always said we'd win, but, to be honest, I thought we'd get a right gubbin'. I can see them yet standing alongside us in the tunnel waiting to go out onto the pitch - Facchetti, Domenghini, Mazzola, Cappellini, all six-footers wi' Ambre Solaire suntans, Colgate smiles and slicked-back hair. They even smelt beautiful.

'And there's us midgets. Ah've got nae teeth, Bobby Lennox hasnae any, either, and old Ronnie Simpson's got the full monty, nae teeth top and bottom. The Italians are starin' doon at us and we're grinnin' back up at 'em wi' oor great, gumsy grins. We must have looked like something oot o' the circus.

'But, somehow, we knew within ourselves, our own ability and we started to believe in ourselves, but we never, ever for a minute thought that we would win the European Cup. Afterwards? We all got drunk, I think. For a week after it, we just got drunk.'

Even today, the mere mention of Jimmy Johnstone brings a beaming smile to the Danny Kaye features of Tommy Gemmell. He recalled, 'Wee Jinky used to tell me how disappointed he was with his own performance in Lisbon. He really wanted to go out there and just take over. As we all know, he was a cocky, capable little character when he was in the mood and he knew this was his sort of platform. The European Cup Final was invented for Jinky; that was his sort of stage. But it is to his eternal credit that he sacrificed himself that day for the team. He roamed here, there and everywhere taking the Italian team's tough guy Burgnich with him. It wouldn't have been how he thought or dreamed how it would turn out, but he saw the team as being a lot more important than himself and he just got on with putting in a marvellous shift.

'Jinky really couldn't fathom what he had given the team against Inter. Their manager, Helenio Herrera, was acclaimed as possessing one of the most tactically astute minds in the game. Unfortunately, it was built solely on defence. He would have plotted and planned for this game as soon as he knew who his team would be facing in that Final. There's little doubt that he believed Jinky would have performed throughout the match wide on the right in his usual position. And no doubt he would still have stuck Burgnich on him and that would have given Facchetti a bit of freedom to race up their left side.

'But Facchetti wasn't afforded the cover his team-mate would have given him and he was pinned back in his own half for virtually the entire game. He might have looked for some help from the other central defenders, but they were getting tied up by the movement and interchanging of Willie Wallace, Stevie Chalmers and Bobby Lennox. Jinky was totally unselfish, but so, too, were those three guys. They were all noted goalscorers, but, like Jinky, they were asked to perform against the Italians in a different manner to confuse the opposition.

'Jock wanted them to make openings for Bertie Auld and Bobby Murdoch, supporting from the midfield, and for me and Jim Craig coming down the flanks. The four of us would pass the ball to feet, take the return and move forward. One quick glance at the statistics will tell you all you need to know. Believe it or not, we had forty-two attempts at the inter goal with twenty-six on the button. I had nine shots on target, Bertie had two, including one that struck the bar, Jinky had two, including a header, and Bobby had four efforts saved by Guiliano Sarti who was having the game of the life. The performance of the keeper would have broken the hearts of other teams. We weren't just any other team, though, and we proved that in Lisbon. And what about the three guys up front, Wallace, Chalmers and Lennox, who had scored nine of our sixteen goals in the competition prior to the Final? Stevie had claimed five while Wispy and Lemon had two to their name.

'As you might expect, I've watched that European Cup Final several times now - if I'm being honest, I think I've worn out about a couple of hundred pairs of specs! - and even I have been surprised to discover that Stevie only had one shot on target - the winner! - Wispy drew one save and, astonishingly, Wee Lemon didn't work the keeper at all! So, if we are just judging the European Cup Final through statistics, then Jock's tactics were absolutely spot-on. But a wee guy called Jinky was instrumental to everything that went on that day. No-one should ever forget that. '

Willie Wallace added, 'Wee Jinky, of course, was an unbelievable character. I've always thought someone should write a Harry Potter-style book about a wee footballer who could do all these magical things as he grows up. You could base it on the life and times of Jimmy Johnstone, I suppose. He was a special player and Lisbon was an ideal setting for him. He told me and all the other Lions afterwards that he wished he could have contributed more that day. We told him to behave himself and stop looking for compliments.

'Inter MIlan stuck a bloke called Tarcisio Burgnich on him that day and he was one of the best man-markers in the world, if not the best. But Jinky stuck at his task throughout the ninety minutes. Burgnich never left his side and Jinky took him into areas that opened up the way for Bobby Murdoch and Wee Bertie to come through. It's not the stuff that is immediately noticeable, or even appreciated by some supporters, but players know what it is all about. Anyway, I will always remember Wee Jinky coming so close that day with a header, which wasn't bad for a bloke who stood 5ft 4in.

'Cairney dinked one in from the right and, for once, Burgnich was nowhere to be seen. Jinky just took off and made perfect contact with his head. The ball was hurtling high into the net until Giuliano Sarti, who might have thought it was going over under its own steam, suddenly reacted to the danger and sprang high to get a hand to the effort to turn it over the crossbar. If he had hesitated, Wee Jinky would have scored. With a header!'

Bertie Auld recalled, 'I could hardly believe my ears when I heard Jinky apologising to us. There was so much going on around me that I thought I had picked up the Wee Man wrong. "What are you saying, Jinky?" I asked. He was an emotional guy and was close to tears as he repeated, "Ah'm really sorry. Ah let youse doon." Celtic had just beaten the famed Inter Milan 2-1 to win the European Cup, the biggest club football prize of them all, and there was Jinky saying he was sorry. I knew him better than most and I realised he wasn't joking, that this was no act. He really meant it. He thought he had failed his colleagues on the day we turned on an illuminating, devastating ninety minutes that blew away the defensive-minded Italians.

'I should have been whooping it up, celebrating with my team-mates and here I was consoling Jinky. "What are you talking about?" I said. "You were one of the best players on the pitch. You and Bobby Murdoch were just brilliant.' " Jinky looked up, "Do ye really mean that, Bert? Ye're no' just sayin' that?" I assured him I meant every word and, even years later, when Jinky and I were on our own, he would still ask, "Me and Bobby, best men on the pitch in Lisbon, Bert? Ye huvnae changed yer mind?" For goodness sake, we had both been out of football for decades and he was still seeking reassurance!

'I'll always remember the laugh we had in the tunnel before the game. There we were lining up and these guys from Inter Milan looked like gods, never mind footballers. I recall they were all immaculate, there wasn't a hair out of place. They oozed glamour. Their blue-and-black tops had been hand-pressed by an expert. A lot of us were standing there minus our false teeth. It didn't look like a fair fight. I looked at Giacinto Facchetti, their world-famous left-back. He was about 6ft 3in and was such an imposing figure. He looked as though he had stepped straight out of a sportswear catalogue.

'I turned to Wee Jinky and motioned towards one of their players with my head at one of their players. "Hey, wee man did I not see that bloke in that movie with Marcello Mastroianni? Did he not get off with Anita Ekberg in La Dolce Vita?" Wee Jinky looked back, puzzled. I indicated another of their players, "Did he not used to go out with that Sophia Loren?" We were all having a good laugh and the Italians simply looked bemused. I heard mutterings of 'loco, loco' among their ranks. They really didn't know what they were up against. "Hail! Hail! The Celts are here," bounced around the walls of the tunnel. We kept it up all the way until we got the okay to, at last, walk out onto the track.

'Big Billy, of course, was first out, chest proudly expanded to its maximum. In order, our captain was followed by Ronnie Simpson, Tommy Gemmell, John Clark, yours truly, Bobby Lennox, Stevie Chalmers, Jimmy Johnstone, Willie Wallace, Jim Craig and Bobby Murdoch. Reserve keeper John Fallon came next with his lucky teddy bear and then out strode Jock Stein alongside Neilly Mochan, our trainer, with assistant boss Sean Fallon and physiotherapist Bob Rooney following on. If you get the opportunity to watch footage of the teams strolling out onto the track and then onto the playing surface have a look at the Italians. A lot of them are actually eyeing us up and down and shaking their heads. They were just a tad bemused. They were going to get a lot more bemused by time-up, that was certain!

'Okay, Wee Jinky thought he under-performed against Inter. Frankly, I knew the Wee Man could be a humble bloke, but I found it simply unbelievable that he would genuinely reckon this was the case. I heard not that long ago that my old team-mate Davie Hay had named me as Celtic's top player that day. Thanks, Davie, but you've got the wrong man; Wee Jinky was streets ahead of anything I conjured up against Inter.

'That Wee Man was different class, on and off the field. That day in Lisbon will be forever remembered for my big pal Tommy Gemmell's spectacular equaliser and Stevie Chalmers' winner five minutes from time, but I thought Jinky was immense in a thoroughly unselfish, totally professional performance. We were all aware of what he could do with a ball. He could take it for a stroll in his early years at the club and no-one else would get a kick for about five minutes. Then he would lose possession and leave everyone sucking out their fillings.

'Against Inter Milan, he put in a wonderfully-disciplined display against one of the toughest defenders in the world, Burgnich, who was also an experienced international. Big Jock had told Jinky to take Burgnich for a walk and drag him all over the place. That would unsettle their defence because he was undoubtedly the rock in their backline. Giacinto Facchetti was supposed to be the greatest attacking left-back on earth back then, but I think we all knew who was the real deal, the genuine article after Lisbon - Big TG, Tommy Gemmell. What a game he had; simply mind-blowing. Cairney, Jim Craig, was like TG, a complete athlete and he was getting up and down that right wing as often as possible as we pounded the Italians. Jinky deserved every accolade and so, too, did my mate Bobby Murdoch. He was a big guy, with that barrel chest of his, but he had the touch of an angel. He didn't kick the ball, he caressed it. He was immense, but, to be honest, we won and lost as a team and we all played our part that day.'

Jim Craig chipped in, 'I don't think Jinky ever received the credit he deserved for his performance against Inter. He didn't appear to be involved in the key points of the game, but, believe me, he pulled their player, Burgnich, all around the pitch to make openings for others. I'm sure if Jinky had hopped on a bus to take him into Lisbon town centre, the Italian would have gone with him! We, the players, knew what he contributed against Inter. Wee Jinky was discipline personified and we all realised he was at his happiest skipping down the wing on one of those unbelievable, hip-swerving runs, leaving distraught defenders tackling fresh air.

'The European Cup Final was his stage, it was his platform to produce another glorious performance of stunning variety that would have undoubtedly mesmerised watching millions on the many TV sets tuned into the game throughout the globe. Without any debate, he possessed the individual skills to take the spotlight in the biggest game of his life. However, he sacrificed all that in Lisbon for the cause of the team. No-one will ever forget that. Nor will we ever forget him.'

Jock Stein once famously said, 'People might say I will be best remembered for being in charge of the first British club to win the European Cup or leading Celtic to nine league championships in a row, but I would like to be remembered for keeping the Wee Man, Jimmy Johnstone, in the game five years longer than he might have been. That is my greatest achievement.'

Jimmy Johnstone, rightly, was voted Celtic's Greatest-Ever Player by the supporters in 2002. With typical humility, he said, 'I thought the honour would go to Henrik Larsson.'

CHAPTER EIGHTEEN
MAY
THE HIRPLING HERO

"We knew it would take something special to beat Sarti and, thankfully, Tommy Gemmell came up with the answer."

- Bobby Murdoch

Bobby Murdoch was a genuine working-class hero from Rutherglen. Not for him the flash cars, the snazzy clothes or the crazy hairstyles. He lived with his family in a comfortable, but hardly ostentatious, home in Cambuslang and shunned the bright lights of nightclubs in preference for a beer with his team-mates and long-time friends at the local.

Months after his mesmerising performance in Lisbon, Argentina's Boca Juniors, one of the biggest clubs in the world at that time, were reported to be getting ready to make a massive bid for his services. In typical Murdoch fashion, he responded, 'Ach, I'm no' interested - no way. I'm staying with the club I love. I'm only interested in playing for Celtic.' And you just knew that he meant every word of it.

One of his prize belongings was a gift from Celtic a couple of months after the victory over Inter Milan in the Portuguese capital. He said proudly, 'Every member of the first team pool that year was given an eight-millimetre colour film of the highlights of our European Cup Final which runs for some forty-five minutes. I regularly run it through at home when friends drop in for a spot of supper or a natter and I never cease to marvel at some of the football the boys turned on. This film is one of my most treasured possessions.'

Murdoch recalled the countdown to that special day in his club's history. He said, 'There was something about Jock Stein leading up to that game in Lisbon that I found impossible to put my finger on. He was a confident individual, of course, but this was different. Our manager looked as though he was utterly convinced we would win the trophy. And, remember, this was the guy who would get all his players around him and insist, "There are no easy games, they all need to be won." It didn't matter who Celtic were playing, he thumped out the same advice. Complacency in the Celtic dressing room was a huge no-no.

'I got the impression Jock genuinely believed he had taken us to a level where we couldn't be beaten. No stone had been left unturned in his preparation for the game. And I mean none. He had gone through the Inter Milan team, man by man, dissected their tactics, told us what every player would be asked to do, how they would set up, which player favoured which foot. The only thing he couldn't have predicted was the performance of their goalkeeper. Many actually thought Giuliano Sarti was the team's Achilles' Heel and, frankly, that made no sense to me. They say a chain is only as strong as its weakest link, don't they? It didn't sound right that Sarti was second rate.

'Inter's obvious strength was their ability to defend in depth. Would a manager such as Helenio Herrera, with his incredible reputation and eye for detail, continually choose a last line of defence who could have been seen as suspect? That went against the very ethos of his thinking. You would have thought his ideal outline would be the spine of the team starting with the goalkeeper, going through his centre-half, central midfielder and through to his centre-forward.

'Sarti was thirty-three at the time of the Cup Final and had played only eight times for Italy. A lot of us had watched the 1966 World Cup Finals in England the previous summer and there had been no sign of Sarti in the squad. Their keeper was Enrico Albertosi, of Fiorentina, and the Inter No.1 hadn't been rated good enough to get a place as one of the two back-up keepers. We weren't fooled, though. We wondered what Inter Milan's players might have thought about our own Ronnie Simpson. A player who cost virtually nothing from Hibs, thirty-six years old - three years Sarti's senior! - and with two international caps. But we all knew how important Ronnie was to Celtic.

'But I have to say Sarti's performance against us in Lisbon bordered on the unbelievable. We bombarded that guy, but he stood up to everything we launched at him. I thought I had scored with a header from about six yards. It looked a goal as soon as it left my forehead, but I couldn't believe it when the keeper caught it in mid-air with one hand. I almost applauded that effort myself. We knew it would take something special to beat him and, thankfully, Tommy Gemmell came up with the answer. It was a long time coming, though - far too long!'

Indeed, there was genuine agony among the ecstasy for Murdoch during the encounter. The midfielder had his right foot stamped on by an Inter Milan defender early in the game. He said, 'The pain shot right through me. It was probably an accident, but it was a dull one. If there had been outfield substitutes available back then, I might have had to go off. However, as it was, we only had stand-by goalkeeper John Fallon on the bench that day. Big Jock told me, "Run it off, Bobby, you'll be fine." As the game progressed towards half-time, I looked down and my right ankle seemed to be twice the size it was at the kick-off.

'People must have wondered why I was favouring my left foot that day. Fortunately, I was two-footed, but my right was undoubtedly the stronger of the two. I even managed to get a couple of left-footed shots on target against Inter, but both were saved.'

Murdoch's midfield ally Bertie Auld remembered, 'I saw Bobby grimace at one point and I asked him what was the matter. He pointed to his right foot and I could clearly see that his ankle was beginning to swell up. I said, "I don't like the look of that, Bobby." "I'm no' too chuffed myself, Bertie," came the reply. What a performance he put in that day on one foot. The Italians got lucky - could you even start to imagine what he would have done to them if he could have used both feet!'

Captain Billy McNeill recalled, 'As Bobby said, we didn't have a substitute to cover for him if he had gone off. Listen, there was no way Bobby was going off that day. No chance. He would have played on with his leg hanging off if need be!'

Bobby Lennox said, 'I thought Bobby was Celtic's best player in Lisbon. I can't give him a higher tribute than that, can I? Of course, he had plenty of competition for that honour with my wee pal Jimmy Johnstone, Bertie Auld, Tommy Gemmell and anyone else you care to mention really turning it on that day. But it was Bobby for me; a real ten out of ten performance.

'He had all the talent in the world and he could also be very aggressive when need be. I mean in a sporting manner, but Bobby was never interested in an opponent trying to boss him around out on the field. That was his domain and he didn't invite anyone in there.

'We all know what he contributed against Inter Milan. That, I swear, was one the most selfless displays I have ever seen. He was carrying that injury, but he was still all over the place trying to galvanise the rest of the team. Just ask Big Billy or John Clark. When they got the ball he wanted it immediately. Luggy seemed to have a lot of the ball that day, as I recall. He would do his sweeping up as Inter's rare attacks came to nothing and he would look around for someone to pass to. Bobby was always there.

'I am sure Bobby was as happy for me as I was for him when we lifted that European Cup. We had grown up together at Celtic Park. I signed two years after him, but, even as a young man, you could see he was going to go all the way to the top. You can't disguise that sort of quality.'

Bobby Murdoch realised a dream that day. He strode the immaculate surface of the Estadio Nacional with a grace and guile that bewildered Inter Milan. He was in the thick of everything. Adding his powerful frame to defensive duties, making himself available for passes from the defence, patrolling the middle of the park with Bertie Auld, spraying the ball around with gravity-defying accuracy and plunging into attack to blitz the overworked Sarti in the Italians' goal. All with one good foot!

It was a truly memorable performance from the masterful Murdoch. Inter Milan, doyens of their defensive craft, had no answer to the gifted linkman. Inevitably, he was involved in both goals that brought the European Cup to Celtic Park. No surprise, really. If you ever want to witness a midfield player in his absolute prime and doing everything with breathtaking precision, just look again at the European Cup Final of 1967. Bobby Murdoch, with one good foot, was in the spotlight and, to everyone's delight, this wonderful and self-deprecating character played a pivotal role in the club's most famous triumph.

Jim Craig said, 'Bobby was known as Chopper for most of his career, but he was also called Sam for a spell - and he didn't like it one little bit! We were down at our usual HQ at Seamill on the Ayrshire coast preparing for an important game and Jock Stein set up a training exercise that saw us dribbling round paint pots.

'Bobby clattered into a few of these obstacles and sent paint flying all over the place. I recall there was a van parked nearby with the name Sam B. Allison emblazoned on its side. He appeared to be the local painter and decorator. Big Jock laughed, "Hey, Bobby, you've spilled more paint than Sam has in a lifetime." So, Bobby instantly became Sam and the nickname stuck for awhile.

'He may not have been able to skip round inanimate objects, but Bobby knew how to get past more orthodox opponents. He had a very graceful, artistic touch. You would sometimes see him going up on his tip-toes, having a wee look around and then arcing a pass about fifty yards or so with uncanny precision.

'His shooting power was fairly devastating, too. He had it all. Another thing you might not know about Bobby was that he was a very emotional character. He would cry if we won. He would cry if we lost. He would even cry if we drew. We just cried when he wasn't in the team!'

John Clark said, 'Bobby was quite a quiet, even reserved, sort of character. What a transformation when he got out on that football field, though. That was his stage and he revelled in that setting. If you asked me to list his strengths, I would say you might as well cut to the chase and try to detect a flaw. If there was one, I didn't see it and I played alongside him often enough.

'Bobby was good with either foot, could shoot from range with equal power and accuracy, could tackle with the best of them and wasn't bad in the air, either. He wasn't the fleetest of foot, but he more than made up for that by his reading of the play. It was actually a pleasure to be on the same pitch as Bobby - especially as he was wearing the same strip as you.

'A lot of teams paid him the compliment of sticking markers on him, but they would simply be undone if Bobby spotted an opening and zapped one of his precision passes through it to a lurking colleague. And, if they weren't sticking the ball in the net, he wasn't adverse to coming forward and rectifying the situation himself.'

Stevie Chalmers laughed, 'Folk have often asked how I celebrated our European Cup triumph. They always looked a wee bit disappointed when I told them I spent it in an empty hotel with Bobby! Let me hastily explain. I roomed with Bobby at our rather splendid hotel in Estoril and after the game we both went back and got ready for the specially-prepared banquet with all the UEFA delegates. The beaten Inter Milan players were there, too, but they really looked as though they would have preferred to be somewhere else. Can't blame them.

'Anyway, our wives had travelled over to Lisbon and were staying in a different hotel from the players. They were scheduled to travel back that night and Celtic were due to fly into Glasgow the following day. Anyway, after the banquet, Bobby and I saw our wives, said our farewells, wished them a safe journey home and then made our way back to our hotel. After a wee while we decided to get some shut-eye. It had been a long and fairly exhausting day and we knew something special would be waiting for us at home. How special we couldn't possibly have known at the time.

'So, we decided to get tucked up in our beds and no sooner had we put our heads on the pillows than there was a banging at our hotel room door. "Hurry, you two, get up," ordered Jock Stein. "There's been a problem with your wives' plane. The flight's been cancelled. The girls have nowhere to stay. You'll have to give them your beds!"

'So, a bleary-eyed Bobby and I dutifully gave up our accommodation for our wives only to find there was no room at the inn for us. And the guys with whom we had made history that same day weren't at all interested in letting us bunk up with them. So, there you have it. Bobby and I were booted out and had an empty hotel foyer to ourselves. I couldn't think of better company.'

Bertie Auld commented, 'I loved playing alongside this boy; he could do everything. He could tackle, he could shoot and he could pass. Everything Bobby Murdoch did was stamped with class and authority. His vision was phenomenal and you would have had to go far to actually meet a nicer bloke.

'Bobby's career really took off when Jock Stein came back to the club. He actively encouraged an individual to play with adventure. Big Jock gave Bobby Murdoch the freedom to express himself and I don't think the player let anyone down. Ever.'

CHAPTER NINETEEN
MAY
ASSAULT COURSE AT THE ESTADIO

"I fought with all my strength to make the tunnel and I made it with my jersey, cap, pants, boots, gloves, hair, false teeth and body intact."

- Ronnie Simpson

'I was crying. I couldn't stop myself. The tears came rolling down my cheeks. I was standing in the lingering sun of Lisbon in the Estadio Nacional, completely helpless in my emotions.'

The words belong to the remarkable Ronnie Simpson, as revealed in his memoirs.

'The European Cup Final of 1967 was over. Referee Kurt Tschenscher, of West Germany, had blown for the last time and Celtic were champions. Champions of all Europe for the first time at their first attempt. And I, Ronnie Simpson, at the age of thirty-six and seven months, had become the first British goalkeeper to win a European Champions Cup medal. I couldn't believe it. I was overcome.

'I wasn't alone for long. In seconds I was smothered in the arms of manager Jock Stein, then reserve keeper John Fallon, the player who had stripped for every European tie and never been called up. The three of us were locked together, crushing each other, scared to open our mouths in case we all burst into tears again.

'Suddenly, I realised there were more people running around us than there should have been. Our supporters were on the field. This was their greatest moment as it had been ours and they were going to make the most of it. But the fastest man of all at that moment was Bobby Lennox. He came sprinting straight at me and I held out my hands, thinking he was coming to join in the goalmouth celebrations. But Bobby kept going right into the back of the net. Then it dawned on me.

'Before a match, I take out my false teeth and stick them in my cap which I keep in the back of the net. It's a habit I have adopted in important matches just in case I have to meet someone at short notice or at the end of a game. Then I can always pop my teeth in. Bobby noticed this habit of mine and, as he also had false teeth, he asked me before the Lisbon Final to keep his set of choppers inside my cap. And this was what Bobby was racing for - and I suddenly knew why!

'The fans, Celtic, Portuguese, Italian and the others were desperate to get some sort of souvenir from this remarkable Final. Players were getting jerseys and pants torn from them bodily, fans were cutting lumps out of the turf, the corner flags were already on their way to places well away from Portugal. My cap, with two sets of false teeth, was too obvious a trophy.

'Bobby won his race, grabbed his teeth and ran for the tunnel leading to the dressing room. I quickly grabbed my cap and teeth and tried to make it - and did so after what seemed an eternity. I was half-strangled and almost crushed as a tug-of-war went on for my jersey. But this was one jersey I was keeping. I fought with all my remaining strength to make the tunnel and I made it with my jersey, cap, pants, boots, hair, gloves, false teeth and body intact.

'I was met in the dressing room by Bob Rooney, our physiotherapist. He threw his arms around me, dumped me on a seat and the two of us burst into tears. We couldn't help it. The happiest moment of my life and I couldn't raise a smile! The joy of beating Inter Milan was a strange experience. Had the tension been so great? Had I put in so much concentration into this match that I had no strength at the finish? Or was it sheer emotion that had made me lose control? I don't really know. But even today I still find it hard to believe I was a member of the Celtic team which won the twelfth European Cup tournament.

'It is wrong to say that we had prepared for this match in the two days we had stayed in Estoril, or the ten days before training at Largs and at Parkhead. I felt we had been preparing for this Final all season. I felt we had been building up for this match from the early days of August.

'I remember well what the Boss said to us after our final training session in Glasgow before we boarded our chartered Dan Air jet aircraft for Lisbon. "Look, boys, I think it can be us. If we play it correctly, we can win." He said it with that dry smile of his which meant he was certain we would win. He talked to us about the method of Inter Milan and their playing strengths. He was convinced that their right-back Tarcisio Burgnich would be given the job of shadowing Jimmy Johnstone. This proved to be correct. He told Willie Wallace to play up front for the first ten minutes, then change over with Stevie Chalmers who would play deep in this early spell. He wanted to confuse the opposition, unsettle them, without upsetting the Celtic team plans. This he succeeded in doing.

'He wanted Jim Craig and Tommy Gemmell to attack freely and run with the ball. And he wanted the ball cut back into the path of running players. And, as the world saw on television, we had ten running players - and all running forward! Our manager never insists on anything. He suggests it. And his suggestions have so often been proved right, that they are now accepted with little, or no, opposition.

'He made one other point. He impressed upon us that should we lose to Inter Milan, we were to lose like true sportsmen. He asked us to play it clean no matter what happened. He wanted Celtic to come out of the Final with credit, no matter whether we won or lost. He didn't dwell too much on this, but he made his point very plainly. With the game on television, to be seen throughout Europe, he wanted Celtic to be seen as a team fit to grace a European Cup Final. Fit to win it – or fit to lose, with dignity.'

Simpson added, 'Inter's manager Helenio Herrera had fought long and hard to get Celtic to some disadvantage. And had failed. He had gone to Portugal some weeks before the Cup Final and appeared on television asking the Portuguese people to support Inter in the game as they, like the Italians, were Latins. He had demanded first choice of the dressing room and had protested when he learned that Celtic wore their numbers on their pants instead of their shirts. He even made sure we would be out first at the interval, so that we would be exposed to the sun longer than Inter Milan.

'Manager Jock Stein held himself in check. He told us, "If I know the people of Portugal, they will support Celtic. We, like the Portuguese side which played in the 1966 World Cup Finals in England, play attacking football. We will win the Portuguese support by entertaining them and by playing the attacking football they enjoy." He was right - as always.'

John Clark said, 'I know Billy McNeill has always stated that he thought the Inter Milan game was the easiest we faced in the European Cup that season. Probably we didn't have to work as hard as we did in the goalless draw against Dukla Prague in Czecholslovakia, for instance, but I still thought it was a tough shift. We all knew about the Italians' attitude to football. They were superb on the counter attack. They didn't waste time or energy coming forward in waves. They were cagey, would keep possession and then suddenly explode into action when they got anywhere near your penalty area.

'They obviously believed in the rapier thrust rather than the almighty bludgeon to get the job done. Thankfully, though, our guys in the middle of the field, Bobby Murdoch and Bertie Auld, and the lads up front kept the Inter back lot occupied throughout huge chunks of the game. Yes, I take on board what Big Billy says, but I have to admit I feared Inter on the rare occasions they tried to get forward. It was a game where you knew one lapse of concentration would bring about disaster.

'I'll never forget that backheel from Ronnie Simpson, for a start. I still break out in a sweat when I think about it. That came from just one long pass from the edge of their own penalty area. Ronnie, as he often did, saw it coming and was off his line swiftly. Their centre-forward, Renato Cappellini, didn't give up the chase, however. He kept on going and, for me, there were danger signals flashing. Ronnie actually turned his back on the Italian and looked as though he was going to run towards his penalty area where he could have picked up the ball. Instead, for absolutely no fathomable reason, he decided to backheel it to me.

'He told me he realised I was there all the time. I'll take his word for it. Anyway, if that had hit the Italian it was goodnight for us. They would have gone 2-0 ahead and I genuinely don't think we would have got three to win in normal time. No-one would have been talking about the Lisbon Lions decades down the line. Or, possibly, I'm just not giving Ronnie the praise he deserves for a bit of off-the-cuff goalkeeping.'

Ronnie Simpson admitted, 'I admit now there is one moment from the game which has given me a couple of sleepless night and has made me think quite a lot. The moment when I backheeled the ball to John Clark across my goal and out of my penalty area. A loose ball had come into our area, some thirty yards from goal and I went for it as almost every other member of our team was up in attack. I had plenty of time, or so I thought, and my intention was to give the ball a good old-fashioned wallop upfield.

'But as I ran towards the ball I could hear an Inter player chasing me from the other side of the field and he was gaining very quickly. It was then that I got it into my head that if I kicked the ball, I might kick it against the Italian and it might rebound towards goal which, of course, was unguarded.

'As I was running, I could see John Clark racing to the other side of the penalty box, obviously to cover the goal. I made my mind up then. As I got to the ball, I threw my left leg over it and backheeled across the penalty area to John Clark. Luggy promptly cleared it and that was that. Since then I have wakened up a few times in the middle of the night and asked myself, What would have happened if that hadn't come off? Supposing I had muffed the kick and Inter had scored? Would I be where I am today? Would I have been able to live it down? Remember, this was the first-half and Inter were already leading 1-0. It would have been a tragedy for me, for Celtic and for Scotland. What a chance to take – but, thankfully, I got away with it.'

Bobby Lennox said, 'We deserved to win in Lisbon. After I scored against Motherwell to make sure we lifted the 1966 league title, our first in twelve years, I recall Big Jock saying, "We mustn't look to the past at the legends who have gone before us – we must build our own legends." How prophetic were those words?

'Yes, it was great to make history in Lisbon. Nothing will ever top that feeling. I will always remember the referee blowing that final whistle and I just turned round to see who was the nearest team-mate. It was John Clark and we just threw ourselves at each other. Honestly, we were like a couple of schoolkids. "We've won! We've won!" We yelled our heads off as Inter Milan players walked disconsolately past us, heads bowed in defeat.

'Then I remembered my false teeth were in Ronnie Simpson's cap in the back of his net. I saw all those supporters racing onto the pitch and I suddenly thought, "I better get my teeth!" I ran to Ronnie, picked up my gnashers and the Lennox smile was ready for the cameras.'

CHAPTER TWENTY

MAY

THE LONELY MAN AND THE IMPOSSIBLE TASK

"The secret of being a good manager is keeping the six players who hate you away from the five who are undecided."

- Jock Stein

He was the individual who possessed the keys to open the gates to hitherto unknown abundances of joy and immeasurable delight for the Celtic support.

For the moment, though, Jock Stein was a man alone.

The Celtic manager had abandoned the touchline bench he had shared with Sean Fallon, Neilly Mochan, Bob Rooney, Jimmy Steele and reserve goalkeeper John Fallon for nudging on ninety epic minutes at the radiant surroundings of the Estadio Nacional in Lisbon on Thursday May 25 1967.

Tension, evidently, possessed qualities to invade even the sternest of facades; suspense had the propensity to penetrate the reserves of the most resolute of characters. With Celtic leading Inter Milan 2-1, the remaining seconds were ticking down agonisingly slowly. Stein, unnoticed in the midst of the increasing anxiety as West German referee Kurt Tschenscher showed no signs of placing the whistle to his lips to bring a halt to proceedings, surreptitiously slid off the seat and began walking along the trackside.

Remarkably, Jock Stein couldn't bear to look and actually turned his back on the action taking place only yards adrift of his left shoulder. He had decided to go walkabout. He strolled down the touchline, his head bowed and his hands clasped in front of him, almost as if in prayer. Celtic were moments away from becoming only the fifth team to win the European Cup while Stein paced steadily forward, his gaze fixed on the track in front of him. A lifetime's achievement was within touching distance; his hard work, toil, graft and genius about to be rewarded. The delay was interminable, verging on the unendurable.

Suddenly, there was the welcoming blast from the match official's whistle and the stress was expunged immediately. Stein spun, brought up his fist in acclaim and yelled, 'Yes!' The job was done; Celtic had made history by conquering Europe, the first British club to achieve what had previously been deemed by so many football experts as an impossible task.

The Celtic bench, thirty yards away, had already joined the cavorting players. There is a famous photograph of the backroom team leaping around with unconfined joy on the touchline seconds after full-time. There is assistant manager Fallon, trainer Mochan, physiotherapist Rooney, masseur Steele and substitute goalie Fallon catapulting to their feet in salute.

There is no sign of the man who masterminded it all, though. Jock Stein absorbed the moment of glory in his own company, alone with his private thoughts for a fleeting second or two. And then the party started.

Back in Glasgow the following evening, the Celtic manager was cornered live on television as his beaming players paraded the newly-won European Cup to the adoring thousands at Celtic Park who had turned out to give a rousing welcome home to their heroes. The BBC commentator, a chap by the name of George Davidson, pushed the microphone towards Stein and said, 'I am told the secret is that Celtic are one big happy family and you keep it that way.'

Stein thought for a moment and replied, 'Actually, there is a better secret than that - we are a good football team.'

The Celtic manager was never known for his under-stated values of his team or its players. Merely good? The team that now ruled European football and who were already being acclaimed as the best in the world? Stein, of course, fully realised Celtic weren't merely a good football team

- they were a magnificent and unique sporting structure who echoed the thoughts, methods and ambitions of their equally progressive manager.

Somehow, Stein had taken a team that had been annihilated 4-0 by MTK Budapest in the second leg of their Cup-Winners' Cup semi-final in Hungary only three years earlier and had shaped them into the best in Europe. And he achieved it with six players who had been on the receiving end of a drubbing in the famous Nep Stadium - Billy McNeill, Tommy Gemmell, John Clark, Bobby Murdoch, Jimmy Johnstone and Stevie Chalmers.

Celtic staggered through a mistake-riddled 1963/64 season routinely being turned over by fairly average opponents such as Falkirk (0-1) and St Mirren (1-2) while Kilmarnock hammered them 4-0 at Rugby Park. They were 4-0 ahead of Third Lanark at the interval in a league game at Parkhead and were pegged back to 4-4. It was goalless at half-time as they struggled to overcome non-league Eyemouth United in the Scottish Cup. They eventually won 3-0 when the gallant part-timers ran out of puff. Even worse, they played Rangers five times - twice in the championship, twice in the League Cup and once in the Scottish Cup - and lost the lot while conceding eleven goals and scoring only one. Grim reading, indeed.

But Stein, with a resolute belief in his self merit, shook a club from its lethargy and navigated a path towards soccer's promised land, vigorously debunking previous long-held theories while doing so.

What motivated the phenomenon that was Jock Stein? There can be no argument that graphic, etched-in-coaldust memories of his early life as a miner, beginning as a sixteen year old at the Earnock pits in Lanarkshire, never left him. He would tell journalists of those days when he fed bread to the rats who awaited his company as he descended 1,000 feet underground on a daily basis to make a living. He would say, 'No-one knows darkness like the darkness inside a mine.' Another oft-used expression was, 'You go down that pit shaft and you can't see a thing. The guy next to you, you don't know who he is. Yet he is the best friend you will ever have.'

Stein wasn't a particularly complex character and had little time for complications while dealing with matters in a basic and practical manner. He could trample on people's sensitivities and he upset more than a few players in his time. There were those who would insist agreeability wasn't exactly his stock in trade. Undoubtedly ruthless, he made decisions that were far removed from popular. Although some former Celtic players of my acquaintance admit to still experiencing traces of bitterness and resentment at the way they were treated, not one of them has even attempted to cast aspersions upon his managerial ability. That aspect of Jock Stein's persona is unchallengeable.

No-one was ever sure whether he was joking or being philosophical when he said, 'The secret of being a good manager is keeping the six players who hate you away from the five who are undecided.'

Jim Craig made this honest observation, 'Jock was not an educated person, in general, but he was a highly intelligent man. He would have sauntered through a university degree course.' To many, the Celtic manager thrived on argument and debate and not just on the topic of football. Craig also pointed out he possessed a general knowledge to enable him to be 'a stimulating conversationalist'.

Sir Matt Busby, the legendary former Manchester United manager, who was a close confidante of Stein, said, 'He had a remarkable eye for detail in football and a memory bank that bordered on the impossible. As history shows, he put it all to a good use.'

On a sun-bathed evening in the Portuguese capital, as far removed from his days of pummeling for coal in the underground gloom, Jock Stein cut a solitary figure. The man who invited Celtic supporters to a destination beyond comprehension was isolated for a moment in time.

In his subconscious, though, he may very well have detected the faint, lilting tones of a well-known Celtic anthem...

'You'll never walk alone.'

CHAPTER TWENTY-ONE
JUNE
THE JIMMY JOHNSTONE SHOW

"Jinky had the Real Madrid fans yelling 'Ole!' every time he touched the ball. Basically, he gate-crashed a legend's party."

- Tommy Gemmell

'Donde esta, Johnstone?' Alfredo di Stefano was clearly perplexed. 'Donde esta, Johnstone?' he repeated, raising the decibel level slightly. The iconic Real Madrid forward, once rated by Pele as 'the most complete footballer in the history of the game', was in a bit of a tizzy.

Di Stefano had assembled a spectacular line-up of legends following the banquet to celebrate his years with the team that conquered Europe five years in succession. Ferenc Puskas, Francisco Gento, Luis del Sol and Jose Santamaria were among a glittering collection of superstars from yesteryear - Cristiano Ronaldo would have struggled for a place on the substitute's bench - who were booted and suited while the official club photographer checked once again to make sure there was film in his Pentax.

But there was no sign of Jimmy Johnstone. And Alfredo di Stefano was determined the Celtic winger would take pride of place in the photograph. He insisted the Wee Man's presence was urgently required to grace the image. *'Donde esta, Johnstone?'* There was a crisp edge to Di Stefano's tone now. Puskas and his exalted former team-mates were beginning to get a bit fidgety. Di Stefano instructed them to calm down; the picture would go ahead as soon as the Celtic player had been located.

At that precise moment, Jimmy Johnstone was propping up the bar in the players' lounge at the Bernabeu Stadium, sipping his favourite tipple of vodka and Coke only an hour or so after spectacularly entertaining an audience of 120,000 in the Testimonial Match for Di Stefano, the sporting artiste who had been a boyhood hero of the football-crazy kid with the explosion of red curls who perfected his art of driving defenders towards a nervous breakdown by dancing round milk bottles on the streets of Uddingston with a ball seemingly glued to his toes.

As he relaxed, he knew his work for the season was done; the following day he and his wife Agnes would be heading for a relaxing fortnight on the beaches of Benidorm.

After wandering around the labyrinthine corridors of the famous old ground, Di Stefano was eventually pointed in the direction of Johnstone and persuaded him to join him and his former Real Madrid colleagues for the historic snap. Tommy Gemmell recalled, 'At first, Jinky thought it was a wind-up. I think he said something to Alfredo like, "Ach, away ye go." Can you imagine it? An assembled company of some of the greatest players the world has ever seen, players who had ruled football for years, and there was Wee Jinky telling the great Alfredo di Stefano to leave him alone?

'When Alfredo managed to convince Wee Jinky he was deadly serious only then did he agree to go and join in for the snap. He was walking on air when he came back to the bar some fifteen minutes later. "I've just got ma picture taken with Alfredo and his mates," he said. Then he laughed, "That'll be something for them to tell their grandweans!" But that was Jinky and nothing fazed him. He had just turned in the performance of a lifetime, had the Real Madrid fans yelling "Ole!" every time he touched the ball and had stolen the spotlight from the fabulous Di Stefano on his big night. Basically, he gate-crashed a legend's party.'

Jimmy Johnstone's illuminating display in the Spanish capital on the evening of June 7 bordered on the magical, eclipsing everyone else on show. Di Stefano, a month before his forty-first birthday, chose the newly-crowned European champions as his preferred opponents for the grand occasion. He had travelled to Lisbon to witness the European Cup Final and turned up at Celtic's hotel in Estoril to ask them to play for him.

Thankfully, the Celtic Board accepted his request.

The players arrived back in Glasgow twenty-fours hours after the historic victory in Lisbon and were given five days off before returning to Parkhead on June 1 for training as they prepared for Madrid. However, this was to be no friendly encounter. As Bertie Auld recalled, 'Alfredo kicked off and was on the pitch for about fifteen minutes and the tempo was hardly above strolling pace. But when he departed, it was a case of, "Let battle commence!" I should know - I was sent off.'

Jim Craig recalled, 'Jinky could do no wrong that night. I well remember a Real Madrid player, Grosso, I think, racing out of defence in an effort to clatter the Wee Man. Clearly, he had had enough of Jinky's one-man show and it was his intention to sort him out. Yes, he did wallop Jinky, but if he thought that was the end of my wee pal's meanderings for the night, he was so wrong. I remember the Real player trotting back into defence, probably thinking to himself, "That takes care of that." His face was a picture, though, when he looked over his shoulder to see the Wee Man bouncing back to his feet to take the free-kick. I suppose he thought his opponent would fold under such treatment, but he didn't know our Jimmy Johnstone. He was unstoppable that evening.'

Gemmell added, 'Jinky was really excited at playing in the Bernabeu for Di Stefano. As soon as the game was announced after Lisbon, it was all he could talk about. I had the feeling the Wee Man might put on something special. Something special? That's a massive understatement. Big Jock sensed it, too. Before the kick-off, he told us, "Get the ball to Jinky. We're here to entertain and win. We want to show these fans that Celtic are worthy European champions. Jinky will be the main man tonight. Make sure he gets that ball." And, if you ever see footage of that game, you'll see that we carried out his instructions. Jinky was given a roving commission for the evening and he was popping up everywhere. There were a couple of occasions when he came deep into our own half just to receive a pass and then take off in the general direction of enemy territory.

'Aye, they tried to kick him, but that never bothered the Wee Man. I never once saw him take a dive. If he went down, you knew he had taken a sore one. But he was always quickly back to his feet. I've said this before and no doubt I'll say it again, but Jinky was incredibly brave. When we talk about Jinky, inevitably we discuss his special talents, his mazy runs that would leave defender after defender in his wake. Rarely, though, does his bravery crop up in these conversations. Let me tell you, he was afraid of no-one or anything. Opponents who threatened him were wasting their time. Jinky would laugh at them and turn to a team-mate and say something like, "Did you hear that, Tam? He's going to break ma fuckin' leg. He's the fifth defender this month who is going to break ma fuckin' leg." And with that, he would continue to take the ball right up to his opponent, swivel those mesmerising hips and take off, either on the outside down the wing or inside into the traffic. I couldn't help but admire that wee chap.'

John Cushley was the player with the most unenviable task at Celtic; trying to dislodge Billy McNeill from the centre-half berth. The no-frills defender was on his last trip with the team before his £25,000 transfer to West Ham United a couple of weeks later. He made only forty-one first team appearances in seven years at Parkhead, but, as Bertie Auld was quick to point out, 'John never complained because he accepted Billy McNeill was one of the best centre-halves in the world.' Cushley was educated at Glasgow University and Celtic put his linguistic skills - he earned a MA in modern languages - to good use on the club's behalf on, at least, two occasions.

McNeill's understudy actually travelled with manager Jimmy McGrory to Spain in 1964 in an effort to persuade the aforementioned Di Stefano to join Celtic. It was a sensational move for a player, who, at thirty-seven years old, was, admittedly, past his best. Cushley, with McGrory's prompting, did his best to convince one of the world's greatest emblematic footballers that he would get a new lease of life in front of the massive Celtic support. Unfortunately, Espanyol also came on the scene and the Buenos Aires-born entertainer agreed a two-year deal to bring down the curtain on his extraordinary career with the Barcelona-based club.

Three years later, Cushley was translating what the Real Madrid players were saying in the newspapers before the confrontation with Celtic. He informed Jock Stein and his team-mates it was more than obvious Real Madrid still saw themselves as the European champions. They had won it the previous year when they had beaten Partizan Belgrade 2-1 in Brussels.

In fact, it was the sixth time they had lifted the trophy in eleven years and, according to what the players were saying in the newspapers, they believed they were still masters of all they surveyed. It was fairly evident they also thought Celtic were Scottish upstarts who had taken everyone by surprise because of their unknown values and alien qualities.

Possibly, the players had conveniently forgotten that the same Inter Milan team that had been taken apart by Celtic were the same set of players who had managed to beat Real Madrid home and away for a 3-0 aggregate triumph in the quarter-finals of the tournament that season.

Billy McNeill added, 'So, every player wearing green and white hoops who stepped onto the Bernabeu pitch that evening knew what to expect. Celtic had to prove to everyone that we were worthy champions of Europe. It wouldn't have looked too clever if we had been turned over 3-0, 4-0 or even worse. But, with Big Cush having told us what was in the newspapers, it was clear that was the aim of the Real Madrid team that evening. Of course, they wanted it to be a memorable farewell to one of the most magnificent players in the club's history, but they wanted to turn us over - and score a few goals, too. However, they reckoned without Jinky. With the Wee Man in that sort of form, Celtic were unbeatable.'

Jock Stein made changes to the line-up that had conquered Europe in the Portuguese capital. He was determined no team would ever beat the formation of eleven Scottish born-and-bred professionals now known worldwide as the Lisbon Lions. John Fallon came into goal for Ronnie Simpson and Willie O'Neill appeared in the old left-half position with John Clark moving to Bobby Murdoch's right-sided slot. Murdoch was pushed slightly forward into the No.8 position and Stevie Chalmers, the matchwinner in Lisbon, made way.

Murdoch also thrived on the incredible atmosphere and, years later, recalled, 'It was amazing. Jinky was unbelievable that night. The supporters were applauding him every time he was on the ball. Remember, those fans were brought up watching teams packed with entertainers, so they knew their stuff and they recognised a showman when they saw one. I'm sure the President of Real Madrid spoke to Big Jock after the game and asked to buy our wee No.7. There would have been something wrong if he hadn't.'

As ever, Bertie Auld, Murdoch's co-conspirator in the cockpit of invention in the heart of the team, has an interesting recollection on the Bernabeu occasion. He recalled, 'Big Jock took me aside and told me, "Real Madrid are desperate to do us. We've just won the European Cup, but they still think they are the best team in Europe. Amancio is their best player - do your best to keep him quiet. Keep an eye on him. I want to win this one."

'It was only thirteen days after our victory over Inter Milan and we had been invited to play for the legendary Alfredo di Stefano in his Testimonial Game at the Bernabeu Stadium. Real Madrid had won the European Cup the previous year and some of their players were making noises that we had merely borrowed the European Cup from Real for a year. Oh, yeah? When we turned up at that magnificent stadium that evening we knew we were not going to be involved in a friendly.

'The great Alfredo, at the age of forty, kicked off and then we got down to the nitty gritty of seeing who was the best team in Europe. Wee Jinky was immense. Di Stefano, along with Stanley Matthews, had been the Wee Man's hero. He decided to put on a show for the Real legend - and what a show it was. The Real players did their best to get the ball off Jinky, but it was one of those nights when it was super-glued to his boot. He would show them the ball, they would lunge in and Jinky would do one of his little serpentine-weaving manoeuvres and they would be left tackling fresh air while he took off on his merry way.

'Even I felt like applauding every now and again as he displayed his awesome talent. Meanwhile, Amancio and I were getting acquainted in the middle of the park. He didn't like the attention I was paying him and we had a couple of kicks when no-one was looking. Nothing too serious, I hasten to add, but enough for him to realise I was there to do a job for Celtic that night. It may have been billed as a friendly, but, please believe me, this was no game where there was anyone on either side pulling out of tackles. They were absolutely determined to hammer us and, equally, we were just as committed to the cause to show we were the best team in Europe.

'Jinky tore them apart in one of the most spellbinding individual shows I have ever had the privilege of witnessing. He actually started to take the mickey at one point which was simply amazing. This wee guy from

Uddingston playing in the most fabulous stadium on earth and giving their players a lesson in how to play football? It could only have been Jinky. Meanwhile, Amancio and I were still having an interesting evening. I don't know if I was marking him or he was marking me, but we weren't far from each other's side for most of the night. Then things got a bit heated. There was a fifty/fifty ball and we both went for it. Crunch! There was a bit of a fracas. He threw a punch at me and I returned the compliment. The referee was far from amused. He didn't hesitate as he pointed to the tunnel for both of us. To be honest, it was a fair decision. As I walked past Big Jock in the dug-out I looked over and said, "Problem solved, Boss." He had the good grace to laugh.

'But it was Jinky's night. It may have been Alfredo di Stefano's final farewell in one of football's theatre of dreams, but I'm sure the name on everyone's lips that evening was Jimmy Johnstone. Jinky, on that form, was irresistible. We played really well that night, despite my absence - possibly because of my absence! Real Madrid knew who were the true masters of European football. To be fair to their support, they started to applaud Celtic and, especially, Jinky. He would sweep past a defender and the fans would shout, 'Ole!' It was a night for our wee magician to show everyone his tricks and flicks. I will never forget that performance. The Wee Man was unstoppable.

'Jinky was going on holiday the following day with his wife Agnes. They left our hotel and the Wee Man jumped into a taxi and said, "Take me to Benidorm, driver." The cab driver asked, "You want to go to the airport, senor?" Jinky replied, "No, I want to go to Benidorm!" Geography might not have been Jinky's best subject at school because Benidorm is about three hundred miles from Madrid as the crow flies. "Are you sure, senor?" asked the driver who must have thought he had won the pools. "Aye," said Jinky and the driver pointed the taxi in the general direction of the holiday resort. Wee Jinky was a one-off, sure enough.'

That evening at the Bernabeu, Johnstone, all 5ft 4in of him, was a mercurial mix of magic and mischief as he dismantled Real Madrid. The only goal arrived in the sixty-ninth minute and there are no prizes for guessing who set it up with utmost perfection for Bobby Lennox to flash a low drive into the far corner of the net. Jinky weaved and waltzed his way forward from the left as he effortlessly skipped past three tackles en route to the danger zone. With devastating timing, he parted with the ball, a threaded pass between two defenders into the path of his best pal. Lennox devoured service like that and he didn't pause as he sent his effort zipping unerringly towards its intended target.

Lennox recalled, 'There were hardly any Celtic fans at that game because the timing didn't give too many the opportunity to make travel arrangements or even attempt to buy a ticket. They had all been snapped up by Real Madrid fans months beforehand, anyhow, as soon as the club announced they were having a testimonial match for the great Di Stefano. When my shot hit the net there was a sudden silence around the great bowl of a stadium. And, then, there was this solitary Scottish voice. "Goal!" There was a Celtic fan in there somewhere in the midst of thousands of Spanish supporters.'

With supreme timing, the shrill sound signalling the completion of the entertainment from the whistle of referee Daniel Zariquliegui saw the ball, fittingly, at the right foot of Johnstone. He lifted the matchball and held it triumphantly above his head like a well-earned trophy. He was afforded a standing ovation while doing so. No wonder Alfredo Di Stefano later described his Testimonial Match as 'The Jimmy Johnstone Show'.

Stevie Chalmers admitted he was desperate to play in the showgame, but acknowledged, 'Big Jock was adamant that the Lisbon Lions would never be beaten; that those eleven players would never taste defeat. So, he rested myself and Ronnie Simpson and brought in Willie O'Neill and John Fallon, our reserve goalkeeper. Actually, he could have rested everyone bar Wee Jinky because he was just out of this world that night in the Spanish capital. I've never witnessed a better individual performance.'

The last word, naturally, has to go to the insuppressible Jinky. Despite his many precious gifts, the wee chap from the working-class housing estate in South Lanarkshire could never be labelled a braggart or a big head.

On this occasion, though, he uttered the memorable words, 'They were frightened to come near me in the last fifteen minutes.'

POSTSCRIPT

FAREWELL, OLD FRIEND

"Joe McBride was a man who would stick the ball in the back of the net when he didn't know what else to do with it."

- Jock Stein

Joe McBride scored his eighty-sixth goal for Celtic against Morton in front of a 23,000 all-ticket crowd on a nondescript, colourless afternoon in Greenock on Saturday October 26 1968. It was enough to give the champions a 1-1 draw, but it was not sufficient to guarantee a future at the club for the diligent centre-forward.

McBride never appeared in the first team again and was sold to Hibs ten days later, exactly two years and five months following his arrival as Jock Stein's first signing for the Parkhead club at £22,000 from Motherwell. It was all too brief a stay in Paradise for an honest, willing professional. And, as Jimmy McGrory pointed out, 'his heart was in the right place.'

It was somewhat ironic for the Govan-born McBride that events at Ibrox hastened his removal from Celtic. The Easter Road side had just accepted a Scottish record bid of £100,000 from Rangers for Colin Stein and urgently required a replacement striker. They turned their attention to the east end of Glasgow and were heartened by the response from Stein: he was ready to do business and allow the thirty-year-old attacker to move on a mere one month and three days after entrusting him with a place in his first team for a crucial European Cup-tie against St Etienne at Parkhead.

With Celtic trailing 2-0 from the first leg in France and their place among Europe's elite in jeopardy, the Celtic manager turned to his tried and trusted marksman, who had become a peripheral figure at the club. McBride scored as the Scottish champions somersaulted the encounter on its head, triumphing 4-0 in rollicking fashion, advancing to the next round and leaving the player with the belief things were beginning to turn around for him at his boyhood favourites. Shortly afterwards, a phone call from a Hibs official to Jock Stein scuppered that notion.

The Celtic boss would never become famous for admitting to an error in judgement, but, later in life and in private moments, those close to Stein would relate tales of the manager accepting he may 'have been a wee bit too hasty' in dispensing with the services of McBride. Certainly, there was no malicious motive in Stein selling the player, not even the merest hint of McBride being pushed towards the Parkhead exit. Such things are daily occurrences at football clubs up and down the country.

There can be little argument, though, the Celtic manager believed the striker's most prolific days were behind him. Records emphasise that wasn't the case and the player was still scoring goals beyond his thirty-fourth birthday. Even early on, Stein must have wondered about the wisdom of allowing McBride to leave when he scored a remarkable eight goals in his first three appearances for the Edinburgh team. He marked his debut with a goal against Rangers at Ibrox on November 9, then rattled in a hat-trick against Lokomotiv Leipzig - the first Hibs player to score a trio in European competition - and rounded off a productive eight days with four against Morton. After leaving Celtic, he claimed fifty-seven goals in one hundred and nine league appearances in total - forty-four for Hibs, eight for Dunfermline and five for Clyde before he called it a day. Joe McBride was simply a phenomenon who would score goals wherever his boots took him.

Stein once put it this way, 'Joe was a man who would stick the ball in the back of the net when he couldn't think of anything else to do with it.'

McBride, in fact, netted four times in three games for Hibs against Celtic during his three years in Edinburgh. His first came in November 30 at Easter Road which made the score 1-1 at half-time before Joe Davis put the home side ahead with a penalty-kick in the seventy-fourth minute. Celtic's reply was emphatic with four goals in an astonishing whirlwind spell with two goals from John Hughes and singles from Billy McNeill and Bobby Lennox making the final score 5-2.

McBride was afforded a standing ovation on his first appearance back at Parkhead on a crisp Monday evening on March 24 1969. The 30,000 home crowd gave him the welcome home he so richly deserved and the player responded by scoring the equalising goal in a 1-1 draw. Willie Wallace gave Celtic an early advantage with a close-range header and it stayed that way with only eighteen minutes remaining. Eric Stevenson, a tricky outside-left, dropped a cross into the box and, unaccountably, McBride, of all people, was left unmarked. He didn't hesitate as he lashed a shot beyond John Fallon.

On Saturday September 19 1970, Celtic arrived at Easter Road for a league meeting with Hibs. It was their fourth game of the campaign and Evan Williams had yet to concede a goal. In their previous match, they had fairly effortlessly beaten Rangers 2-0 with goals from John Hughes and Bobby Murdoch. They could even afford a squandered second-minute penalty-kick by Jim Brogan, replacing the injured Tommy Gemmell, with the ball going closer to Bridgeton Cross than Peter McCloy's goal. A week later, the winning sequence was obliterated with the Edinburgh side winning 2-0 and Joe McBride plonking two into the net after the turnaround, a stunning volley followed by a trademark tap-in.

Billy McNeill, who, ironically was McBride's partner in hotel and restaurant businesses, faced his former colleague on all three occasions. 'Joe wasn't out to prove anything in these games,' the legendary captain recalled. 'Anyone who knew Joe would realise that was the only way he knew how to play - it was always one hundred per cent effort from him. The afternoon we lost at Easter Road, was a particularly sore one for us. Apart from beating Rangers 2-0 the previous Saturday, we had also scored nine in a midweek European Cup-tie against a Finnish team by the name of Kokkola. We were in a confident mood travelling through to the capital, but we were turned over and we could have no complaints or excuses.

'Joe made it as difficult for me as I did for him and neither of us would have expected or wanted it to be any other way. Big Jock took the decision to allow my pal to move on and people may have expressed doubts at the time, but you couldn't argue with the Boss when you looked at the reserve team back then and saw the likes of Kenny Dalglish, Lou Macari and Vic Davidson desperate to get into the team. He saw them as the future of Celtic and, of course, he was right. Joe McBride may have left and scored goals against Celtic, but, rest assured, no matter where he played or for whichever club, he was always one of us.

'Joe McBride was a Celt at heart right to the very end.'

PLAYER PROFILES

RONNIE SIMPSON

BORN: 11.10.30, Glasgow; **DIED:** 20.4.2004
POSITION: Goalkeeper
SIGNED FOR CELTIC: 3.9.64
PREVIOUS CLUBS: Queen's Park, Third Lanark, Newcastle United, Hibs.
DEBUT: 18.11.64 (against Barcelona)
RETIRED: 7.5.70
APPEARANCES: 188; Shut-outs: 91
INTERNATIONAL HONOURS: 5 Scotland caps
MEDALS: League Championship: 4 (1966,67,68,69)
SCOTTISH CUP: 1 (1967)
LEAGUE CUP: 3 (1965,66,67)
EUROPEAN CUP: 1 (1967)
(**FA CUP** with Newcastle United: 2; 1952,55)

JIM CRAIG

BORN: 7.5.43, Glasgow
POSITION: Right-back
SIGNED: 7.1.65
PREVIOUS CLUBS: Glasgow University
DEBUT: 7.10.65 (against Go-Ahead Deventer, Holland)
LEFT CELTIC: 6.5.72 (Hellenic, South Africa)
APPEARANCES: 231; Goals: 6
INTERNATIONAL HONOURS: 1 Scotland cap
LEAGUE CHAMPIONSHIP: 7 (1966,67,68,69,70,71,72)
SCOTTISH CUP: 4 (1967,69,71,72)
LEAGUE CUP: 3 (1967,68,69)
EUROPEAN CUP: 1 (1967)

TOMMY GEMMELL

BORN: 16.10.43, Craigneuk, Lanarkshire
POSITION: Left-back
SIGNED: 25.10.61
PREVIOUS CLUBS: Coltness United
DEBUT: 5.1.63 (against Aberdeen)
LEFT: CELTIC: 12.12.71 (for Nottingham Forest)
APPEARANCES: 418; Goals: 64
INTERNATIONAL HONOURS: 18 Scotland caps, 5 Scottish League caps
LEAGUE CHAMPIONSHIP: 6 (1966,67,68,69,70,71)
SCOTTISH CUP: 3 (1965,67,69)
LEAGUE CUP: 4 (1965,66,67,68; excluding 1 with Dundee; 1973)
EUROPEAN CUP: 1 (1967)

BOBBY MURDOCH

BORN: 17.8.44, Rutherglen, Lanarkshire; Died: 15.5.2001
POSITION: Right midfield
SIGNED: 23.10.59
PREVIOUS CLUBS: None
DEBUT: 11.8.62 (against Hearts)
LEFT CELTIC: 17.9.73 (for Middlesbrough)
APPEARANCES: 484; Goals: 105
INTERNATIONAL HONOURS: 12 Scotland caps, 5 Scottish League caps, 1 Scotland Under-23 cap
LEAGUE CHAMPIONSHIP: 8 (1966,67,68,69,70,71,72,73)
SCOTTISH CUP: 4 (1965,67,69,72)
LEAGUE CUP: 5: (1965,66,67,68,69)
EUROPEAN CUP: 1 (1967)

BILLY McNEILL

BORN: 2.3.40, Bellshill, Lanarkshire
POSITION: Centre-half
SIGNED: 20.8.57
PREVIOUS CLUBS: Blantyre Vics
DEBUT: 23.8.58 (against Clyde)
RETIRED: 3.5.75
APPEARANCES: 790; Goals: 34
INTERNATIONAL HONOURS: 29 Scotland caps, 9 Scottish League caps, 5 Scotland Under-23 caps
LEAGUE CHAMPIONSHIP: 9 (1966,67,68,69,70,71,72,73,74)
SCOTTISH CUP: 7: (1965,67,69,71,72,74,75)
LEAGUE CUP: 6 (1965, 66, 67, 68, 69, 74)
EUROPEAN CUP: 1 (1967)

As a manager:

LEAGUE CHAMPIONSHIP: 4 (1979,80,82,88)
SCOTTISH CUP: 3 (1980,88,89)
LEAGUE CUP: 1 (1982)

JOHN CLARK

BORN: 13.3.41, Bellshill, Lanarkshire
POSITION: Left-side defence
SIGNED: 8.10.58
PREVIOUS CLUBS: Birmingham City, Larkhall Thistle
DEBUT: 3.10.59 (against Arbroath)
LEFT CELTIC: 12.6.71 (for Morton)
APPEARANCES: 318; Goals: 3
INTERNATIONAL HONOURS: 4 Scotland caps, 2 Scottish League caps
LEAGUE CHAMPIONSHIP: 3 (1966,67,68)
SCOTTISH CUP: 3 (1965,67,69)
LEAGUE CUP: 4: (1965,66,67,68)
EUROPEAN CUP: 1 (1967)

JIMMY JOHNSTONE

BORN: 30.9.44, Uddingston, Lanarkshire; Died: 13.3.2006
POSITION: Outside-right
SIGNED: 8.11.61
PREVIOUS CLUBS: Blantyre Vics
DEBUT: 27.3.63 (against Kilmarnock)
LEFT CELTIC: 9.6.75 (for Hamilton Accies)
APPEARANCES: 515; Goals: 129
INTERNATIONAL HONOURS: 23 Scotland caps, 4 Scottish League caps
LEAGUE CHAMPIONSHIP: 9 (1966,67,68,69,70,71,72,73,74)
SCOTTISH CUP: 4 (1967,71,72,74)
LEAGUE CUP: 5 (1965,66,68,69,74)
EUROPEAN CUP: 1 (1967)

WILLIE WALLACE

BORN: 23.6.40, Kirkintilloch
POSITION: Striker
SIGNED: 6.12.66
PREVIOUS CLUBS: Kilsyth Rangers, Stenhousemuir, Raith Rovers, Hearts
DEBUT: 10.12.66 (against Motherwell)
LEFT CELTIC: 19.10.71 (for Crystal Palace)
APPEARANCES: 234; Goals: 135
INTERNATIONAL HONOURS: 4 Scotland caps, 4 Scottish League caps
LEAGUE CHAMPIONSHIP: 5 (1967,68,69,70,71)
SCOTTISH CUP: 3 (1967,69,71)
LEAGUE CUP: 2 (1967,68: excluding 1 with Hearts 1962)
EUROPEAN CUP: 1 (1967)

STEVIE CHALMERS

BORN: 26.12.36, Glasgow
POSITION: Striker
SIGNED: 6.2.59
PREVIOUS CLUBS: Kirkintilloch Rob Roy, Newmarket Town, Ashfield
DEBUT: 10.3.59 (against Airdrie)
LEFT CELTIC: 9.9.71 (for Morton)
APPEARANCES: 405, Goals: 228
INTERNATIONAL HONOURS: 5 Scotland caps, 4 Scottish League caps
LEAGUE CHAMPIONSHIP: 4 (1966, 67, 68, 69)
SCOTTISH CUP: 3 (1965, 67, 69)
LEAGUE CUP: 4 (1966, 67, 68, 69)
EUROPEAN CUP: 1 (1967)

BERTIE AULD

BORN: 23.3.38, Glasgow
POSITION: Left-side midfield
SIGNED: 2.4.55
PREVIOUS CLUBS: Panmure Thistle, Maryhill Harp
DEBUT: 1.5.57 (against Rangers)
LEFT CELTIC (first time): 1.5.61 (for Birmingham City)
RE-SIGNED: 14.1.65 (from Birmingham City)
LEFT CELTIC (second time): 6.5.71 (for Hibs)
APPEARANCES: 279; Goals: 85
INTERNATIONAL HONOURS: 3 Scotland caps, 2 Scottish League caps
LEAGUE CHAMPIONSHIP: 5 (1966, 67, 68, 69, 70)
SCOTTISH CUP: 3 (1965, 67, 69)
LEAGUE CUP: 4 (1966, 67, 68, 69)
EUROPEAN CUP: 1 (1967)

BOBBY LENNOX

BORN: 30.8.43, Saltcoats, Ayrshire
POSITION: Striker/outside-left
SIGNED: 5.9.61
PREVIOUS CLUBS: Ardeer Recreation
DEBUT: 3.3.62 (against Dundee)
LEFT: 10.5.78 (for Houston Hurricane)
RETURNED: 25.8.78 (from Houston Hurricane)
RETIRED: 8.11.80
APPEARANCES: 571; Goals: 273
INTERNATIONAL HONOURS: 10 Scotland caps, 3 Scottish League caps
LEAGUE CHAMPIONSHIP: 10 (1966, 67, 68, 69, 70, 71, 72, 73, 74, 79)
SCOTTISH CUP: 8 (1965, 67, 69, 71, 72, 74, 75, 80)
LEAGUE CUP: 4 (1965, 66, 67, 68)
EUROPEAN CUP: 1 (1967)

JOHN HUGHES

BORN: 3.4.43, Coatbridge
POSITION: Striker/outside-left
SIGNED: 3.10.59
PREVIOUS CLUBS: Shotts Bon Accord
DEBUT: 13.8.60 (against Third Lanark)
LEFT CELTIC: 19.10.71 (for Crystal Palace)
APPEARANCES: 416, Goals: 189
INTERNATIONAL HONOURS: 8 Scotland caps, 6 Scottish League caps
LEAGUE CHAMPIONSHIP: 6 (1966,67,68,69,70,71)
SCOTTISH CUP: 1 (1965)
LEAGUE CUP: 4 (1965,66,67,69)

CHARLIE GALLAGHER

BORN: 3.11.40, Glasgow
POSITION: Midfield
SIGNED: 20.9.58
PREVIOUS CLUBS: Kilmarnock Amateurs, Yoker Athletic
DEBUT: 22.8.59 (against Raith Rovers)
LEFT CELTIC: 1.5.70 (for Dumbarton)
APPEARANCES: 171; Goals: 32
INTERNATIONAL HONOURS: 2 Republic of Ireland caps
LEAGUE CHAMPIONSHIP: 3 (1966,67,68)
SCOTTISH CUP: 1 (1965)
LEAGUE CUP: 1 (1965)

JOE McBRIDE

BORN: 10.6.38, Glasgow; Died: 11.7.2012
POSITION: Striker
SIGNED: 5.6.65
PREVIOUS CLUBS: Kilmarnock Amateurs, Shettleston Town, Kirkintilloch Rob Roy, Kilmarnock, Wolves, Luton Town, Partick Thistle, Motherwell
DEBUT: 21.8.65 (against Dundee)
LEFT CELTIC: 5.11.68 (for Hibs)
APPEARANCES: 94; Goals: 86
INTERNATIONAL HONOURS: 2 Scotland caps, 4 Scottish League caps
LEAGUE CHAMPIONSHIP: 2 (1966,67)
LEAGUE CUP: 1 (1966)

JOHN FALLON

BORN: 16.8.40, Blantyre
POSITION: Goalkeeper
SIGNED: 11.12.58
PREVIOUS CLUB: Fauldhouse United
DEBUT: 26.9.59 (against Clyde)
LEFT CELTIC: 29.2.72 (for Motherwell)
APPEARANCES: 184; Shut-outs: 61
INTERNATIONAL HONOURS: None
LEAGUE CHAMPIONSHIP: 2: (1969,70)
SCOTTISH CUP: 2 (1965,69)
LEAGUE CUP: 2 (1968,69)

IAN YOUNG

BORN: 21.5.43, Glasgow
POSITION: Right-back
SIGNED: 28.6.61
PREVIOUS CLUB: Neilston Waverely
DEBUT: 5.5.62 (against Third Lanark)
LEFT CELTIC: 1.5.68 (for St.Mirren)
APPEARANCES: 164; Goals: 3
INTERNATIONAL HONOURS: None
LEAGUE CHAMPIONSHIP: 1 (1966)
SCOTTISH CUP: 1 (1965)
LEAGUE CUP: 1 (1965)

DAVID CATTENACH

BORN: 27.6.46, Falkirk
POSITION: Right-sided defender
SIGNED: 19.8.63
PREVIOUS CLUBS: Stirling Albion
DEBUT: 9.4.66 (against St.Mirren)
LEFT CELTIC: 20.1.72 (for Falkirk)
APPEARANCES: 19; Goals: 1
INTERNATIONAL HONOURS: None
MEDALS: None

WILLIE O'NEILL

BORN: 30.12.40, Glasgow; Died: 28.4.2011
POSITION: Left-back
SIGNED: 12.10.59
PREVIOUS CLUBS: St.Anthony's
DEBUT: 26.4.61 (against Dunfermline)
LEFT CELTIC: 13.5.69 (for Carlisle)
APPEARANCES: 86; Goals: 0
INTERNATIONAL HONOURS: None
LEAGUE CHAMPIONSHIP: 1 (1967)
LEAGUE CUP: 1 (1966)

JIM BROGAN

BORN: 5.6.44, Glasgow
POSITION: Left-side defence
SIGNED: 11.9.62
PREVIOUS CLUB: St.Roch's
DEBUT: 21.9.63 (against Falkirk)
LEFT CELTIC: 4.6.75 (for Coventry City)
APPEARANCES: 339; Goals: 9
INTERNATIONAL HONOURS: 4 Scotland caps, 1 Scottish League cap
LEAGUE CHAMPIONSHIP: 7 (1968,69,70,71,72,73,74)
SCOTTISH CUP: 3 (1969,71,74)
LEAGUE CUP: 4 (1968,69,72,74)

JOHN CUSHLEY

BORN: 21.1.43 , Hamilton; Died: 24.3.2008
POSITION: Centre-half
SIGNED: 7.7.60
PREVIOUS CLUBS: Blantyre Celtic
DEBUT: 27.3.63 (against Kilmarnock)
LEFT CELTIC: 17.7.67 (for West Ham)
APPEARANCES: 41; Goals: 0
INTERNATIONAL HONOURS: None
LEAGUE CHAMPIONSHIP: 1 (1966)

BENT MARTIN

BORN: 19.2.43, Sonderborg, Denmark
POSITION: Goalkeeper
SIGNED: 4.2.1966
PREVIOUS CLUB: AGF Aarhus.
DEBUT: 10.10.1966 (against Queen's Park)
LEFT: 23.12.1966 (for Dunfermline)
APPEARANCES: 1 (one shut-out).
INTERNATIONAL HONOURS: None

THE GAMES, THE TEAMS, THE RESULTS...THE GLORY

FIRST DIVISION

September 10: CLYDE 0 CELTIC 3
(Chalmers, McBride, Hughes)
Simpson; Gemmell, O'Neill; Murdoch, McNeill, Clark; Chalmers,
Lennox, McBride, Auld, Hughes.

September 17: CELTIC 2 RANGERS 0
(Auld, Murdoch)
Simpson; Gemmell, O'Neill; Murdoch, McNeill, Clark; Johnstone,
Lennox, McBride, Auld, Hughes.

September 24: DUNDEE 1 CELTIC 2
(Penman - Lennox, Chalmers)
Simpson; Gemmell, O'Neill; Murdoch, McNeill, Clark; Johnstone,
Lennox, McBride (sub: Chalmers), Auld, Hughes.

October 1: CELTIC 6 ST JOHNSTONE 1
(Johnstone (2), Lennox (2), McBride (2) - Kilgannon)
Simpson; Gemmell, O'Neill; Murdoch, McNeill, Clark; Johnstone,
Lennox, McBride, Auld, Hughes

October 8: HIBS 3 CELTIC 5
(Cormack, Davis pen, McGraw - McBride 4, Chalmers)
Simpson; Gemmell, O'Neill; Murdoch, McNeill, Clark; Johnstone,
McBride, Chalmers, Auld, Hughes.

October 15: CELTIC 3 AIRDRIE 0
(Lennox (2), McBride)
Simpson; Young, Gemmell; Clark, McNeill, O'Neill; Chalmers,
Lennox, McBride, Gallagher, Hughes.

October 24: CELTIC 5 AYR UNITED 1
(Lennox, Hughes, Johnstone 2, Gemmell - Black)
Simpson; Gemmell, O'Neill; Murdoch, McNeill, Clark; Johnstone,
Lennox, Chalmers, Auld, Hughes.

November 2: CELTIC 7 STIRLING ALBION 3
(Johnstone, McBride (3), Chalmers (2), Auld - McGuinness, Reid, Kerray)
Simpson; Gemmell, O'Neill; Murdoch, McNeill, Clark; Johnstone, Gallagher (sub: Craig), McBride, Chalmers, Auld.

November 5: CELTIC 1 ST MIRREN 1
(Gemmell - Treacy)
Simpson; Craig, O'Neill; Murdoch, Gemmell, Clark; Johnstone, McBride, Chalmers, Auld, Lennox.

November 12: FALKIRK 0 CELTIC 3
(McBride (2, 1 pen), Auld)
Simpson; Gemmell, O'Neill; Murdoch, McNeill, Clark; Chalmers, Gallagher, McBride, Lennox, Auld.

November 19: DUNFERMLINE 4 CELTIC 5
(Robertson, Delaney, Paton, Ferguson - Murdoch, Johnstone, Auld, McBride (2, 1 pen))
Simpson; Gemmell, O'Neill; Murdoch, McNeill, Clark; Johnstone, Chalmers, McBride, Auld, Lennox.

November 26: CELTIC 3 HEARTS 0
(Miller og, McBride (2, 1 pen))
Simpson; Gemmell, O'Neill; Murdoch, McNeill, Clark; Johnstone, Chalmers, McBride, Lennox, Auld.

December 3: KILMARNOCK 0 CELTIC 0
Simpson; Gemmell, O'Neill; Murdoch, McNeill, Clark; Johnstone, Chalmers, McBride, Lennox, Auld.

December 10: CELTIC 4 MOTHERWELL 2
(Chalmers (3), Murdoch - Murray, Lindsay)
Simpson; Gemmell, O'Neill; Murdoch, McNeill, Clark; Johnstone, Wallace, Chalmers, Lennox, Auld.

December 17: CELTIC 6 PARTICK THISTLE 2
(Wallace (2), Murdoch, Chalmers (2), McBride - Duncan, Gibb)
Simpson: Gemmell, O'Neill; Murdoch, McNeill, Clark; Chalmers, Wallace, McBride, Lennox, Auld.

December 24: ABERDEEN 1 CELTIC 1
(Melrose - Lennox)
Simpson; Gemmell, O'Neill; Murdoch, McNeill, Clark; Chalmers,
Auld, McBride, Wallace, Lennox.

December 31: DUNDEE UNITED 3 CELTIC 2
(Dossing, Gillespie, Mitchell - Lennox, Wallace)
Simpson; Gemmell, O'Neill; Murdoch, McNeill, Clark; Chalmers,
Lennox, Wallace, Auld, Hughes.

January 7 1967: CELTIC 5 DUNDEE 1
(Wilson (og), Gallagher, Wallace (2), Johnstone - Cameron)
Simpson; Craig, Gemmell; Murdoch, McNeill, Clark; Johnstone,
Wallace, Chalmers, Gallagher, Lennox.

January 11: CELTIC 5 CLYDE 1
(Chalmers (2), Gallagher, Gemmell, Lennox 1 - Gilroy)
Simpson; Craig, Gemmell; Murdoch, McNeill, Clark; Johnstone,
Wallace, Chalmers, Gallagher, Lennox.

January 14: ST JOHNSTONE 0 CELTIC 4
(Johnstone (2), Chalmers, Lennox)
Simpson; Craig, Gemmell; Murdoch, McNeill, Clark; Johnstone,
Wallace, Chalmers, Auld, Lennox.

January 21: CELTIC 2 HIBS 0
(Wallace, Chalmers)
Simpson; Craig, Gemmell; Murdoch, McNeill, Clark; Johnstone,
Wallace, Chalmers, Auld, Hughes.

February 4: AIRDRIE 0 CELTIC 3
(Chalmers, Johnstone, Auld)
Simpson; Craig, Gemmell; Murdoch, McNeill, Clark; Johnstone,
Wallace, Chalmers, Auld, Hughes.

February 11: AYR UNITED 0 CELTIC 5
(Johnstone, Hughes, Chalmers (3))
Simpson; Craig, Gemmell; Murdoch, McNeill, Clark; Johnstone,
Wallace, Chalmers, Gallagher, Hughes.

February 25: STIRLING ALBION 1 CELTIC 1
(Peebles - Hughes)
Simpson; Craig, Gemmell; Murdoch, McNeill, Clark; Johnstone,
Wallace, Chalmers, Auld, Hughes.

March 4: ST MIRREN 0 CELTIC 5
(Wallace (2), Hughes, Lennox, Gemmell (pen))
Simpson; Craig, Gemmell; Murdoch, McNeill, Clark; Hughes,
Gallagher, Wallace, Lennox, Auld.

March 18: CELTIC 3 DUNFERMLINE 2
(Chalmers, Wallace, Gemmell (pen) - Ferguson (2))
Simpson; Gemmell, O'Neill; Murdoch, McNeill, Clark; Hughes,
Gallagher, Chalmers, Wallace, Lennox.

March 20: CELTIC 5 FALKIRK 0
(Chalmers (2), Auld, Hughes, Gemmell (pen))
Simpson; Craig, Gemmell; Murdoch, McNeill, Clark; Johnstone,
Wallace, Chalmers, Auld, Hughes.

March 25: HEARTS 0 CELTIC 3
(Auld, Wallace, Gemmell (pen))
Simpson; Craig, Gemmell; Murdoch (sub: Lennox), McNeill,
Clark; Johnstone, Wallace, Chalmers, Auld, Hughes.

March 27: PARTICK THISTLE 1 CELTIC 4
(Flanagan - Lennox, Chalmers 2, Wallace)
Simpson; Craig, Gemmell; Wallace, McNeill, Clark; Johnstone,
Gallagher, Chalmers, Lennox, Auld.

April 8: MOTHERWELL 0 CELTIC 2
(Wallace, Gemmell (pen))
Simpson; Craig, Gemmell; Wallace, McNeill, Clark; Hughes,
Lennox, Chalmers, Gallagher (sub: Brogan), Auld.

April 19: ABERDEEN 0 CELTIC 0
Simpson; Craig, Gemmell; Murdoch, McNeill, Clark; Johnstone,
Wallace, Chalmers, Auld, Lennox.

May 3: CELTIC 2 DUNDEE UNITED 3
(Gemmell (pen), Wallace - Hainey, Gillespie, Graham)
Simpson; Craig, Gemmell; Murdoch, McNeill, Clark; Johnstone,
Gallagher, Wallace, Lennox, Hughes.

May 6: RANGERS 2 CELTIC 2
(Jardine, Hynd - Johnstone (2))
Simpson; Craig, Gemmell; Murdoch, McNeill, Clark; Johnstone,
Wallace, Chalmers, Auld, Lennox.

May 15: CELTIC 2 KILMARNOCK 0
(Lennox, Wallace)
Fallon; Craig, Gemmell; Murdoch, Cushley, Clark; Johnstone,
McNeill, Wallace, Auld, Lennox.

LEAGUE CUP

GROUP STAGES

August 13: HEARTS 0 CELTIC 2
(McBride (2, 1 pen))
Simpson; Gemmell, O'Neill; Murdoch, McNeill, Clark; Johnstone,
McBride, Chalmers, Lennox, Auld.

August 17: CELTIC 6 CLYDE 0
(Lennox (2), McBride (3, 1 pen), Chalmers)
Simpson; Gemmell, O'Neill; Murdoch, McNeill, Clark; Johnstone,
McBride, Chalmers, Lennox, Auld.

August 20: CELTIC 8 ST.MIRREN 2
(Lennox (2), McBride (4, 1 pen), Auld, Chalmers - Treacy (2))
Simpson; Gemmell, O'Neill; Murdoch, McNeill, Clark; Johnstone,
McBride, Chalmers, Lennox, Auld.

August 27: CELTIC 3 HEARTS 0
(McBride (2, 1 pen), Chalmers)
Simpson; Gemmell, O'Neill; Murdoch, McNeill, Clark; Johnstone,
McBride, Chalmers, Hughes, Auld.

August 31: CLYDE 1 CELTIC 3
(Gilroy - McBride (2, 1 pen), Gemmell)
Simpson; Gemmell, O'Neill; Murdoch, McNeill, Clark; Johnstone,
McBride, Chalmers, Lennox, Auld.

September 3: ST MIRREN 0 CELTIC 1
(Murdoch)
Simpson; Craig, Gemmell; Murdoch, McNeill, Clark; Johnstone
(sub: O'Neill), McBride, Chalmers, Lennox, Gallagher.

September 14: Quarter-finals: 1st leg:
CELTIC 6 DUNFERMLINE 3
(McNeill, Johnstone, McBride (pen), Auld (2), Hughes - Ferguson 2,
Hunter)
Simpson; Gemmell, O'Neill; Murdoch, McNeill, Clark; Johnstone,
McBride, Chalmers, Auld, Hughes.

September 21: 2nd leg: DUNFERMLINE 1 CELTIC 3
(Fleming - McNeill, Chalmers (2))
Simpson; Gemmell, O'Neill; Murdoch, McNeill, Clark; Johnstone,
Chalmers, McBride, Auld, Hughes.

October 17: Semi-final: CELTIC 2 AIRDRIE 0
(Murdoch, McBride)
Simpson; Gemmell, O'Neill; Murdoch, McNeill, Clark; Johnstone,
McBride, Chalmers, Auld, Lennox.

October 29: Final: CELTIC 1 RANGERS 0
(Lennox)
Simpson; Gemmell, O'Neill; Murdoch, McNeill, Clark; Johnstone,
Lennox, McBride, Auld, Hughes (sub: Chalmers).

SCOTTISH CUP

January 28: First Round: CELTIC 4 ARBROATH 0
(Murdoch, Gemmell, Auld, Chalmers)
Simpson; Craig, Gemmell; Murdoch, McNeill, Clark; Gallagher,
Wallace, Chalmers, Auld, Hughes.

February 18: Second Round: CELTIC 7 ELGIN CITY 0
(Chalmers, Lennox (3), Hughes, Wallace (2))
Simpson; Cattenach, Gemmell; Murdoch (sub: Wallace), McNeill,
Clark; Johnstone, Lennox, Chalmers, Gallagher, Hughes.

March 11: Third Round: CELTIC 5 QUEEN'S PARK 3
(Gemmell (pen), Chalmers, Wallace, Murdoch, Lennox - Gemmell (og),
Hopper (2))
Simpson; Cattenach, Gemmell; Murdoch, McNeill, Clark;
Johnstone, Wallace, Chalmers, Auld, Lennox.

April 1: Semi-final: CELTIC 0 CLYDE 0
Simpson; Craig, Gemmell; Wallace, McNeill, Clark; Johnstone,
Auld, Chalmers, Lennox, Hughes.

April 5: Semi-final replay: CELTIC 2 CLYDE 0
(Lennox, Auld)
Simpson; Craig, Gemmell; Wallace, McNeill, Clark; Johnstone (sub:
Hughes), Gallagher, Chalmers, Auld, Lennox.

April 29: Final: CELTIC 2 ABERDEEN 0
(Wallace (2))
Simpson; Craig, Gemmell; Murdoch, McNeill, Clark; Johnstone,
Wallace, Chalmers, Auld, Lennox.

EUROPEAN CUP

September 28: First Round: 1st leg: CELTIC 2 ZURICH 0
(Gemmell, McBride)
Simpson; Gemmell, O'Neill; Murdoch, McNeill, Clark; Johnstone,
McBride, Chalmers, Auld, Hughes.

October 5: 2nd leg: ZURICH 0 CELTIC 3 (Agg: 5-0)
(Gemmell (2, 1 pen), Chalmers)
Simpson; Gemmell, O'Neill; Murdoch, McNeill, Clark; Johnstone,
Lennox, Chalmers, Auld, Hughes.

November 30: Second Round: 1st leg: NANTES 1 CELTIC 3
(Magny - McBride, Lennox, Chalmers)
Simpson; Gemmell, O'Neill; Murdoch, McNeill, Clark; Johnstone,
Chalmers, McBride, Lennox, Auld.

December 7: 2nd leg: CELTIC 3 NANTES 1 (Agg: 6-2)
(Johnstone, Chalmers, Lennox - Georgin)
Simpson; Gemmell, O'Neill; Murdoch, McNeill, Clark; Johnstone,
Gallagher, Chalmers, Auld, Lennox.

**March 1: Quarter-final: 1st leg: VOJVODINA NOVI SAD 1
CELTIC 0**
(Stanic)
Simpson; Craig, Gemmell; Murdoch, McNeill, Clark; Johnstone,
Lennox, Chalmers, Auld, Hughes.

March 8: 2nd leg: CELTIC 2 VOJVODINA 0 (Agg: 2-1)
(Chalmers, McNeill)
Simpson; Craig, Gemmell; Murdoch, McNeill, Clark; Johnstone,
Lennox, Chalmers, Gallagher, Hughes.

April 12: Semi-final: 1st leg: CELTIC 3 DUKLA PRAGUE 1
(Johnstone, Wallace (2) - Strunc)
Simpson; Craig, Gemmell; Murdoch, McNeill, Clark; Johnstone,
Wallace, Chalmers, Auld, Hughes.

April 25: 2nd leg: DUKLA PRAGUE 0 CELTIC 0 (Agg: 3-1)
Simpson; Craig, Gemmell; Murdoch, McNeill, Clark; Johnstone,
Wallace, Chalmers, Auld, Lennox.

May 25: Final: CELTIC 2 INTER MILAN 1
(Gemmell, Chalmers - Mazzola (pen))
Simpson; Craig, Gemmell; Murdoch, McNeill, Clark; Johnstone,
Wallace, Chalmers, Auld, Lennox.

GLASGOW CUP

August 23: First Round: RANGERS 0 CELTIC 4
(McNeill, Lennox (3))
Simpson; Gemmell, O'Neill; Murdoch, McNeill, Clark; Johnstone,
Gallagher, McBride, Auld, Lennox.

October 10: Semi-final: CELTIC 4 QUEEN'S PARK 0
(McBride (2), Lennox, Gallagher)
Martin; Young, Gemmell; Murdoch, McNeill, Clark; Johnstone,
Lennox, McBride, Gallagher, Hughes.

November 7: Final: CELTIC 4 PARTICK THISTLE 0
(Chalmers, Lennox (3))
Simpson; Gemmell, O'Neill; Murdoch, McNeill, Clark; Chalmers,
Gallagher, McBride, Lennox, Auld.

CHALLENGE GAMES

August 6: CELTIC 4 MANCHESTER UNITED 1
(Lennox, Murdoch, McBride, Foulkes (og) - Sadler)
Simpson; Gemmell, O'Neill; Murdoch, McNeill, Clark; Johnstone,
McBride, Chalmers, Auld, Lennox.

February 7: CELTIC 0 DINAMO ZAGREB 1
(Zambata)
Simpson; Cattenach, McNeill, Clark; Hughes, Murdoch, Auld,
Gemmell; Chalmers, Wallace, Lennox (sub: Johnstone)

ALFREDO DI STEFANIO TESTIMONIAL

June 7: REAL MADRID 0 CELTIC 1
(Lennox)
Fallon; Craig, Gemmell; Clark, McNeill, O'Neill; Johnstone,
Murdoch, Wallace, Auld, Lennox.

AUTHOR'S END NOTE

Over the years, I have read several irresponsible stories and heard far too many inaccurate tales of Celtic taking advantage of an ageing Inter Milan team to lift the European Cup in Lisbon on May 25 1967.

This is a monumental fallacy and, I believe, it's a misrepresentation that is long overdue being corrected once and for all.

If the myth was ever designed to take the gloss off Celtic's marvellous accomplishment, I think it's had a boomerang effect and, if anything, attracts attention to the historic feat of Jock Stein's team.

Four of the Inter Milan players who faced Celtic in the Portuguese capital were so 'over the hill' they were still deemed good enough to represent Italy in the memorable World Cup Final against Brazil in Mexico - THREE years after the European Cup spectacle.

Tarcisio Burgnich had sufficiently recovered from his exertions against Jimmy Johnstone at the Estadio Nacional to line up against Jairzinho in the Azteca Stadium in front of 107,412 spectators on Sunday June 21 1970. He was thirty-one years old. On the left defensive flank was Giacinto Facchetti, his nation's captain. He was twenty-seven years old. On the right wing was Tommy Gemmell's old mate Angelo Domenghini. He was twenty-eight years old. Lending assistance in the midfield and attack was Inter's astute penalty-kick expert Sandro Mazzola. He was twenty-seven.

So, no-one needs a degree in maths to realise they were all three years younger in Lisbon! And yet that quartet pravided the backbone of their national team in Mexico. By the way, it was a team good enough to beat West Germany, Franz Beckenbauer, Gerd Muller et al, in the semi-final after extra-time. Of course, the history books will show the Brazilians claimed the old Jules Rimet trophy by dint of their 4-1 triumph over the Italians in Mexico City, but, remember, Pele and his pals were in their pomp at the time. It was no disgrace to be turned over by this mesmerising mixture of skills and talents.

And just to keep the observation going, Burgnich, Facchetti and Mazzola were all in the Italian World Cup Finals squad for the tournament in West Germany in 1974. Before that competition, the Inter trio had amassed over two hundred caps among them. Not bad for has-beens.

On May 25 1967, Burgnich was twenty-eight, Domenghini twenty-six and Facchetti and Mazzola both twenty-four.

Goalkeeper Guiliano Sarti was the oldest Inter player in Lisbon at the age of thirty-three - three years younger than Ronnie Simpson. Second oldest was defensive midfielder Mauro Bicicli at thirty-two. The only other player in his thirties was captain Armando Picchi at thirty-one. Central defender Aristide Guarneri was twenty-nine, Mario Corso twenty-five, Renato Cappellini twenty-three and Gianfranco Bedin was the youngest at twenty-one.

The average age, therefore, was a shade under twenty-seven. Hardly ancient. World-class midfielder Luis Suarez would have played against Jock Stein's team had he been fit. I've been assured he had reached veteran status. Just for the record, he celebrated his thirty-second birthday twenty-three days before Lisbon.

Contrast that with the ages of the Celtic performers. The most senior member of the Lions was, of course, goalkeeper Ronnie Simpson at thirty-six. Then came goal hero Stevie Chalmers at thirty-one, Bertie Auld twenty-nine, Billy McNeill twenty-seven, John Clark and Willie Wallace, both twenty-six, Jim Craig, Tommy Gemmell and Bobby Lennox, all twenty-three, and Bobby Murdoch and Jimmy Johnstone, both twenty-two. The youngest of the iconic Celts was Murdoch, forty-four days the junior of Johnstone. The average age was a mere fraction over twenty-six.

So, arithmetically, there wasn't much in it. In footballing terms, though, they were worlds apart.

So, please, let's have no more erroneous histrionics about Celtic walking all over a pitiful collection of decrepit footballing geriatrics in Lisbon. No more dastardly slurs and outrageous innuendo. Give credit where credit is due.

Celtic were crowed the Kings of Europe on May 25 1967 in Lisbon purely on merit.

And how they deserved That Season In Paradise.

I T I N E R A R Y .
- - - - - - - - -

European Cup Final Glasgow Celtic -v- Inter Milan.

23rd May.

Report	GLASGOW	Abbotsinch Airport,	09.30.
Depart	GLASGOW	For flight DA.6793 Abbotsinch Airport,	10.30.

A meal will be served during the flight.

Arrive	LISBON	Lisbon Airport,	14.00.

On arrival you will be transferred from the airport to the hotel in Estoril, where accommodation has been reserved on a full board basis from arrival on 23rd May until departure on 26th May.

24th May.

Free for private arrangements.

25th May.

Football match -Glasgow Celtic -v- Inter Milan.

We have arranged coach transfer for all passengers from the hotel to the stadiu in Lisbon for the match.   After the game the coach will then return you back t the hotel in Estoril.

26th May.

You will be transferred from your hotel in Estoril to Lisbon airport for departure of your flight.   Coach departure time approximately 13.00.

Report	LISBON	Lisbon Airport,	14.15.
Depart	LISBON	For flight DA.6793 Lisbon Airport,	15.00.

A meal will be served during the flight.

Arrive	GLASGOW	Abbotsinch Airport,	18.30.

- - - - - - - - - - - - - - - - - -

N.B. If you wish any further information please contact our representative

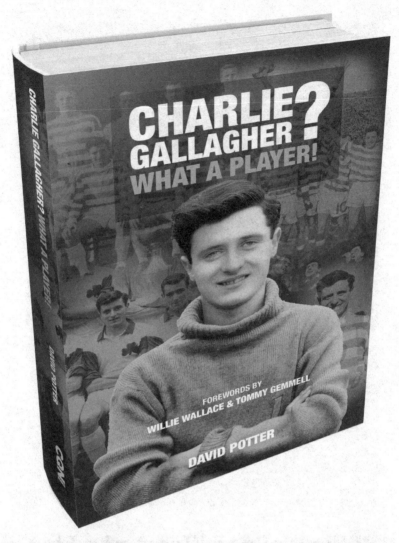

Charlie Gallagher? What a Player!

Charlie Gallagher was at Celtic Park for over 10 years. Encompassing the 1960s, his career was an eventful one, touching the depths of despair and the ultimate triumph. Although never a permanent fixture in the Celtic first team, his memory is much revered by the Celtic support. Slightly-built, he seemed to lack the necessary robustness. But appearances can be very deceptive. Behind the easy-going exterior lurked a tremendous football brain, with the ability to spray passes which fast-running forwards would relish. Charlie Gallagher starred in one of Celtic's best performances in years as MTK Budapest were beaten 3-0 in the European Cup-Winners' Cup semi-final at Celtic Park.

Available at CQNBookstore.com

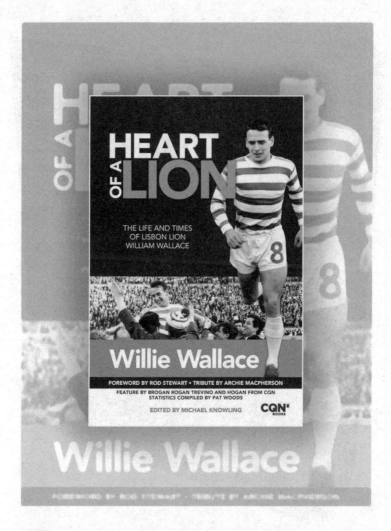

Willie Wallace. Heart of a Lion

Join Willie Wallace on a journey of a lifetime. And a trip it has been, as you'll find out, in 'Heart of a Lion'.

This is Willie's own story, from boyhood in Kirkintilloch, to the life of a professional footballer criss-crossing Scotland and Europe as part of the all-conquering Celtic squad of the late 1960s, to the decision to make a post-retirement home under the warm Australian sun.

Scotland has had two famous men named William Wallace. Heart of a Lion reveals the journey of today's Wallace to be no less colourful, courageous and loyal than his predecessor!

Available at CQNBookstore.com

YOGI BARE
The Life and Times of a Celtic Legend JOHN HUGHES

John Hughes, known as Yogi Bear to his adoring Celtic legions, was one of the most explosive and spectacular players in the club's history.

Now, for the first time, this true legend has decided to lift the lid on his remarkable career. It's a book that is as powerful as one of his blockbusting shots that became a famous trademark on his way to becoming one of the highest scoring Celtic players of all time.

His forthright views hit the target with all the shuddering force of one of his 'Yogi Specials'. It's an unmissable chronicle from a genuine Celtic icon from the sixties, an extraordinary decade in the club's proud history...

Available at CQNBookstore.com

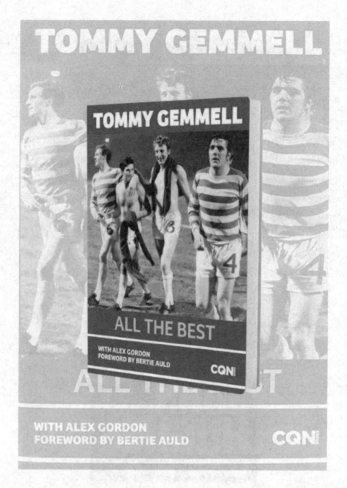

Tommy Gemmell. All the Best

Tommy Gemmell scored perhaps the most significant goal in the history of Celtic FC on that beautifully sunny day in Lisbon on 25th May 1967. Here in his final book Tommy looks back with Alex Gordon, on a lifetime in the game and selects the players he rates as the best he's played with or watched.

The events in South America when Celtic participated in the Inter-Continental Cup against Racing Club of Argentina. From the beauty of Celtic's attacking play in Lisbon to the farce of facing these cheats from Argentina - Tommy tells us about every kick, and not just of the ball!

All The Best is a book that every Celtic supporter will want to own. Lisbon Lion, Celtic legend and the man who scored for Celtic in not one but two European Cup Finals – no wonder he was called The Big Shot!

Available at CQNBookstore.com

A South American Liberty!

Tommy Gemmell wrote his first book, The Big Shot, when he was at the height of his career as a professional footballer. The Big Shot was a best seller when it was first published in 1968. In The Big Shot, Tommy told for the first time his side of the story regarding the notorious incidents that occurred in Montevideo in a play off match against Racing Club of Argentina. Much has been written about these matches in later years but Tommy's account, written so close to the matches, gives a real insight into what actually happened and what drove Tommy to make that most famous of well aimed kicks to the tender regions of the Racing No.11. Raffo apparently squealed like a pig! Here is how Tommy described these matches with Racing Club in The Big Shot...

Ever since 1960 the European champions have met the top team in South America for a trophy called the Inter – Continental Cup. That name is hardly ever used, however, as everyone accepts that this home and home fixture is for the World Championship – the supreme status symbol in club football. So I imagine there ate lots of youngsters in many countries who dream of playing in these very special show games.

Frankly, my advice to them all is...FORGET IT! Aim as high as you like in football but don't worry if you never get to play for that World title because then your dream might just become a nightmare – and as a Celtic player I can speak from bitter experience. We were the first British club ever to play for the Inter-Continental Cup and naturally it was a terrific honour. It was a great feeling too to be going forward as Europe's champions, knowing that only one team stood between you and the World title.

In 1967 we thought we could win that title. We were playing good football and we were a better side than the South Americans. But that was before we knew very much about our opponents, Racing Club of Argentina. Later, we were to discover that their plans for winning the World Crown had very little to do with football.

These Argentinians were like no team I had ever encountered before. Indeed, I think it is fair to say that they were the dirtiest, most ruthless, and despicable bunch of soccer hatchet-men ever gathered together under the one set of jerseys. In all grades of football you'll find the tough guy and the 'fly' man. But Racing Club were in a class of their own.

They were the masters at heel-clicking and catching you with their elbow when the ball was well away and they had long since perfected every other dirty trick known in football, including a fair amount of spitting. I'm not saying they took us by surprise. The Boss, Jock Stein, had compiled a pretty thick dossier on them before they reached Scotland and he warned us that in the first leg at Hampden they would be a certain amount of trouble, as the best way to slow any game down is to commit as many fouls as possible. We were just as determined not to let them knock us out of our stride.

The Hampden tie worked out as anticipated. They played a purely destructive game and we refused to be upset. Self-discipline was easy for us on that October evening because as far as behaviour was concerned this game was no different from any other. Every player at Parkhead knows he will get no sympathy if he is guilty of field offences. In fact, although it was well into the second half before Billy McNeill headed the winner I think we all gained confidence from this match because Racing did not appear to have much to offer in the finer points of football, although they gave us one or two hints that they knew a thing or two about unarmed combat.

It was not until the second leg in Buenos Aires, however, that we fully realised why Racing are known as the 'dirtiest team in South America'. The astonishing thing is that their coach, Jose Pizzuti, is a most pleasant wee man off duty and was a really skilful player in his day. You would think he would seek the same kind of reputation for his team. Instead, when he went for that coaching certificate, he must have studied under SMERSH!

Ten days after the Hampden game we were flying in over the skyscrapers of Buenos Aires to prepare for the second leg. At that time we were an optimistic outfit because we sensed that the Boss believed we were capable of getting the draw, which would be enough to give us the World title. We moved out immediately to the luxurious Hindu Club and on that first Sunday we got off to a light-hearted start.

As it was a day of Obligation most of our party went off to find the nearest Catholic church. That left the Boss, Bertie Auld, Willie Wallace, Ronnie Simpson and myself. So we headed for the golf course. And what a start the

Boss made. Over the first none holes he played as if he had been searching for that course all his life. No wonder all the wee local boys skipped around his heels and fought to pull his clubs. They knew class when they saw it and the Boss looked at us as if we were lucky to be playing with him. He was in a great mood and, like any golfer who thinks he has suddenly found the secret; he could hardly keep the smile off his face.

Then the bubble burst. After the turn the Boss's ball began to go in all directions and the wee boys retreated to a safe distance. Even the smallest member of the gallery soon realized that old man Simpson, commonly known as 'faither', was the real golfer in the company. By the eighteenth he had the gallery to himself and the Boss was pulling his own caddie-car.

Yet I think I remember that round of golf because it was the only time during our stay in South America that I saw him looking really relaxed. Usually he hides his feelings well, especially in the tension before a big game, but he was obviously concerned about these matches with racing Club.

The strain the Boss was under would show through during training sessions. Usually, as we train, a lot of cross-talk goes on and the Boss is liable to take as much a part in it as anybody, but in those days before the tie in Buenos Aires he would turn on anyone who was capering about and tell them: 'That's enough. We are here to work'...or words to that effect. So we were all on our best behaviour while we stayed at the Hindu Club. Even if we thought we were good enough to get the draw, which would give us the title, we sensed it was going to be no picnic.

And when we reached the Avellanda Stadium our worst fears were justified. Even before the game started, as we loosened up and hit a few shots t goal, Ronnie Simpson suddenly staggered and put his hands to his head. He had been hit. A narrow rectangular piece of iron, about two inches long, had been thrown through the fence, which is supposed to protect the players.

Boy, were we angry! It was ridiculous that a think like that should happen to any player before such a big game. Ronnie, dazed, shocked, and obviously in pain couldn't possibly play and it meant our reserve John Fallon suddenly found himself playing in a World tie at two minutes' notice. At least he hardly had time to get nervous, but I could not help thinking this was one time when fate wasn't working for Celtic.

Yet despite Ronnie's injury and despite all the unfriendly Argentinians in that stadium, we actually came very near to victory in Buenos Aires. In fact, we scored first. With what was virtually his last gesture of neutrality, the referee awarded us a penalty. I never took a kick with more determination and it was worth a guinea a box to see the expressions on the faces of racing Club. The turning point came, however, when Jimmy Johnstone scored what looked like a perfectly good second goal, only to have it chalked off. Racing equalized after that, yet at the interval we still thought we had a chance. The Boss urged us, as he had done before kick-off, not to 'annoy' either racing or their supporters. He couldn't have guessed how difficult this was going to be!

For racing got their second goal soon after the interval and from there on they decided to take no chances. Their tackling became worse and worse and after a while you didn't need to decide whether to pass or hold the ball, because if you did not get rid of it immediately, someone was sure to send you sprawling. Jimmy Johnstone suffered more than most of us, but we all had to remember, firstly, not to annoy the Argentinians.

Well, we didn't annoy them. Instead they hacked, tripped and pushed their way to a 2-1 victory, which earned them a third-game play-off for the title, which they were obviously determined to get at all costs. We trooped back to our dressing room, disgusted. I'll never forget it. We were so incensed at the treatment we had had to take from these South American soccer gangsters. Nobody made a dive for the bath as they would normally do. We just sat there trying to think of words bad enough to describe Racing Club who had obviously been confident the Uruguayan referee would let them away with anything.

Then we were joined in the dressing room by our own officials. Chairman Bob Kelly told us he would not allow us to play a third game against these opponents. I think that cheered most of us up because we were so fed up with the whole affair we would have like nothing better than to grab the first plane back to Glasgow.

Half an hour later we would have been happy to settle for a 'pass out' from that dressing room. The atmosphere had become chaotic. Argentinian and Uruguayan officials poured in when they heard we did not want to play a third in Montevideo, and they were followed by Press men, photographers, police, and anyone in Buenos Aires who had nothing better to do at the time.

At least, that's how it seemed because there was simply no room to move and most of us had still not changed.

As the flash-bulbs went off and interpreters tried to sort out the various arguments, it was difficult to know whether our next destination would be Scotland or Uruguay. At one stage the Boss asked us if we were prepared to play Racing Club again and we said 'Yes', mainly because we could tell from his attitude that he thought we could still win the third game if we got protection from the referee. The Uruguayans assured us the next game would be strictly controlled, and finally Mr. Kelly took their word for it.

I didn't know then, of course, that if the Chairman had been adamant and refused to play in Montevideo I would have been spared the most embarrassing football experience of my career…but I'll tell you about that later.

We had cheered up a lot by the time we flew out to Uruguay the next day. We had heard that the fans in Montevideo didn't like racing Club at all and were sure to be behind us. And any doubts we may have had about this story were quickly dispelled at the airport. We got a great reception; the crowds were shouting 'Celtic, Celtic' and that really gave our morale a boost. It pleased us even more when we were visited at out hotel by the Penarol players, the former World Champions who had played us in a friendly at Parkhead. They confirmed that Racing Club had a reputation for being a really nasty bunch, hut they were sure we could beat them.

The Boss must have been cheered by all this too because there were two occasions when he showed how quick he can be with the gags. There was a phone call and one of the waiters in the hotel came up to him and asked: 'Are you Stein?' In the local accent, however, it sounded like 'Are you stayin'? – and quick as a flash the Bog man replied: 'No, I'm leaving on Sunday.'

Outside the hotel the following day he really had us rolling about. We had been invited to go to a nearby shop where we could get some bargains in clothes. The proprietor was delighted to see us. He wore a broad smile and, like me, he had the kind of nose, which leaves very little room for the rest of your face. "This is wonderful,' he said. To think you come all the way from Glasgow to my shop. And you know what? I've got a cousin in Glasgow. Maybe you know him. His name is Levy.'

The rest of us smilingly shook our heads. Our clothier friend didn't realise how many people there are around Glasgow with a name like Levy. But the Boss had the answer. After a moment he said 'Levy? Sure I know him. Your cousin must be Betting Levy!'

As the rest of us nearly choked trying not to laugh, the Montevideo man could hardly contain himself. 'Sure, sure', he cried, 'that sounds like him. But is he doing well?'

Back came the deadpan reply: 'Doing well? He takes a fortune every week!'

That was the news this leading light in Montevideo Menswear had been waiting for. He could hardly serve us after that because he was obviously bursting to spread the word among his relations that their nearly forgotten cousin in Scotland was making a fortune and seemed to be a household name.

This little bit of kidding by the Boss gave the clothier a great deal of pleasure – and it helped the Celtic camp a lot too. It gave us something to look back and laugh about for the rest of the day and as the 'decider' approached our mood of optimism was increasing. Yet at the same time our preparations were deadly serious – so serious that Bertie Auld and I were nearly thrown out of the team altogether!

It happened like this. On the afternoon before the game Bertie and I sat in the hotel lounge chatting to some Press men. Time passed quickly and it was a long while before we realised we were the only players around. No wonder. Up in one of the rooms the Boss was holding his final tactics talk and nobody had noticed we were missing. By the time we sheepishly put our heads round the door the meeting was almost over. Later the Boss had a few things to say to both of us and he finished by telling us very frankly that if the next day's game had been anything less important than a World tie we would have been out of the team and in the grandstand.

Since we were in we were able to join the rest of the boys in a search for a Uruguayan flag. It had been decided that since the local fans were supposed to be on our side they would back us even more if we went out with their flag. So about twenty minutes before the kick-off we all strolled on to the field, waved, acted like a most friendly bunch of fellas, then unfurled the flag. The fans seemed to like the gesture, but their response wasn't quite as enthusiastic as we had hoped. Back in the pavilion we soon found the answer. Someone told us that ten minutes earlier the Racing Club party had been waving an even bigger Uruguayan flag than ours!

Yes, one up to the Argentinians – and a lesson to us all that no matter how smart you may think you are in these top international competitions you should always remember that the other fellow is thinking too and he may come up with an even better idea than you. It's this kind of thing, no doubt, which puts an extra strain on managers.

Before the game the Boss warned us, as usual, of the need for self-control. He no doubt hoped, as we all did, that the assurances given about firm refereeing would keep the wild men of racing Club in check. Yet I'm sure he sensed our mood that if the South Americans kicked, hacked and spat at us any more we would do a wee bit of Scottish 'sorting out'.

It was obvious, after hardly any time at all, that Racing had no intention of altering their tactics. Our appeals to the referee were a pure waste of time and after one particularly vicious foul on Jimmy Johnstone I think we all decided that was the last straw. I could see our blokes were no longer holding back and the game became nothing more than an exhibition of unarmed combat.

The Paraguayan referee was not slow, however, to spot crimes committed by anybody in a Celtic jersey and as the game went on John Hughes, Jimmy Johnstone and Bobby Lennox were all ordered off and Racing had the one goal lead which they no doubt felt justified all their diabolical tactics.

So, as near as I can guess, there would be about ten minutes to go when I decided that justice had to be done. After the umpteenth incident players and officials were gathered round the referee and Bertie Auld. It was all very heated and everyone was trying to see what was happening...but one player was standing apart. He was making sure he wouldn't be involved. I wasn't surprised because he had managed to stay out of all the real trouble throughout the tie. This was Raffo, wearing a No.11 jersey and looking quite pleased with himself. It made me so annoyed to think that the tie was nearly over and this man looked like finishing it unscathed, yet of all the members of the ruthless Racing team he had been the most consistently dirty. Yet he was crafty enough to do all his spitting and kicking when the referee was looking the other way. Nobody had been able to get their own back on him because he jumped high in the air every time you tried to tackle him. As I looked at him I thought: 'I bet he's thinking the Scots are a soft lot because he's "given us stick" all that time and got away with it.' All this had gone through my mind in a matter of seconds and in sheer temper I decided to hand out justice myself. I ran quickly round to where he was standing and kicked him. The swing was well timed, the aim was good too, and my boot landed on a very tender spot. Mr. Raffo squealed like a pig and went down in a heap. I quickly returned to my previous stance feeling very, very pleased with myself. Because of the fuss round Bertie hardly anyone had seen my little deed and it did my heart good to know that Raffo had got what was coming to him.

Now, I'm not going to defend myself. I'm not suggesting this was a nice thing to do. If another player annoys you it is no solution to kick him deliberately. But in this instance it seemed the only way to deal with him. Racing Club had set their own standards in these matches and to get down to them you had to stoop pretty low.

Mark you, I had no idea what an infamous kick that was to become. I certainly never dreamed I would have to spend days, even weeks, explaining it when I got back to Glasgow.

The trouble began when, on the Wednesday evening after we returned home from South America, the BBC showed a film taken during the game in Montevideo. I never saw it so I was completely taken by surprise when I arrived at Parkhead on the following morning and the first people I met said:

'You're some guy you…what a daft thing to do in front of the cameras! What a fool you are!' And I couldn't even start to print some of the other things, which were said to me in the days that followed.

It seemed that the BBC had managed to get hold of a film which highlighted most of the fouls committed by Celtic and somehow missed the dirty work done by the Argentinians. And I was assured that by far the most dramatic shots were of a bloke called Gemmell kicking a bloke who was standing minding his own business.

Yes, while I had been getting my revenge on Raffo a TV camera high in the stands had followed my every move. I haven't seen that particular film yet, but I've been told often enough that my hasty retreat after delivering the blow did not look particularly dignified on the screen. I thought I was just helping the cause of justice… but I never thought justice would be seen to be done by about ten million British viewers, including my family and friends. I was widely criticised, of course, especially by English critics who had been waiting on an opportunity to knock Celtic. They had been shocked when we won the

European cup; annoyed that we had done so much more than any of their teams.

Even my mother said to me the first time I visited her after the TV film had been shown: 'Why did you have to go and kick that man?' I explained, as I've tried to explain here, and I think she understood. Many other people still think what I did to Raffo was outrageous, but I think they will understand the atmosphere in Montevideo better when I tell this story, which has never been told before.

The fact is, the most amazing thing about that game, as far as I was concerned, happened as I was walking off the field, Raffo ran over to me... and was smiling. He made signals and at first I thought he was looking for a fight! Then I realised he wanted to swap jerseys with me. Swapping jerseys is an international football custom, of course, but you tend to do more of it in a game where relations have been good. It seemed strange to me in that situation and I admit I was suspicious. I thought: 'This bloke probably wants me to pull the jersey over my head so he can belt me one when I can't see him.'

But Raffo looked so darned friendly I felt I could hardly turn him down. So I warily got out of one sleeve first, then the other, then, stepping back quickly, I whipped my jersey over my head. His smile became even broader, and as we swapped jerseys he warmly shook my hand. Indeed, as he ran towards the tunnel he had a grin on his face and, in English, he shouted a little remark about the accuracy of my kick.

In the game of football as we know it, it seems unlikely that Raffo should have anything to do with me. But at home, among my other souvenirs, I have a neatly pressed Racing Club jersey with vertical blue and white stripes and a No. 11 on the back which proves that its former owner was less upset by that kick than the millions of TV fans who saw it in Britain.

Players like him kick – and expect to be kicked. It is the way some of them play the game. Referees in most European countries would not stand for that behaviour. That's why I started off warning youngsters that playing in the World Championship is an experience they can probably do well without. I feel certain Celtic would not take part again in similar circumstances. It is a good idea that the European Champions should meet the Champions of South America each year, but these games are going to get out of control too often unless these is a neutral venue.

I would play the World final in New York. It might deprive the clubs of a financial bonanza, but if the referee was a thoroughly reliable man, carefully selected, then we could be sure the winners would be worthy champions. I certainly think no British team should ever agree to a World series in which two of the three matches could be played in South America. If the 1967 title had been decided over ninety minutes in a neutral country there is no doubt we would have been able to take it back to Parkhead.

As it was, our encounter with Racing Club brought us nothing but trouble. After we got home, and even after the TV film, another shock awaited those of us who had played in Montevideo.

One morning during training we were told the Chairman wanted to meet us at 11.30. The Boss admitted that it had to do with our behaviour in that third game in Uruguay. Celtic through the years had always had a good reputation for discipline on the field and it certainly been tarnished in Montevideo. There had to be a punishment and the Boss wanted our opinion on whether it should be spread over the entire team or merely those who had been sent off. We immediately said it should be a team affair. He had known what our answer would be anyway.

So there were eleven very shocked individuals in Parkhead that morning when Mr. Kelly announced that the Board had decided to fine each of us £250!

There were those who thought this was just a gesture to impress the public and that we would never really have to pay all that money. But they didn't know Bob Kelly. He doesn't do things like that – and every penny of the fine was deducted from bonuses, which we had earned previously in other matches.

Mr. Kelly was also ready, however, to accept part of the responsibility. As he announced the fines he confessed that he should have stuck to his original decision in Buenos Aires. He said he ought never to have allowed us to play in that third game and that he had no doubt in his own mind that he had made a mistake.

I think everyone would agree with him now. If we had refused to play the third game, especially after what happened to Ronnie Simpson, football people everywhere would have been on our side. Many would have regarded us as the best team in the world even if we had no official title. But it is easy to be wise after the event.